PLAYING

WITH

PURPOSE

PLAYING

WITH

PURPOSE

Inside the Lives and Faith of
Tim Tebow, Jeremy Lin,
and Today's Top Athletes

MIKE YORKEY

BARBOUR
PUBLISHING

© 2012 by Mike Yorkey

ISBN 978-1-61626-942-5

The author is represented by WordServe Literary Group, Ltd., Greg Johnson, Literary Agent, 10152 S. Knoll Circle, Highlands Ranch, CO 80130

Published by Barbour Publishing, Inc., P.O. Box 719, Uhrichsville, Ohio 44683 www.barbourbooks.com

Our mission is to publish and distribute inspirational products offering exceptional value and biblical encouragement to the masses.

ecpa Member of the
Evangelical Christian
Publishers Association

Printed in the United States of America.

CONTENTS

INTRODUCTION

Perhaps you've heard of A.C. Green, who holds the NBA record for consecutive games played at 1,192—but he's probably best known for his stand on purity during his days with the Los Angeles Lakers. Although his career has been over for more than a decade, A.C.'s boldness in speaking up for biblical values means he was playing with purpose during all those years he chased loose balls and grabbed rebounds.

Today, there are dozens of NBA players—as well as guys in the NFL and Major League Baseball—trying to make a difference in the lives of those around them and in the lives of the fans looking on. In the pages to follow, you'll learn about several of them:

- Tim Tebow
- Jeremy Lin
- Luke Ridnour
- Stephen Curry
- Nenê
- Reggie Williams
- Nick Collison
- Kevin Durant
- Greivis Vasquez

- Clayton Kershaw
- Albert Pujols
- Josh Hamilton
- Mariano Rivera

Each of these talented players wants his career to count for something more than championship rings, individual awards, and hefty paychecks. You'll love their faith stories—which are just as powerful as their athletic achievements.

1.

TIM TEBOW
THE CHOSEN ONE

Here we go again.

Tim Tebow, who—according to a *Sports Illustrated* cover headline, "demands that you watch"—finds himself starting all over now that he's donning the hunter-green No. 15 jersey of the New York Jets for the 2012 NFL season.

We all wonder what will transpire—but half the fun of sports is not knowing the outcome. When Tim has the ball in his hands, anything can happen. He certainly grabbed our attention as the biggest football story of 2011, taking the reins of a 1–4 Denver team headed for oblivion and single-handedly spearheading the Broncos to their first AFC West division title in six years—plus an incredible playoff win against the Pittsburgh Steelers.

The Broncos leadership was so thrilled by the turnaround that they went out and signed free agent Peyton Manning to quarterback the team in 2012.

Don't let the door hit you on your way out of town, Tim. But thanks for the memories, especially that sweet pass you threw to

Demaryius Thomas against the Steelers.

Now he's taking his act to Broadway, playing in America's biggest city, the epicenter of the media universe. He's always worn his Christian faith on the sleeve of his football jersey, and that won't change in New York. Will the Jets' prickly fans and wise-guy New York media mock him, respect his faith, or just be apathetic? Nobody knows which direction the wind will blow—but it was revealing that Virgin Airlines quickly offered Tim unlimited free flights to London, as long as he remains sexually pure. (A *virgin*, get it?)

Whatever happens in the 2012 season, you can figure that Tim will continue to be one of the most talked-about football players in America. And if he gets a chance to play—or even leapfrogs Mark Sanchez for the starting job—watch out. He'll once again become the most discussed, dissected, and debated athlete on ESPN, the arbiter of what's important in the sports world.

This fishbowl existence has been part of Tim's world since he burst on the scene in 2006 as a true freshman quarterback at the University of Florida. When he's in public, he's a compelling figure who draws stares from bystanders, screams from fans, and clicks from cell phone cameras. He's been called the NFL version of a total solar eclipse, blotting out nearly every other name or topic in the football world.

His smile melts hearts. His demeanor is humble and earnest. His attitude is respectful to elders and authority figures (like coaches), and his faith moves mountains. His work ethic is off the charts. He's so good-natured and likable that you want to bottle him up and take him home to the family.

Admit it—you can't keep your eyes off him. The camera loves

Tim Tebow. His emotions on the field run the gamut: full-throated exhortations to his teammates, fist pumps and bear hugs after big plays and touchdowns, broad smiles and gracious interviews after victories, and emotional on-the-field meetings with youngsters fighting a terminal disease or physical disfigurement.

If football was show business (and, in many ways, that's a good metaphor for a city with Times Square and the Great White Way theater district), Tim's charisma and poise—that special "it"—defines his uniqueness, fortitude, determination, and belief in himself. He has an amazing presence on and off the field as well as a wonderful alliterative roll to his name.

Tim Tebow generates so much heat and attention because his outsized personality broke the mold for the quarterback position during a four-year career at Florida. Things haven't changed since he's been in the NFL. Once he plants his feet under or behind the center, he plays QB like it's his personal fiefdom. He's as relentless as Attila the Hun, as unstoppable as a Mack truck plowing through a roadblock. Now if he could just pass a little better.

His agent, Jimmy Sexton, has predicted that Tim will become the most marketable athlete in history—and that seems more likely now that he's playing for a New York team. Even before he was traded to the Jets, however, the endorsement deals piled up like snowdrifts along Fifth Avenue. Jockey underwear. Nike shoes. FRS energy drinks. During his rookie year with Denver, his No. 15 Broncos jersey led the league in sales in 2010 and was second last season to the forest green jersey belonging to the Green Bay Packers' Aaron Rodgers, another Christian quarterback who's at the top of his game.

"But nobody seems to have popped out quite like Tebow," said

Darin David, account director for The Marketing Arm agency.

Everyone wants to be associated with him. Jockey, the underwear company, featured Tim in catalogs and TV and print advertisements because "Jockey's interest in Tim goes beyond football," the company announced. "He is dedicated to community service, and his work ethic, positive attitude, and leadership skills are unquestionable."

Expect more companies like Jockey to launch Tim Tebow campaigns in the future—or maybe we'll see some type of film endeavor. Following the 2011 season, he signed with William Morris Endeavor, one of Hollywood's top talent agencies. WME will be the point for any of Tim's off-the-field pursuits, such as endorsements, books, personal appearances, and any television or movie roles pitched his way.

But don't worry—Tim hasn't gone Hollywood on us. It's not in his DNA or his upbringing.

IN THE BEGINNING

Timothy Richard Tebow was born August 14, 1987, in the Philippines.

In a manger.

Because his parents were told there was no room at the inn.

The part about Tim being born in the Philippines is true, but we're just having fun with his "nativity story." But this is the sort of mythmaking that happens when they start calling you "The Chosen One"—in high school.

Tim was born in Makati City, part of metro Manila, because his parents, Bob and Pam Tebow, were living in the Philippines as missionaries at the time. Bob and Pam met at the University of Florida in 1967, when Bob was a sophomore and Pam was a freshman. Even back then, Bob knew his life's goal: to share the message of Jesus Christ with others.

That was certainly a different goal than the one set forth by his father, whom Bob described as a workaholic who moved the family from Alabama to California to Florida as he developed a business in sales and finance. "Growing up, I knew my goal was to get a job and make a million dollars," Bob said.

That desire evaporated during a high school ski trip organized by Young Life, a ministry that reaches out to adolescents. The slopes were bare from warm weather that winter, which kept the Young Life group indoors for presentations and lectures. There, Bob heard the gospel message and became a Christian, a choice that would shape the rest of his life.

When Bob started attending the University of Florida, he and a close friend, Ander Crenshaw (who in 2001 began a career as a member of the U.S. House of Representatives, representing Florida's 4th congressional district) started a Campus Crusade for Christ chapter on the Gainesville campus.

Bob met Pam when he was publicizing a Campus Crusade event. She was the daughter of a U.S. Army colonel who moved frequently, with many of his postings beyond U.S. borders. Pam settled in Tampa during her high school years.

Bob and Pam became friends, and their first date came a year later, when Bob invited Pam to join him at. . .a football game between the University of Florida and the University of Georgia. The rivalry game was played each year at a neutral site: Jacksonville. The Gators won, which may have been a sign of good things to come.

Their love blossomed, and they graduated together from the University of Florida in 1971—he with a degree in health and human performance, and she with a degree from the College of Journalism and Communications. They married that summer and moved to Portland, Oregon, where Bob enrolled at Western Seminary to earn master's degrees in divinity and theology.

The extra schooling took five years. When Bob was finished, he and Pam moved back to Florida, where he became the area representative for the Fellowship of Christian Athletes (FCA) in the northeastern part of the state. Even though Bob had to raise his own support, he and Pam felt financially secure enough to start a family. After their first child, Christy, arrived in 1976, the parents spaced out Katie, Robby, Peter, and the family caboose—Tim—over the next 11 years.

Beginning in 1976, the Tebows started making major moves every three years. After a three-year stint with the FCA (1976–1979), Bob moved into church ministry at Southside Baptist Church in Jacksonville, where he was the associate pastor for three years until 1982. Then, for the next three years, he served as pastor of Cornerstone Community Church, also in Jacksonville.

While at Cornerstone, Bob embarked on a life-changing missionary trip to the Philippines. During the visit, he received what he believed was a summons he could not deny: God was calling him to become a missionary in the Philippines.

Bob and Pam believed then, as they do now, that God had been preparing their hearts for the mission field. Though they had been praying He would open this door, think about how difficult the undertaking must have been for the family, especially Pam: she had three children, ages eight, six, and four, as well as an infant son, Peter, who was born in 1984. To pull up stakes in Jacksonville, where her husband was a respected pastor with a bright career ahead, and resettle the family in a Third World country must have bordered upon the unreal for her.

They would move 12 time zones and almost exactly halfway around the world to Southeast Asia, a 19-hour plane trip that would take her far from the comforts of home. The logistics had to be daunting, the heartbreak of leaving behind friends and family gut-wrenching. They would have to sell most of their personal belongings. But to her credit, Pam never blinked. Living abroad as a young girl had certainly prepared her for this time in their lives. Besides, she was convinced this was God's will for the family, and she was fine with that.

The Tebows settled outside Manila, capital city of the Philippines, and the transition went as smoothly as they dared to hope. Filipinos were being trained as pastors, and countless locals were embracing the Christian faith. The Tebow kids—who had yet to reach their teenage years—acclimated well. "It wasn't always easy, but it was a wonderful time for our family," Pam said. "We learned a lot—you always learn a lot when you [live in] a Third World country."

A year after their arrival, Bob was in a remote village in the mountains in Mindanao, playing *The Jesus Film* on a white sheet that hung between two coconut trees. "I was showing a film and preaching that night," he told *Sports Illustrated*. "I was weeping over the millions of babies being [aborted] in America, and I prayed, 'God, if you give me a son, if you give me Timmy, I'll raise him to be a preacher.'"

The previous sentence is taken word-for-word from a *Sports*

Illustrated article that ran in the summer of 2009. Did you notice the editorializing? Writer Austin Murphy and/or the SI editors inserted the word "aborted" in brackets to signify that the magazine was not using the original word Bob said (or, in this case, wrote, because Bob Tebow was responding to questions that had been e-mailed to him).

What do you think Bob originally typed? Since he is ardently pro-life, you have to figure he tapped out this sentence on his computer screen:

I was weeping over the millions of babies being killed in America. . . .

That's how strongly he—and Pam—felt about abortion, which stops a beating heart and ends the life of a growing human being. Their hearts wept at the carnage of 4,000 abortions that happen every day—1.5 million each year—in the United States.

Sports Illustrated—and the Tebows would tell you the world feels the same way—didn't like the starkness or the reality of the word *killed*. So they chose to insert *aborted* instead. More clinical. Easier to brush off, sweep under the rug.

And then Pam got pregnant with Tim, and she and Bob suddenly had to confront their beliefs about the sanctity of life and the sovereignty of Almighty God.

A CHOICE

When Pam became pregnant with Tim, she was 37 years old, living 9,000 miles from home, the mother of four energetic children, and the wife of a missionary pastor.

The pregnancy was not unexpected. In fact, she and Bob very much desired to have a fifth child. They had been praying for

Timmy by name—to this day, they still call him "Timmy," not "Tim"—before she conceived. They wanted to name their son after the young church leader named Timothy, who received a pair of letters from the apostle Paul that now appear in the New Testament.

Just before she became pregnant, however, Pam contracted amoebic dysentery, a disease caused by bacteria transmitted through contaminated drinking water. Dysentery is common in developing and tropical countries like the Philippines and is not to be taken lightly—between 40,000 and 100,000 people die worldwide each year of amoebic dysentery. The disease causes inflammation of the intestines and bloody, severe diarrhea. Dysentery was the leading cause of death in the Philippines.

Pam fell into a coma and was treated aggressively with a series of strong antimicrobial drugs. As she came out of the coma and her condition stabilized, she continued to take the powerful medications.

Then, when she took a pregnancy test, the stick turned blue.

Pam recalled reading a label on her prescription warning that the antimicrobial drug could cause "severe birth defects." She immediately discontinued the treatment protocol, fearing harm had already been done to the life growing inside her. When she told her doctor what had transpired, her worst fears were confirmed—she heard that her "fetus" had been irreversibly damaged. That being the case, the doctor recommended that she "discontinue" the pregnancy—in other words, have an abortion.

Actually, "They didn't recommend," Pam said. "They didn't really give me a choice. That was the only option they gave me."

To Pam and Bob, there was a lot more than a "fetus" growing

inside her womb. This was a life, not a glob of tissue or a "product" of conception. Since the Tebows believed God was the author of life—and death—there was no doubt in their minds that they would trust Him in this perilous situation for both Pam *and* the unborn child.

Pam and Bob's decision was set in concrete, and their determination to see the pregnancy through didn't waver when Pam's doctor said that her placenta had detached from the uterine wall—a dangerous development known as placental abruption. Pam was a high-risk patient living in the Philippine countryside, and a severe condition like this one could have easily killed her. Once again, she was counseled to abort—to save her own life. Certainly she would be justified in taking this measure. But Pam wouldn't consider it.

"We were determined to trust the Lord with the children He would give us," she said in an interview with Focus on the Family president Jim Daly, taped after she and Tim completed filming their Super Bowl commercial in 2010. "And if God called me to give up my life, then He would take care of my family."

Bottom line: Pam Tebow wasn't just *willing* to risk her life for Timmy; she actually *chose* to risk her life so her son might live.

At the seventh month of her crisis pregnancy, Pam traveled to Manila, where she went on bed rest and received around-the-clock care from an American-trained physician. It was a touch-and-go pregnancy the entire way, and she and Bob prayed earnestly that God would give them the chance to raise the son they would name Timmy.

On her due date, August 14, Pam gave birth to Tim—and the family learned just how serious the placental abruption had been.

"There was a great big clump of blood that came out where the placenta wasn't properly attached, basically for the whole nine months," Bob said in an interview with Focus on the Family. "He was a miracle baby."

He was also skinny and long—like the malnourished newborn he was. The Tebows asked friends and family to pray that their newborn son would grow up big and strong. "It was amazing that God spared him, but we knew God had His hand on his life," Bob said. "We all, through the years, have told Timmy that."

BACK IN THE USA

When Tim was three years old, the Tebows decided to move back to Florida, closer to home and family. After laying a strong foundation and sending pastors out into the fields, Bob felt he could run the Bob Tebow Evangelistic Association from a distance while making periodic trips to the western Pacific. He could also better organize short-term and summer mission trips to the Philippines while living stateside.

The family moved back to the Jacksonville area, to a 44-acre farm tucked between the city and the tranquil setting of Baldwin. When Tim was a kindergartner, he joined his four older sisters and brothers at a special school with a limited enrollment—the Tebow Homeschool.

Homeschooling was becoming better known to the general public in the 1980s, thanks to pioneers like Dr. Raymond Moore and his wife, Dorothy—educators who became vocal advocates for homeschooling, particularly among Christian families. Parents purchased curriculum packages and teaching aids geared to their children's ages. The Tebows were early adopters, beginning in 1982 with Christy.

Let's face it: homeschooling was a radical idea back then, and it's still looked upon in many circles as strange. How can children learn enough to get a good education or get into college if they don't receive instruction from trained teachers in public and private school classrooms?

The Tebows had some clear ideas about how they wanted to raise their children. They were wary of worldly influences intruding upon their five offspring—outside influences that would smack them the moment they stepped on the school bus. They were also greatly concerned about the moral and cultural values conveyed in the public school classrooms.

So Bob and Pam sought a different approach. They wanted to inspire their children to love God, live excellently, be humble, and serve their fellow man. As hands-on parents who would alone be responsible for their children's formal educations, they would closely monitor what came into the home and be intentional about the lessons their children would learn.

"If I could get my kids to the age of 25 and they knew God and served God and had character qualities that pleased God, then I knew God would be happy and I would be happy," Bob said. "The only way I could do that was to do it myself, commit to God that this is my job. Traditional academics had to take a backseat to God's Word and character-building."

They started homeschooling Christy, Katie, Robby, and Peter before the family moved to the Philippines. Pam taught them the Three R's—reading, 'riting, and 'rithmetic—plus other subjects as they got older. Everything their children learned would be taught through the prism of the Bible, with an emphasis on learning how to speak in public. Bob and Pam wanted each of their children to feel comfortable and confident in communicating their beliefs.

Memorizing Bible verses, as well as life lessons, were foundational to learning in the Tebow home. For instance, Proverbs 27:2 (New King James Version) taught the children not to brag on themselves:

> *Let another man praise you, and not your own mouth;*
> *A stranger, and not your own lips.*

Bob and Pam believed humility was one of the greatest measures of a person's character, so they constantly had their children memorize Bible verses on humility, such as:

> Remember how the LORD your God led you all the way
>   in the desert these forty years, to humble you and
>   to test you in order to know what was in your heart,
>   whether or not you would keep his commands
>   (Deuteronomy 8:2).
> You save the humble, but your eyes are on the haughty to
>   bring them low (2 Samuel 22:28).
> When pride comes, then comes disgrace, but with
>   humility comes wisdom (Proverbs 11:2).
> The fear of the LORD teaches a man wisdom, and
>   humility comes before honor (Proverbs 15:33).
> Humility and the fear of the LORD bring wealth and
>   honor and life (Proverbs 22:4).

When the children weren't memorizing Bible verses or doing schoolwork, they learned discipline through chores like taking out the trash, vacuuming, making their beds, and washing dishes. That was just the beginning, since there was always work to do on such a large property dotted with pines and grassy fields—mowing the grass, building fences, feeding the cows.

The parents turned a half-acre plot behind the house into a vegetable garden, and the children learned the value of stoop labor. They weeded with hoes and planted and cared for the vegetables that fed their family of seven year-round. They slaughtered and ate the cows they raised. Bucking fallen trees in the "back 40" was another way Bob instilled the value of physical labor in his sons.

Bob and Pam had a firm rule in the Tebow household: no complaining. That rule must have stuck because you can't call Tim Tebow a grumbler or whiner today. The characteristic has shown itself on the football field. While Tim deeply hates losing at anything, he's never been one to offer excuses.

NO GRAND PLAN

It's a great quip, a superb sound bite, and something Bob Tebow has repeated many times over the years. It goes like this:

"I asked God for a preacher, and He gave me a quarterback."

There was no grand plan in the Tebow family to raise a great athlete, let alone a star quarterback who would become an NFL starter. In the Tebow household, sports were low-key. They had to be, if you think about it. During their five years in the Philippines, there was no such thing as Little League or AYSO soccer for Tim's older brothers and sisters. The kids played outside, ran around, did things that kids do. But there were no "travel teams" in the Philippines.

After the Tebow family returned to Florida, Christy played some tennis, and Katie was a runner. Tim's older brothers Robby and Peter got into youth baseball and football. The parents kept everything in perspective; they knew getting exercise was good for the body, but they didn't want their schedules revolving around sports. The Tebows *were* into competition, though. "There was no mercy in our family," Bob said. "Katie, every once in a while, would show you mercy, but everyone else would cut your throat."

The Tebow family's competitive streak extended beyond sports. Board games like Monopoly quickly deteriorated into overheated emotions when a simple roll of the dice landed one of the Tebow kids on Boardwalk or Park Place teeming with red hotels. And woe to the Risk players when their territories were captured. When Bob taught each of his children how to play chess, the sparks would fly following a checkmate.

Bob said he never let any of the children beat him at chess— and no one can topple his king to this day. The last time he challenged anyone to take him on, there were no takers. "It's pretty dog-eat-dog around here," he said. "They know the outcome."

With that thought in mind, Bob noticed something about Tim, even when his son was a five-year-old: he had a tremendous arm and impressive hand-eye coordination—as well as the Tebow competitive streak. Tim threw left-handed, but that was his natural side, so Bob didn't try to change him.

Tim could throw a football with excellent velocity for a pint-sized tyke, and when he had a bat in his hand, he could swing and hit the ball squarely. His parents thought he'd have fun playing

T-ball, the pressureless entry point for youth baseball, so they signed him up. There's no live pitching in T-ball; each batter steps up to the plate and swings at a ball placed on a plastic tee. Once the player hits the ball into fair territory, he starts running.

Many five-year-olds are clueless about how baseball is played, and some prefer to lie down in the outfield and watch the clouds roll by. Not Tim, who played second base for the White Sox. If he had another gift besides pure athleticism, it was awareness of his surroundings. He would get perturbed when the other kids didn't know what was going on, as Guerry Smith described on Rivals. com:

> Some of his teammates were picking at the ground without even paying attention. *How is that possible?* he wondered. *There's a game going on. Focus on the game.* He heard players say they were out there for the snow cone they would get when the game was over. Not Tebow. The competition was all that mattered at the moment. He heard his coach say, "You don't have to play to win. Just play to have fun," and he could not comprehend the mindset. *It's not fun if you don't win*, he said to himself. He was dumbfounded. He was also five years old.

Tim also played Pop Warner football. As one of the bigger kids on the team, he played tight end on offense and linebacker on defense. Then one day, when he was 11 years old, his coach, David Hess, watched him practice and said to himself, *This kid is such a talented athlete. He'd make a good quarterback.*

Hess asked Tim to get down on one knee and throw the ball

as far as he could. The youngster heaved the ball 30 yards in the air. After that, Tim was lining up behind center. "Guess that's my claim to fame," Coach Hess said years later.

People who knew Tim during his Pop Warner days are still telling Tebow stories—like the time he lined up behind center on his team's 20-yard line and saw the tackles cheating a bit. Instead of taking the snap and tossing the ball to the tailback—the play called in the huddle—Tim ran a quarterback sneak . . . all the way into the end zone, 80 yards away.

When Tim wasn't flying past defenders, he was running over players who dared get in his way. Linebackers who searched for Tim in the open field to deliver a hit stopped searching after the first time they collided with him.

Then there was the tremendous arm strength his father first saw back on the farm. Tim was heaving the ball 50 yards in the air as a sixth grader, and everyone who saw him throw thought, *Wait until he gets to high school.*

Except Tim was homeschooled. How was he going to play high school football when he wasn't even going to *go* to high school?

LOOKING UP TO A HERO

When he was young, Tim's parents encouraged him to pick a hero who modeled humility and modesty. They suggested just the person for the nine-year-old to emulate: Danny Wuerffel, the University of Florida quarterback who would win the Heisman Trophy in 1996 and lead the Gators to a national championship the same season.

Dad and Mom both graduated from the University of Florida,

so the Tebows were Gator fans who occasionally attended some games. Older sister Katie was making plans to enroll there in the fall of 1997. Tim, who slept under a Gator bedspread and had a bathroom that sported a Gator shower curtain, tacked a giant color poster of Danny Wuerffel to his bedroom wall. Before the start of the 1996 season, young Tim enjoyed seeing his hero at Gators Fan Day.

Tim liked how the Florida QB was quick to give God credit and living his life to bring honor to Him. Danny loved quoting Proverbs 3:5–6 to the media: "Trust in the Lord with all your heart and lean not on your own understanding; in all your ways acknowledge him, and he will make your paths straight."

So Tim wanted to be like Danny Wuerffel—and to play quarterback like him. Would he get his chance?

The answer was yes, thanks to a new Florida law that allowed homeschooled children to take part in interscholastic sports. A homeschooling mom named Brenda Dickinson spearheaded a two-year battle in the Florida legislature that ended in 1996 with the passage of a law providing home-educated students with the opportunity to participate on athletic teams at their local schools. In other words, if a child was schooled at home, he or she had to be "accommodated" and couldn't be kept off the interscholastic playing field.

Florida became one of 16 states that allowed homeschooled kids to play varsity sports at a traditional high school. Robby and Peter Tebow took advantage of that opportunity and played high school football at Trinity Christian Academy in Jacksonville, a K–12 school with 450 high school students.

When Tim reached ninth grade, he was itching to play at

Trinity as well. But Tim didn't start out playing quarterback. The Trinity Christian coach, Verlon Dorminey, looked at Tim's broad-shouldered build and lined him up on the varsity team at tight end on offense and linebacker on defense.

That was okay for his freshman year, but Tim wanted to play quarterback. Quarterbacks were the playmakers, the center of action. If you were going to *beat* the other team, you needed a quarterback who could make plays. Tim wanted to *lead* his team to victory, not depend on someone else making plays.

Coach Dorminey was open to the idea, but he had installed a Wing-T offense that relied heavily on the run. In his system, the quarterback made a lot of handoffs or ran off the option play. Little or no passing. This run-centered offense worked for Dorminey and the team: Trinity Christian won the Florida state championship in its division in 2002.

That's not what Bob Tebow wanted for his son, though. He knew Tim had a special gift for throwing the ball and that he needed to be on a team where he could shine as quarterback. He didn't want his son typecast at tight end or linebacker—grunt positions that take size. Quarterback—the position with the ultimate skill set—was where he needed to be.

If Tim was ever going to play quarterback in high school, he had to make his move. That's because quarterbacks establish themselves on the varsity team during their sophomore seasons. Maybe they don't play that much because a senior or a junior is ahead of them—but they take their place on the depth chart and learn the position on the practice field.

Since Trinity Christian didn't throw the ball—and since Tim didn't go to school there anyway—the Tebows starting shopping around. They found a public high school in nearby St. John's County where the coach, Craig Howard, ran a spread offense and liked to see the ball in the air.

The school was Nease High, and the football team hadn't been winning much. In fact, the Panthers were 2–8 the season before Tim arrived, 1–9 the year before that.

In other words, the perfect situation for Tim Tebow.

"We wanted to give Tim the opportunity to develop his God-given talent and to achieve his lifelong dream of playing quarterback," Bob said. "It wasn't that we were leaving an unsuccessful program to go to a successful one; it was the other way around."

There was one hitch, though: Tim had to live in the Nease High School district. The Tebow farm was situated in nearby Duval County.

The Tebows overcame that hurdle by renting an apartment close to Nease High in Ponte Vedra Beach. They put the family farm up for sale and signed up Tim to play football at Nease High. Pam and Tim did Bible studies and worked through his home school curriculum in the morning and early afternoon, then it was off to football practice at Nease High. The family farm never sold, so the Tebows eventually kept their homestead. But as Bob said, "We were willing to make that sacrifice. We made sacrifices for all our children."

Nease High—named after Allen Duncan Nease, a pioneer of Florida's reforestation and conservation efforts in the mid-twentieth century—was a public high school of about 1,600 students that played in Florida's 4A division. In Florida—a hotbed of high school football talent—schools competed in one of eight classifications, all based on enrollment. The largest classification in the state was 6A, and the smallest was 1B, so there were some schools in Florida classed higher than Nease and many classed lower.

Tim's talent could not be denied nor his work ethic overlooked. Coach Howard certainly noticed. "People can always lead with words but not always with actions," he said. "Timmy was the hardest worker I've ever been around. His work ethic was uncompromising, and all of those around him were affected by it."

Tim won the starting quarterback role in his sophomore season. Based on their history of losing, though, the Panthers figured to be the patsy on other teams' schedules. "We had six road games my sophomore year, and we were the homecoming game for all six of them," Tim said. "Talk about embarrassing."

But the Panthers, with their sophomore quarterback making throws, bullying his way through the line, and never giving up, acquitted themselves well during Tim's first season. Nease High finished 5–5 in 2003, a turnaround that portended better things to come.

BREAKOUT TIME

Tim had a big junior season in high school football. He enjoyed a strong cast around him to block, catch the ball, and stop the other team from scoring. In that respect, he was in the right place at the right time.

But Tim didn't go to school with his teammates. No friendly banter between classes or hanging out in the cafeteria during lunchtime. No horseplay or kidding around while gathering for a school assembly.

Yet Tim won over his teammates with his hard work on

the practice field, his unyielding determination to win, and his respectful attitude toward players and coaches. His teammates saw him as a nice, fun-loving guy—as one of them, even though he didn't go to classes during the school day.

For Tim, all the pieces were in place for a successful 2004 season. He was big and brawny, pushing past 6 feet, 2 inches tall, and weighing in north of 215 pounds. He single-handedly, by force of will and great talent, took a nothing team and turned it into an 11–2 powerhouse that advanced to the third round of the state playoffs.

If Tim wasn't pile-driving his way through the line like a determined fullback, he was hitting receivers between the numbers and lofting bombs into the end zone. Suddenly, rival schools didn't want anything to do with Nease High on homecoming night.

Coach Howard saw that he had a thoroughbred in Tim, and he let him run—and throw and throw and throw. Before the season was over, Tim had set the state record for total yards in a season with 5,576—of which 4,304 yards came from passing, for an average of 331 yards per game. He was also responsible for 70 touchdowns in 13 games—and that's not a typo: he tossed 46 touchdown passes (more than three per game) and ran for 24 more, making himself the ultimate "dual-threat" quarterback. He threw just six interceptions all season.

NO FACE IN THE CROWD

The honors rolled in for Tim Tebow following his junior season: Florida Dairy Farmers Player of the Year, All-State, and a third-place finish in Florida's Mr. Football balloting. He rose up the college recruiting Web sites such as Rivals.com and

SuperPrep.com like a hit song on a Top 40 chart. Scout.com even ranked him third nationally among high school quarterback prospects.

Sportswriter John Patton of the *Gainesville Sun* called Tim "the best high school football player I have ever seen"—even though he still had another season of high school ball left. Then, at the end of his junior season, *Sports Illustrated* printed his smiling mug in the magazine's "Faces in the Crowd" section.

The hype machine was pulling out of the driveway.

College coaches descended upon the Tebow family like solicitous salesmen carrying briefcases filled with wares. Eighty schools offered him scholarships and pleaded with him to come play for State U—but the only ones the Tebows actively considered were Miami, Michigan, Southern California, Alabama, and Bob and Pam's alma mater—the University of Florida.

But the Tebow parents didn't want Tim to make a verbal commitment to any college at the end of his junior year. They weren't ready yet; they wanted to take their time.

As word got around about this Tebow kid in Florida, an ESPN producer smelled a good story and sent a camera crew from Murrah Communications to Nease High during the summer of 2005. Coach Howard gave the film crew full access throughout the 2005 season—training camp, locker room, practice field, and the sidelines during the games. The coach even allowed himself to be miked.

This would be an ESPN *Faces in Sports* program, and the title of the hour-long documentary was *The Chosen One*. The storyline was Tim's record-setting career at Nease, his senior season, and the team's drive toward a state championship. The program ended with Tim's postseason announcement in December of which school he had chosen to attend.

The Chosen One is still worth watching. (It's readily available in five segments on YouTube.) It's a chance to watch a youthful Tim—wearing a No. 5 jersey—not only develop as a player but also into a young man learning to deal with intense media scrutiny. He handled everything with aplomb. There are many amazing scenes:

- Tim and his dad sitting at the dinner table in their ranch house, sifting through a mound of recruiting letters from the nation's top college football coaches—many handwritten—informing Tim that he'd be a "welcome addition" to their program.

- Pam perched at a small table with Tim in their Ponte Vedra apartment, working through a home school lesson together.

- Bob and Pam talking about their years in the Philippines and a clip of Tim preaching before hundreds of Filipino kids when he was only 15 years old.

- Tim in the locker room, firing up his team before a big game like it was the end of the world.

- Tim suffering a broken leg but refusing to be pulled out of the game, and later hobbling 29 yards into the end zone on sheer guts.

- Bob standing in a grassy field, reading Proverbs
  22:6 from his Bible ("Train a child in the way he
  should go . . .").

THE NEXT BIG THING

The cameras were there when Nease High opened the 2005 sea-son with a road game against highly regarded Hoover High in Hoover, Alabama, which aired *nationally* on ESPN. Even though Nease lost 50–29, everyone agreed that Tim put on quite a show.

The national media had now officially anointed Tim as the Next Big Thing. Tim backed that up by putting together another record-breaking season and leading Nease to its first state championship, which the Panthers took home after beating Armwood High 44–37 in the state final. Tim's stats: 237 yards and four touchdowns in the air, 153 yards and two touchdowns on the ground . . . and jokes about selling popcorn at halftime.

All that was left for Tim to do was to announce which college had won his heart. The family narrowed down the choices to Alabama or Florida, then Bob and Pam stepped aside. *It's your decision, son. You're the one who's going to be playing there. You pray about it and let the Lord guide your steps.*

Three days after pocketing the state championship, Tim—dressed in a dark coat, blue shirt, and white tie—took the podium at the Nease High Performing Arts Center. He stood before an auditorium packed with hundreds of screaming teenagers and Gator partisans. ESPN's cameras were there—live.

That morning, Tim and his golden lab, Otis, had gone for a long walk among the pine trees and oaks that outlined their homestead. He sat next to a lake and thought and prayed about what he should do. He and his parents liked both coaches; Urban Meyer at Florida and Mike Shula at Alabama were God-fearing men of strong character. Both schools were capable of winning the national title. This was one of those win-win decisions.

In the end, the edge went to Florida. Coach Meyer ran a spread offense, just like Coach Howard did at Nease, and the family's deep roots at the University of Florida couldn't be glossed over. Mom and Dad went there, and Pam's father had played basketball there. Tim had grown up in Gator Nation. The school was close to home, which meant his parents and siblings—Team Tebow—could watch him play at Ben Hill Griffin Stadium, also known as "The Swamp."

Bob and Pam held their breath as Tim straddled the podium, looked straight into the camera, and said, "I will be playing college football next year at the University of Florida."

THE GREEN SHIRT AT GATOR NATION

How do you describe the four-year college career that launched Tebowmania and lifted Tim into the living rooms of millions of Americans?

Do you start with Tim's freshman year and his double-pump "jump pass" for a one-yard touchdown against LSU that had announcers raving about his originality? Or was it the *Braveheart* scene at Florida State—when Tim's face and white jersey were smeared in reddish "war paint" from the end zone? Or how about the controversy when he started inscribing Bible verses on his eye black?

When Tim announced, "I will be playing college football next year at the University of Florida," he was talking about playing the very *next* season, not kicking back and enjoy a low-stress redshirt year. In January 2006, within a few weeks of his announcement, Tim enrolled at Florida. He didn't have to wait to graduate with his high school class—he *was* the class.

Tim was eligible to enroll in college because he had completed his studies and had taken an SAT test in ninth grade. By becoming a University of Florida student, Tim made himself eligible to participate in spring football practice—the rehearsal time for the fall season.

In the college football lexicon, he was not a red shirt but a "green shirt"—green as in "go early." A green-shirt athlete is someone who graduates from high school in December of his senior year and immediate enrolls in college so he can participate in spring practice—and get a head start on learning the system and moving up the depth chart.

Chris Leak was a senior and a three-year starter for the Gators, so he was the No. 1 quarterback. But Tim wasn't willing to rock on his cleats on the Florida sidelines, helmet in hand, waiting for his chance to play. He was going to *compete* for the job, even as a true freshman.

At the annual Orange and Blue scrimmage game, which ended three weeks of spring practice, Tim looked sharp in leading his Orange team to a 24–6 victory. "Chris Leak is our quarterback, and Tim Tebow is a guy who is going to play," Coach Meyer said afterward. "There is no quarterback controversy. There are two great young men who we are going to build an offense around to be successful."

Translation: *We're going to start Chris Leak so our freshman quarterback doesn't have the pressure of being the starter, but he's going to be playing a lot.*

Tim did play a lot as a true freshman in 2006, even though Florida had arguably the toughest schedule in the nation. He scored the first time he touched the ball in a Florida uniform—on a goal-line keeper against Southern Mississippi. Coach Meyer continued to play Tim in spot situations, bringing him along slowly. But in the third game of the season, against Tennessee—in Knoxville, before 106,818 rabid Volunteer fans—Meyer threw Tim into the fire. In the fourth quarter, with the Gators trailing by six points, Florida faced a fourth-and-one inside Tennessee territory. Meyer flung Tim into the game, Tim punched out two yards to keep the drive alive, and Chris Leak took his place and led the Gators to the winning score.

Against Southeastern Conference opponents, Florida fell into a familiar pattern throughout the season—fall behind early, then claw its way back. Against LSU, Tim unveiled his first "jump pass." With Florida knocking on the door at the one-yard line, Tim took the snap five yards behind center, ran toward the pile, then suddenly leaped and lobbed a rainbow pass to his tight end, Tate Casey. Touchdown!

It was a clever gadget play—known in the Florida playbook as Trey Left, 341 Stop Bend X Fake—that hadn't been seen since the days of Bronko Nagurski and leather helmets. With retro panache, Tim would make two more jump passes in his career at Florida.

After defeating LSU, Florida—now ranked No. 2 in the country—suffered its first hiccup of the season—against Auburn in a 27–17 road loss in an ESPN *GameDay* match-up. A controversial fourth-quarter fumble by Chris Leak, with Florida trailing 21–17 but driving for the potential win, sealed the Gators' fate.

That was the only smudge on an otherwise golden 2006 Florida football season. The Gators ran the table the rest of the way, beating Georgia, Florida State, and Arkansas (in the SEC Championship Game) to climb back to No. 2 in the polls and into the BCS National Championship Game—played at the new University of Phoenix Stadium in Glendale, Arizona—against top-ranked Ohio State.

Florida thrashed the Buckeyes 41–14 to win its second national football championship in school history—the other one happening in 1996 when Danny Wuerffel was the Gator quarterback. The victory also helped mark the first time in college sports history that the NCAA college basketball and football titles rested in the same trophy case—the Gator men's basketball team having won the national championship in the spring of 2006. Chris Leak played clutch football, and when Tim spelled him, he found the soft spots in the Ohio State defense with his power running, scoring one touchdown and throwing for another on college football's biggest night.

At a well-attended victory celebration at Ben Hill Griffin Stadium a few days later, a special guest was invited onstage to hand Chris Leak the Most Valuable Player trophy. Who was the surprise invitee?

Danny Wuerffel, Tim's boyhood hero.

After telling Chris they were now the only starting Gator quarterbacks in Florida football history to wear national championship rings, Danny paused for a moment and turned to the freshman quarterback standing nearby. Everyone wondered what Danny Wonderful would say.

"There's room for another one next year, Timmy Tebow," he said.

The baton had been officially passed.

IT'S TIM'S TEAM NOW

With Chris Leak graduated, the Florida Gators were now Tim Tebow's team. Everyone knew it. A FLORIDA FOLK HERO PREPARES TO FACE REALITY read a preseason headline in the *New York Times,* which knew an important story when it saw one.

The story noted that during the offseason, Tim had sung "She Thinks My Tractor's Sexy" onstage with country singer Kenny Chesney, preached in two prisons "so convincingly" that 200 hardened criminals began weeping and became Christians, and dealt with coeds camping outside his apartment—some who asked him to autograph their underwear.

Saying that Tim had a big year in 2007, after having just turned 19, would be like saying the New York Yankees and Murderer's Row had a big year in 1927. In the season opener against Western Kentucky, Tim led the Gators to touchdowns on their first four possessions. He finished his first career start by going 13-for-17 for 300 yards with three touchdown passes and one rushing touchdown in a 49–3 wipeout. Another warm-up game against Troy was also a Tebow gem.

Tim's first big test was the 2007 SEC opener against Tennessee, which was played before 90,707 hot and sticky fans at The Swamp. Tim was unstoppable, running and throwing the ball up and down the field almost at will. When he scored on a seven-yard touchdown run in the second quarter, CBS cameras caught safety and roommate Tony Joiner planting a kiss on Tim's left cheek as a reward.

The lovefest continued until Tim's first interception of the season, which resulted in a 93-yard Volunteer touchdown to pull Tennessee to within 28–20 in the third quarter. After that, though, the rout was on—31 unanswered Florida points as Tim racked up 61 yards on the ground and 299 yards through the air.

HE15MAN TIME

This amalgamation of Joe Montana and Jim Brown added up to two words: *Tebow hysteria*. Some zealous Florida fans created TimTebowFacts.com, where fans could contribute a list of Tim's most legendary, Paul Bunyanesque accomplishments. T-shirt makers started silk-screening "He15man" on Gator blue shirts, and the ESPN and CBS football pundits declared that Tim was the early-season favorite for the Heisman Trophy, even though they were careful to insert a "but"—*but a sophomore has never won the Heisman, Lou.* They pointed out that ex-Gator quarterback Rex Grossman didn't win one in 2001 and running back Darren McFadden of Arkansas didn't pick up the Heisman in 2006, even though both players had superb seasons—so it was likely never to happen.

Tim's legend expanded the following week against Ole Miss when he took over a road game in Oxford, Mississippi, that Florida looked destined to lose. The Gators struggled most of the game until five consecutive Tebow runs set up a short field goal that gave the Gators a 30–24 lead with less than five minutes to play. After a stop, when Florida needed to run time off the clock, Tim carried the ball six consecutive times to secure a victory and keep the No. 3 Gators undefeated for the season. In all, Tim accounted for all four Gator touchdowns and 427 of his team's 507 total yards.

But the Gators lost three of their next four games, falling to Auburn at home, LSU in Baton Rouge, and Georgia at the neutral Jacksonville site. Tim didn't do much against Georgia because of a right shoulder contusion he suffered the previous week against Kentucky. When he was in the game, the Georgia rush menaced him the entire afternoon, sacking him six times. It seemed like he was running for his life the entire game.

Tim, who had wiped tears from his face after walking off the field at LSU, had to fight back moisture in his eyes at the postgame podium as he faced the media following the tough loss to interstate rival Georgia. "I do take them [the losses] hard," he said, "but that's because I am so passionate."

Listening to the Georgia game on her computer, via the Internet, was his sister Christy. It was the middle of the night in Bangladesh, where she had recently moved with her husband, Joey, and their one-year-old daughter, Claire, to do missionary work.

After the game, Tim spoke by phone with Christy, who told him how she and her family were adjusting to life in one of the poorest countries of the world. He felt chastened. "It makes you realize that everything that happens in this game doesn't really mean that much in the grand scheme of things," Tim said. "Losing to Georgia is not the biggest thing in the world."

The Gators—and Tim—bounced back and played a perfect November, even though his shoulder bruise still bothered him. He shook off the pain and ran for five touchdowns against South Carolina, set a career-best in passing yards with 338 against Florida Atlantic, and dominated intrastate rival Florida State at

The Swamp, despite suffering a displaced fracture on his non-throwing right hand. He played 30 downs with the busted hand and laid out his final argument to win the Heisman Trophy. In the closing moments of a one-sided 45–12 victory against the Seminoles, Gator cheerleaders struck Heisman poses—carriage slightly bent, leg up, right arms thrust out to stiff-arm a tackler—on the sidelines.

Florida finished the season a respectable 9–3 and earned a January 1, 2008, date with Michigan at the Citrus Bowl. But the big story in Gator Nation was whether Tim would capture the Heisman Trophy.

In the 72-year history of the award, Heisman voters—sportswriters and past winners—had never handed the award to a sophomore, reserving the honor for upperclassmen. It seemed to be one of those unwritten rules.

Wait your turn, son.

But who had played better than Tim Tebow in 2007? Some said Arkansas running back Darren McFadden deserved it after failing to strike the pose in 2006, or that University of Hawaii senior quarterback Colt Brennan should win because of his outlandish passing stats—but no one played better than Tim in 2007.

In early December, Tim and his family flew to New York City for the Heisman Trophy ceremony at the Nokia Theatre in Times Square. It turned out to be a family reunion when Christy and her family flew to New York from Bangladesh.

When he heard his name announced as the winner, a beaming Tim sprang out of his chair and hugged his parents, then Gator coach Urban Meyer. Standing on the stage with all the surviving Heisman winners since 1935 was his boyhood idol, Danny

Wuerffel, who greeted him with another hug.

After first thanking God for the ability to play football, Tim thanked his teammates back home, his coaches, and especially his parents: "I want to thank my dad, who taught me a work ethic every day growing up, and my mom, who instilled in me so many great characters."

It's okay, Tim. This was live TV before millions of viewers. We know what you meant: Mom instilled in you so many great characteristics.

Football commentators agreed that being the first NCAA Division 1 quarterback ever to have a "20/20" season—22 rushing touchdowns and 29 touchdown passes—sealed the deal with Heisman voters. Tim, the youngest Heisman winner ever at 20 years of age, accepted the trophy with a blue cast on his right hand.

The 2007 season ended with a 41–35 loss to Michigan on New Year's Day. Tim played with a soft cast to protect his mending right hand. Although the defeat was disappointing to the Gators and their fans, they knew Tim would return the following season—all healed up and with a talented, more experienced team surrounding him.

Deep within, a passion burned within Tim for a national championship ring—the one Danny Wuerffel said there was room for.

PROMISE MADE, PROMISE KEPT
In Gator lore, it's called "The Promise."

Here's the situation. Through the first three games of the 2008 season, Florida was pancaking opponents. Victories over Hawaii,

Miami, and Tennessee were as lopsided as some girls' basketball games. The talk in Gator Nation was that this team could go undefeated—something never before done in the history of Florida football.

Ole Miss was coming to Gainesville a decided underdog—22 points according to the oddsmakers. Quarterbacking the Rebels was Jevan Snead, who (1) "decommitted" to Florida after Tim announced he would become a Gator and (2) enrolled at Texas but transferred to Ole Miss after getting beat out by Colt McCoy. So you could excuse Snead if he had a bit of an inferiority complex playing in Tim Tebow's house.

But Snead was a gamer, as was the entire Rebel team. They made plays, recovered fumbles from Tim and star running back Percy Harvin, and "hung around"—football-speak for a team that should have been put away after falling behind 17–7.

The game was tied 24–24 midway through the fourth quarter when the Rebels—playing with house money since they were still in the game—got lucky (if you're a Gator fan) or made a great effort (if you're an Ole Miss fan). Snead found Shay Hodge all alone on the sideline for an 86-yard scoring play to give Ole Miss a 31–24 lead with 5:26 to play.

Tim and the Gators hitched up their pants and scored quickly when Percy Harvin scooted 15 yards for a touchdown. The extra point attempt, however, was foiled when an Ole Miss player hurdled a blocker to tip the kick—an illegal tactic in organized football. Coach Meyer argued his case to no avail.

Disaster! Instead of being tied, Florida was down 31–30. With 3:28 left, the Florida defense needed a quick stop, which it got. Tim had the offense driving, but the Gators faced a fourth-and-one on the Ole Miss 32-yard line. Do you go for a 49-yard field goal to win the game or get the first down and try to get closer?

The Gators were going for it—but the Rebel defense stuffed Tim at the line of scrimmage.

Game over.

When Tim faced the media afterward, he was asked if he wanted to forget the loss. "I don't want to," an emotional Tim replied. "I want it to stay in our hearts and keep hurting so that we'll never let this happen again."

Then he paused and gathered his thoughts. What spilled forth came to be known as "The Promise":

> "I just want to say one thing" . . . *deep breath* . . . "to the fans and everybody in Gator Nation" . . . *pause, sniffle* . . . "I'm sorry. I'm extremely sorry. We were hoping for an undefeated season. That was my goal, something Florida's never done here.
>
> "I promise you one thing: a lot of good will come out of this. You will never see any player in the entire country who will play as hard as I will play the rest of the season. You will never see someone push the rest of the team as hard as I will push everybody the rest of the season.
>
> "You will never see a team play harder than we will the rest of the season. God bless."

With that, Tim exited the post-game podium—and Florida didn't lose another game the rest of the 2008 season.

THREE-SECOND EVANGELISM

Two weeks after the Ole Miss debacle, Tim took the field against LSU suited up like he always was for a home game: blue-jersey-and-white-pants Gator uniform, football pads, cleats, and a helmet. Underneath his eyes, on his upper cheeks, were two black rectangular patches.

Called "eye black," this dark mixture of beeswax, paraffin, and carbon is applied under the eyes to reduce glare. Sunlight or stadium lights can impair the view of an airborne ball.

Tim began wearing smudges of eye black during Florida day games, but before this important test against the defending national champion LSU Tigers, he had someone in the locker room use a white grease pencil to print **PHL** on top of the black strip underneath his right eye and **4:13** under the left eye. The idea was an out-of-the-box, genuine, clever way to share the biblical message of Philippians 4:13—"I can do all things through Christ who strengthens me"—with millions of football viewers.

Remember, the camera loved Tim Tebow. Throughout the game, TV producers in the truck inserted as many close-up "cutaways" of Tim as they could—like when he was barking out signals in the shotgun or swallowing a spritz of Gatorade on the Florida sideline with his helmet off.

The eye-black-with-a-Bible-verse-story took on a life of its own after the LSU victory, and in every game for the rest of his college career, Tim "shared" a Bible verse with his football-watching audience.

Talk about three-second evangelism. These spiritual billboards sent millions to their Bibles or computers to find out what the verse of the week said. What Tim did with his eye black messages was share his Christian faith, jumpstart a national conversation—and add to his legend.

Tim took some hits from the media, though. "There's something strange about the alliance of modern sports and religion," a columnist with *The Tennessean* opined. Others felt religion and sports should not mix. "Why must he rub it in my face?" was the sentiment of *Orlando Sentinel*'s David Whitley.

None of the potshots fazed Tim or changed the way he played through the rest of the 2008 season. After "The Promise," he actually accomplished what he pledged to do: grab his team by the scruff of the neck and yank them over the national championship goal line with an eight-game winning streak that earned fourth-ranked Florida a date with No. 1-ranked Alabama for the SEC Championship. Alabama was a solid 10-point favorite for this monster match-up in Atlanta.

With star running back Percy Harvin out of the game, an even heavier offensive load fell on Tim's shoulders. The way he took over in the fourth quarter with his team down 20–17, engineering two touchdown drives, ranked right at the top of the Tebow highlight reel. He kept the chains moving by throwing into tight spots and battering the 'Bama defense with muscular runs.

"You knew he was going to lead us to victory," said receiver Carl Moore following a 31–20 triumph that catapulted the Gators into the BCS National Championship Game against top-ranked Oklahoma. "You looked into his eyes, and you could see he was intense. We were all intense."

A HEISMAN REPEAT?

After the Alabama conquest, Tim learned he was again a finalist for the Heisman Trophy—so he and his family repeated the trip to Manhattan. This time at the Nokia Theatre, he was the first to hug Sam Bradford after the Sooner quarterback's name was announced as college football's most outstanding player.

Tim did receive plenty of recognition for his stellar 2008 season—like the Maxwell Award and the Manning Award—but none meant more to him than taking a phone call from Danny Wuerffel, who informed Tim that he'd won the 2008 Wuerffel Trophy, presented annually to the college football player who combines exemplary community service with athletic and academic achievement.

After retiring from professional football in 2004, Danny and his family joined Desire Street Ministries in one of New Orleans' toughest and poorest neighborhoods.

"He's just an amazing young man, an amazing football player," Danny said. "It's funny how things go back and forth. Maybe one day my son will win the Tebow Trophy."

CHAMPIONSHIP GAME MOTIVATION

Florida had one month to prepare for the national championship game, which felt very much like a home game to the Gators since they would be playing the Sam Bradford-led Oklahoma Sooners at Dolphins Stadium in Miami. What made the matchup even more intriguing was that Florida and Oklahoma had *never* played each other before.

Tim didn't have to reach too deep to summon pregame motivation. The acrid smell of the September defeat to Ole Miss still singed his nostrils, and losing the Heisman Trophy vote—despite winning more first-place votes, 309 to 300—certainly smarted.

When Sooners cornerback Dominique Franks popped off that Tim would probably be the fourth-best quarterback in the Big 12 Conference—well, that's all the incentive Tim needed in his wheelhouse.

Properly inspired, Tim decided to forgo **EPH 4:31** and inscribe his eye black with the most widely quoted Bible verse—and one considered the summary of the central doctrine in Christianity—**John 3:16**:

> "For God so loved the world that he gave his one and only Son, that whoever believes in him shall not perish but have eternal life."

Once the BCS championship game started, though, Tim was out of sync. Two interceptions came on balls he shouldn't have thrown. The Oklahoma defense swarmed the line of scrimmage and shut down Tim as well as the Gator ground game. Florida scored only one touchdown in the first half, which would normally put a team in a big hole against a team like Oklahoma, a juggernaut that averaged 50 points a game and rarely had to send their punt team onto the field. But the Gator defense was up to the challenge, and the score was tied 7–7 at halftime.

The Florida defense continued making big stops after intermission, and then Tim got into the flow, converting several big third downs by running and throwing, staking Florida to a small lead. Tim then put a cherry atop the BCS championship sundae when he lobbed a four-yard jump pass to David Nelson with 3:07 left in the game, giving Florida a commanding 24–14 lead.

After a four-down stop, all the Florida offense had to do was run out the clock. An exuberant Tim got a bit over-the-top when he celebrated a big 13-yard rush by aiming a "Gator Chomp" at Oklahoma's Nic Harris. Tim fully extended his arms, one above the other, then moved them together and apart to symbolize the opening and closing of an alligator's mouth. An official threw a yellow flag for taunting, and Florida was penalized 15 yards.

"I was pretty excited," Tim said after the game. "Just gave it a little Gator Chomp, and it was also for the fans. I think they kind of enjoyed it." Gator fans also enjoyed how Tim made "The Promise" come true. Everyone on the Florida team believed the Ole Miss loss turned around the season.

Funny how a loss can turn out to be a blessing in more ways than one.

And on a side note, Google reported that searches for "John 3:16" totaled 93 million during and immediately after the BCS victory by Florida.

"I'M COMING BACK"

After the national championship-clinching win over Oklahoma, a plaque was affixed to the James W. "Bill" Heavener Football Complex outside The Swamp. Entitled "The Promise," the silver tablet immortalized Tim's emotional post-game speech following the Ole Miss loss.

The idea to mount Tim's heartfelt declaration came from Coach Meyer, who thought Tim's words would inspire future generations of Gators, much the same way Knute Rockne's "Win one for the Gipper" speech back in 1928 had ignited Notre Dame teams over the decades.

Quite an honor—especially for a college football player with one season left to play. Or was Tim bolting to the NFL? He was eligible to turn pro.

"Let's do it again!" he shouted to an estimated 42,000 Gator fans celebrating the team's national championship at The Swamp three days after the victory in Miami. "I'm coming back!"

A few days later, *Sports Illustrated*'s cover showed Tim about to slap his palms in that infamous Gator Chomp against Oklahoma. The headline: NOT DONE YET: TWO TITLES IN THREE YEARS, AND TIM TEBOW IS COMING BACK FOR MORE.

Tim never thought seriously about passing up his senior year to play in the NFL, but he *did* start giving a great deal of thought to what Bible verses he would inscribe on his eye black during his final season in college. Before each game in 2009, Tim lettered a new Bible verse on his eye black, sending millions of fans to their computers to do a Google search.

It turned out Bob Tebow got a preacher after all.

A FAREWELL AT THE SWAMP

For Tim's final home game, against Florida State—Senior Day— Gator fans were urged to wear eye black, with or without an inscribed Bible verse. After Florida whipped its intrastate rival, the Gators had a sparkling 12–0 regular season record, had been ranked No.1 all season, and were two games away from completing the program's first-ever perfect season.

The stage was set for back-to-back national championships, but first there was some business to conduct against Alabama in the SEC Championship Game, a rematch from the year before held in Atlanta's Georgia Dome.

This time, it was all Crimson Tide. The Florida defense

allowed Alabama to convert 11 of 15 third-down opportunities, which kept the Tide rolling down the field and chewing up the game possession clock. Alabama's offense was on the field for 39 minutes, 27 seconds, 20 minutes longer than Florida's.

Instead of giving the Tide a hard-fought game early on, the Gators went meekly into the night, losing 32–13. Their 22-game win streak was toast, the dream of a perfect season rudely ended.

The enduring image from the game is Tim on one knee with his team hopelessly behind as the clock ticks away, tears streaming through his eye black and down his face. He barely held it together during a post-game interview with CBS' sideline reporter, Tracy Wolfson.

"Tim Tearbow" is how some bloggers lit him up, but Tim had one game left in his college career—a January 1 date with No. 5 Cincinnati in the Sugar Bowl.

LOW THROW

If you look at Tim's performance at the 2010 Sugar Bowl, you would think he single-handedly destroyed the Bearcats. He put on a passing exhibition, completing his first 12 passes and going 20-for-23 in the first half for 320 yards and three touchdowns. When it was all over, he had torched Cincinnati for 482 passing yards and supplied the perfect ending to a storied four-year career. The 51–24 annihilation of the previously unbeaten Bearcats left Florida as the only BCS team ever to win at least 13 games in back-to-back seasons.

You'd think Tim would be carried off the field and hailed by the media as one of the greatest college quarterbacks ever. Team Tebow, however, woke up the next day to a media drumbeat that started as a whisper but gained concussive force almost overnight: *Tim Tebow is not first-round draft material for the National Football League. In fact, he should consider a position change to tight end.*

In other words, back to the future.

Here's what happened:

With the Sugar Bowl game out of hand, the Fox commentators in the booth, Thom Brennaman and former Baltimore Ravens coach Brian Billick, tossed the topic of Tim's future into the air and batted it around between beer commercials—oops, during lulls in the action.

Does Tim have what it takes to "play at the next level" and become an NFL quarterback?

Cue up the slo-mo of Tim dropping back to pass.

Using a telestrator, Billick dissected Tim's passing motion like a high school biology teacher peeling back the innards of a frog. "You're going to have to change everything he does," the former Ravens coach declared. "He has a windup delivery. He carries the ball too low. And he needs to read his progressions. He's a heck of a player, but how do you make him a first-round pick when you have to change so much?"

Billick's critique certainly made for interesting TV: a former NFL coach slicing up a legendary college player in the midst of the most dominating performance of his career. But what Billick did was bring to light the whispering campaign among NFL general managers and their coaching staffs about Tim's throwing motion—the elongated swoop of his left arm prior to releasing the ball.

The conventional wisdom among NFL cognoscenti was

hardening like spackling compound. If Tim wasn't worth a first-round pick in the 2010 NFL draft, was he capable of even playing quarterback at the professional level?

PLENTY OF PREDRAFT DRAMA

The instant the 2010 Sugar Bowl game clock struck 00:00, Chase Heavener, who was standing on the floor of the New Orleans Superdome, turned on his Canon 5D Mark II camera—capable of shooting high-quality digital video.

Chase, the son of Bill Heavener (after whom the Heavener Football Complex next to The Swamp is named), was initializing work on a documentary about Tim's road to the NFL. Filming couldn't start until Tim's college career was officially over—to preserve his amateur status—so Chase and his small film crew waited patiently for the final seconds to tick off the Superdome scoreboard. The young filmmaker planned to produce a film about Tim's life from the end of the Sugar Bowl through his first game in the NFL.

It looked like there would be enough drama between the Sugar Bowl and the 2010 NFL draft to fill a miniseries. Tim's opening episode began with the Senior Bowl—a postseason college football exhibition game for graduating seniors played in Mobile, Alabama, in late January. With National Football League coaches and personnel monitoring a week of practices as well as the game, the Senior Bowl would be a showcase for the best prospects in the upcoming NFL draft.

Tim opted to play in the Senior Bowl because he wanted to improve his deteriorating draft standing. Following the Sugar Bowl, NFL scouts were telling reporters—anonymously—that

Tim figured to go in the third round and might have to think about playing tight end or H-back, a combination tight end/full-back position. Since Tim wasn't ready to abandon his dream of playing quarterback in the NFL—a yearning of his since he was six years old—he didn't shy away from a week of Senior Bowl practices . . . or from working on his ball placement, footwork, and release.

Team Tebow was aware of the NFL's reservations about his mechanics and loopy throwing motion. In fact, he made the decision to reinvent himself *before* the Senior Bowl by attending the D1 Sports Training facility in Cool Springs, Tennessee, outside Nashville. Tim was one of 18 former college players working out with D1's coaches and trainers.

Tim had visited several other training facilities before deciding on D1, which was co-owned by quarterback Peyton Manning. (Now isn't that ironic?) Waiting for him were several experienced coaches: Marc Trestman, a former quarterbacks coach with Tampa Bay, Cleveland, and Minnesota; Zeke Bratkowski, a longtime NFL coach; former NFL head coach Sam Wyche; and Arizona State University offensive coordinator Noel Mazzone.

The D1 coaches worked Tim hard: two hours in the weight room, two hours on the field doing speed work, two hours on quarterback-specific drills, and two hours watching film and studying NFL terminology. Capturing it all was Chase Heavener and his film crew, and the D1 staff downloaded their super slow motion footage into their computers and used the film to show Tim how he could improve his five-step drop, seven-step drop, and throwing motion.

After spending a week in Cool Springs working on his

fundamentals, Tim flew to Mobile for the Senior Bowl. He was far from 100 percent: he was battling strep throat, a 103-degree temperature, and a skeptical football media that smelled blood in the water.

When the Senior Bowl was over, Tim can be excused for wishing he'd never played in Mobile. What a dreary late afternoon for No. 15: two fumbles (one lost), four yards rushing on four attempts, and 50 yards passing on 12 attempts, although he did complete eight of his throws. His critics were waiting with long knives.

"It's simple," said one NFL scout. "He's just not a very good quarterback prospect." Scouts Inc. gave Tim a D+ grade, noting that he "put all his weaknesses on display in a setting that did nothing but magnify them." Todd McShay, one of ESPN's NFL draft gurus, was more muted, declaring that Tim "is just not comfortable as a pro-style quarterback."

Only one voice wasn't pessimistic—the one belonging to a feeling-under-the-weather quarterback from Florida. Tim said he improved every day in practice and that his decision to play in the Senior Bowl was proof of his willingness to work hard on his fundamentals. Yet his subpar performance was enough for many NFL coaches and GMs to sell their stock in Tebow, Inc.—despite Tim's 66 percent college career passing percentage, the dozens of passing records he had set in high school and college, and his unworldly 88–16 touchdown-to-interception ratio as a Gator quarterback.

The fact that Tim had been a winner while playing a hybrid style of running back/passing quarterback—where he punished defenses with his left shoulder as well as with his left arm—didn't count for much in the minds of NFL brass or the draft experts.

COMBINE TIME

Tim returned to Cool Springs, still working to get rid of his swooping windup to pass the ball more quickly.

Was he overhauling his throwing motion? Not really, he said.

"It's more of a tweak," Tim told the press. "It's not necessarily changing my whole motion, just the way I'm holding the ball and kind of how I'm getting to where I'm throwing it. That's kind of the biggest problem we've seen, so that's what we're working on the most."

Tim practiced over and over holding the football higher—at shoulder height—after he received the snap. That movement effectively cut the loop from his throwing motion.

B-roll from Chase Heavener's film crew was released to ESPN and other media outlets showing Tim—under the gaze of his D1 coaches—dropping back seven steps with his left arm cocked high before delivering a tightly thrown pass. Even casual fans could tell his throwing motion was more compact and that he was "getting" to his releases quicker.

Between working on this throwing motion and hopping on private planes to make appearances at the Super Bowl, the Daytona 500, and the National Prayer Breakfast in Washington, D.C., Tim worked insanely hard during the month of February.

Kurt Hester, the corporate director of training at D1, said Tim's work ethic was a problem—"he just goes all-out all the time." Working around all the out-of-state appearances had been tough, Hester said, "but he won't quit. If I told him to get here at three in the morning, he'd get here at three in the morning."

Coming up during the first week of March was the National Invitational Camp, otherwise known as the NFL Combine, which is named after three scouting camps that "combined" or merged in 1985. More than 600 NFL personnel, including head coaches, general managers, and scouts, converged on Indianapolis for the camp.

The 329 players who expected to be drafted were invited to Lucas Oil Field to be weighed and measured and to participate in six measurable drills—40-yard dash, 225-pound bench press repetitions, vertical jump, broad jump, three-cone drill, and shuttle run—as well as individual drills. There would also be psychological evaluations and an IQ exam known as the Wonderlic Test.

The process can be dehumanizing; some call the NFL Combine the "Underwear Olympics" and compare the physicals to being poked and prodded like steers on a hoof. The extensive medical exams, which could last up to eight hours, had players clad only in undershorts, standing in a room full of NFL team doctors and scouts as they were weighed, measured, and subjected to a battery of tests—MRIs, EKGs, CT scans, X-rays, and more.

Aspiring NFL players dare not skip the Combine, and Tim flew to Indianapolis to participate, even though he said he would not participate in individual throwing drills. Tim said he would instead wait until the pro day at his alma mater to put his arm to the test in front of NFL evaluators.

Pro days are held at each university under conditions thought to be more favorable for the players. At their pro days, quarterbacks participate in passing drills, and position players run the 40-yard dash, make a vertical jump, do the three-cone drill, and undergo other physical tests in front of an array of NFL coaches and scouts.

The NFL Combine—an entirely different bird—is a four-day process that begins with a preliminary medical examination and orientation. During his first night in Indianapolis Tim went through a process called "speed dating"—where representatives of every NFL team sit at tables inside small rooms and conduct 10-to-15-minute interviews with each of the players.

If a prospect isn't in good shape physically, the NFL has a way of finding out. The second day is reserved for four extensive medical exams—eight doctors at a time, one from each of the 32 NFL teams. If players, especially quarterbacks, had fudged on their height and weight, it was now out in the open.

Here's how Tim Tebow measured up: 6-2¾, 236 pounds. Tim was usually listed at 6-3, so he wasn't too far off the mark.

For quarterbacks, the 40-yard dash ranks far down on the list of priorities; height, arm strength, quick release, escapability, leadership skills, and football knowledge are what matter to the NFL. Ditto for the standing broad jump, a drill where former Texas QB Colt McCoy excelled, vaulting nine feet, six inches, but Tim just beat him out, clearing nine feet, seven inches. Tim also wowed the scouts with his 38.5-inch vertical leap, which tied him for the Combine's all-time record for quarterbacks, held by Josh McCown. By way of comparison, Tim's leap was a half-inch higher than Michael Vick's in 2001. He completed five of the six measurable drills, passing on the 225-pound bench press repetitions so he could protect his throwing arm.

There was one individual drill Tim performed at the NFL Combine, however, where you could say his time was a revelation: in the three-cone drill, Tim ran a hell-blazing 6.66 seconds, which showed he was a real speed demon.

PRO DAYS AHEAD

With so much at stake—draft position, which team would pick them, and millions of dollars—quarterbacks aspiring to an NFL career leave little to chance. Very few throw at the NFL Combine because they will be passing to unfamiliar receivers at an unfamiliar venue. NFL coaches can also dictate which passing drills they would like to see at the Combine.

As they say at golf's biggest tournaments, you can't win a major on the first day, but you sure can lose it with a poor outing.

Tim was into his second month of working to get rid of his below-the-belt throwing motion and to perfect the above-the-shoulder delivery NFL coaches like to see in their quarterbacks. The more time he had to practice and improve his new technique, the better chance he had to impress coaches and scouts when it came time to throw at his pro day.

Tim was first to fire up for pro day, and as you would expect, the March 17 event at the University of Florida was a circus. "For all the television time, Internet bandwidth, and newsprint used to discuss Tim Tebow's new throwing motion, anything short of the southpaw walking onto Florida Field and throwing right-handed was found to be a bitter disappointment," wrote *Sports Illustrated*'s Andy Staples.

More than 3,000 spectators and 100 NFL personnel were on hand at The Swamp, including five head coaches and a couple of general managers. Tim wasn't the only Gator athlete under the microscope; teammates Carlos Dunlap, Joe Haden, Aaron Hernandez, and Maurkice Pouncey—all potential first-rounders—

were going through their pro day paces as well.

Tim threw for 45 minutes—outs, curls, hitches, posts, comebacks, and gos. He cocked the ball closer to his ear, released the ball much more quickly, and delivered tight spirals where they needed to be. He hit receiver David Nelson on a 45-yard post pattern—in stride. Next throw, the same 45-yard post but to the opposite side of the field, where the deep pass landed in Riley Cooper's arms in full gait.

Tim looked flat-out impressive. The backpedaling on his seven-step drops was an athletic work of art, his command of the field was sure, and his passing was on the money. The debut of his new throwing motion went off without a hitch.

Like the opening of a hit show on Broadway, Tim's new act drew raves. The consensus in the media was that he had shown "ridiculous" improvement. In less than an hour on his favorite field, Tim successfully pushed back a tide of coaching opinion that had threatened to sink his chances of ever playing quarterback in the NFL. He was once again a viable NFL quarterback prospect.

Between pro day and NFL draft day five weeks later, Tim scheduled private workouts with several NFL teams, including Seattle, Washington, and New England.

Tim also hoped to get a closer look from the Denver Broncos. During one of the "speed dates" at the NFL Combine, he had sat in a meeting room just a few feet apart from Josh McDaniels, the boyish-looking 33-year-old head coach of the Broncos. They were talking football, and the energy level rose as their eyes locked and their ideas spilled forth. In a word, they *clicked*.

The 15 minutes passed by way too quickly. Tim felt jacked as he left the room. He had met someone with the same passion for football that he had himself. Coach McDaniels was just as intense, just as juiced about finding a way to win in the NFL. He understood where Tim was coming from.

Tim stood up and shook hands with the Broncos coach and left the meeting not wanting to visit with another team.

THE 2010 NFL DRAFT

It used to be that character didn't count for much in the National Football League.

As long as you could deliver blistering hits in the open field, create a hole in the line, make a catch in traffic, or run the two-minute offense, you pretty much got a free pass.

Back in the day, fans were amused by the antics of Broadway Joe Namath—he of the white llama rugs and "bachelor pad" fame who titled a chapter in his 1970 autobiography "I Like My Girls Blonde and My Johnny Walker Red."

Those relatively innocent days are as long gone as love beads and incense sticks.

Between January 2000 and the spring of 2010, arrests, citations, and drunk-driving charges involving NFL players piled up—495 according to an investigative article in the *San Diego Union-Tribune*. It seems like there's a report every week about an NFL player arrested for public intoxication, driving under the influence, brandishing a weapon, battering a girlfriend, getting caught in a bar fight, or being charged with sexual assault.

One of the most scandalous affairs was an alleged sex party early in the 2005 season involving hookers and 17 Minnesota Viking football players—including the team's starting quarterback—

aboard a pair of chartered boats on Lake Minnetonka.

For years, some NFL teams have closed one eye to character issues in their evaluation of draft prospects. The St. Louis Rams drafted running back Lawrence Phillips in 1996 despite the fact that he received a six-game suspension during his senior year at the University of Nebraska for dragging his girlfriend by her hair down a flight of stairs. The Rams believed the on-the-field reward of playing Phillips in the backfield outweighed any off-the-field risk. Bad call. Phillips was arrested three times in two seasons before the Rams released him . . . for insubordination.

When quarterbacks Peyton Manning and Ryan Leaf were in the running to be selected first in the 1998 NFL draft, Indianapolis Colts president Bill Polian made appointments to meet with both at the NFL Combine. Manning showed up on time, groomed and mature, while Leaf blew off the appointment.

Small actions make big impressions, and the Colts took Manning as the No. 1 pick and were richly rewarded. The Chargers followed with Ryan Leaf, who quickly unimpressed his teammates and coaches with a lousy work ethic, surly attitude, and profane outbursts at members of the media. Leaf was one of the more remarkable flameouts in NFL history, and many point to his character, or lack of it, as the main reason why.

Then came a disturbing period between April 2006 and April 2007, when the NFL realized it had a serious problem with players of poor conduct and character. At least 79 incidents, including a series of high-profile arrests involving Tennessee Titans cornerback Adam "Pacman" Jones and Cincinnati Bengals wide receiver Chris Henry, prompted Commissioner Roger Goodell to decree a tough personal conduct policy.

When it seemed like NFL rookies stood a better chance of making the police blotter than the team that drafted them, Goodell and the league had to look at a different way of doing things. The commissioner's personal conduct policy spurred NFL front office personnel to rethink the criteria they used when considering a professional football player.

"CHARACTER GUYS"

In recent years, the buzzword in NFL draft war rooms—thank goodness—has been *character*. These days, you're apt to hear GMs say, "He's a character guy," for someone on their draft board, or "He had character issues" for a player they passed on.

Character is one of those intangibles that may be hard to define but is easy to recognize. As someone once pointed out, character means having the inward motivation to do what's right even when nobody is looking. Character means practicing self-restraint regardless of the circumstances. In light of that, it might be a good idea for every football player to memorize this observation from nineteenth-century American newspaper editor Horace Greeley: "Fame is a vapor, popularity an accident, riches take wing, but only character endures."

Going into the 2010 NFL draft, coaches and team personnel were paying attention to character more than ever in making their player evaluations. That's part of why many teams thought so highly of Sam Bradford, Colt McCoy, and Tim Tebow, who were all outspoken about their faith. While there were internal debates about Sam's right shoulder, Colt's height, or Tim's throwing motion, there was a league-wide consensus that these three quarterbacks were "character guys"—upstanding young men with a strong moral compass.

When the 2010 NFL draft arrived, it turned out that character played a huge role for Sam, Colt, and Tim. Their attitude, work ethic, disposition, and respect for authority were the determining factors in where the Three QBs landed during the draft. Bradford went number one overall to the St. Louis Rams. McCoy, not expected to be a first rounder, went to the Cleveland Browns with the 85th pick.

And then there was Tebow. . .

TIM TEBOW: THE FIRST-ROUND SHOCKER

Tim Tebow was in New York City, too, but not for the NFL draft. He had traveled to Manhattan a couple days earlier to promote *NCAA Football 11*, EA Sports' new college football video game. After making an appearance at an upscale restaurant on lower Broadway and playing his brother Robby in the football video game—Tim was Virginia Tech and Robby was Florida—Tim announced he would fly back to Jacksonville to accompany his family for the draft, even though he was one of 18 players the NFL had invited to attend.

"It would have been exciting to be here, to hold your jersey up with the commissioner. That's always something every athlete wants to do," Tim told NFL Network's Charles Davis the day before the draft. "But it's going to be special being at home. Being with my family, my friends, my best friends, my high school teammates, people like that that I know couldn't make their way up here, that I wanted to be able to spend this moment with. That's what it's truly about for me."

The prospect of sitting in the Radio City Music Hall green

room—with TV cameras recording every nose twitch until his name was called—understandably lacked appeal in the Tebow camp. Who wants to squirm on national TV as the pressure mounts when you're passed over?

Tim and his parents had no idea whether Tim would be picked in the first round or drop ingloriously to the second, third, or—gasp!—fourth. From the going-out-on-top Sugar Bowl victory to the Senior Bowl washout to the raves he received for his revamped throwing motion at pro day, Tim's stock among NFL teams fluctuated like the Dow Jones average.

Throughout the spring of 2010, one of the biggest stories in sports remained: *Where will Tim Tebow be drafted?* If an NFL player or coach wanted to get some face time with the media, all he had to do was venture an opinion on Tim's draft day prospects.

Tim's former teammate at Florida, Cincinnati Bengals wide receiver Andre Caldwell, said the right spot to draft the Gator quarterback would be "late second round," adding that the former Heisman winner would need significant time to adjust to life in the NFL. Following Tim's pro day, Miami Dolphins quarterback Chad Henne bluntly told WQAM radio in Miami, "My judgment is that he's not an NFL quarterback. I'll leave it at that."

That's precisely what draftnik Mel Kiper Jr. had been saying since the end of Tim's junior year, when he began ringing the town bell, proclaiming that Tim wasn't NFL quarterback material—and would be better suited to playing professional football as a tight end or H-back. The helmet-haired analyst dissed everything about Tim's quarterbacking skills.

To his credit, Tim did an interview on ESPN Radio with host Freddie Coleman and Kiper at the end of his junior season. The

Florida quarterback showed he could think on his feet just as quickly as he could move them after a snap count. "You tell me this," Tim said during his radio exchange with Kiper. "What do you think I need to do to be an NFL quarterback? You tell me that."

Kiper backpedaled like an All-Pro cornerback and mumbled something about the NFL being a "flip of the coin" and that Peyton Manning had his detractors when he came into the league. Said Kiper, "You're too good with the ball in your hands not to think, *Could he be Frank Wycheck? Could he be Chris Cooley?* That's why," Kiper said. "You're too good, doing what you do, Tim, running with the football."

Wycheck and Cooley were NFL tight ends, but in this context, the comment was a thinly veiled insult since Tim's peers were quarterbacks like Sam Bradford and Colt McCoy, not journeymen tight ends.

After hearing Kiper out, the Florida quarterback replied, "The quarterback has the ball in his hands every play."

Touché, Tim . . .

In the weeks leading up to the 2010 NFL draft, Tim's name was nowhere to be found on Kiper's "Big Board" of Top 25 picks, but "he's the story of the draft, like him or not," said Peter King of *Sports Illustrated.* For every Tebow doubter, though, there was a Tebow booster. Perhaps the biggest voice in his corner was former Tampa Bay coach Jon Gruden, who had worked out Tim as part of *Gruden's QB Camp* specials that ran on ESPN leading up to draft day. Gruden told anyone who would listen that Tim could very well crack the first round.

"If you want Tim to be on your football team, if you want him bad enough, you're going to have him in the first round or the second," Gruden said. "If you want Tim in your locker room, on your football team, and you can see a little down the road, a team like that is going to take him earlier than some people expect. I'm very confident in this guy."

Preceding the draft, five NFL teams requested private individual workouts with Tim, including the Denver Broncos, whose young head coach, Josh McDaniels, was said to be intrigued with Tim—even though the club had recently traded for Cleveland's Brady Quinn, a third-year pro out of Notre Dame. In the week preceding the draft, the Broncos visited and worked out Tim twice in a five-day span.

Kiper and his ESPN sidekick, Todd McShay, stuck to their guns regarding Tim's draft prospects. "I think Tim has got to develop into a starting quarterback to be worth being a second-round choice," said Kiper, showing his belief that the first round was beyond the realm of reason for Tebow. "I don't think he can be. Others do. We'll see . . . I'll root for Tim to prove me wrong on that one."

McShay called Tim a "project" and said he'd be surprised if any team parted with a cherished first-round pick for him. "I would not draft Tebow in the first two rounds. My philosophy is you draft people who have a legitimate shot to be a starter right away."

Through it all, Tim's faith and confidence never wavered. On the morning of the NFL draft, he told *USA Today*, "I believe I'll be drafted as a quarterback and used as a quarterback."

Tim watched the draft unfold at a private residence at Jacksonville's Glen Kernan Country Club, surrounded by two or three dozen family members, close friends, and others in the Tebow camp, including his agent, Jimmy Sexton. Sitting in the corner of the living room was a cardboard box stuffed with Denver Broncos hats.

They knew.

But you need a flow chart to follow the Broncos' crazy route to using the No. 25 pick to select Tim Tebow.

> First, the Broncos traded their No. 11 pick to the San Francisco 49ers for the Niners' first-round pick (No. 13) and a fourth-round pick.
>
> Next, the Broncos sent the No. 13 pick to Philadelphia in exchange for the Eagles' first-round pick (No. 24) and two third-rounders.
>
> Then the Broncos traded the No. 24 pick (as well as a fourth-round choice) to New England for the Patriots' first-round pick (No. 22), which they used *not* to draft Tim Tebow but Georgia Tech receiver Demaryius Thomas. (Keep track of this name.)
>
> Three picks later, the Broncos grabbed the No. 25 pick from Baltimore in exchange for Denver's second-, third-, and fourth-round picks. The Broncos also received the No. 119 pick in the deal.

All this shuffling momentarily confused the ESPN talking heads. Could it be that Denver . . . ?

And that's when Tim's cell phone rang with a 303 area code. "Should I answer it?" he asked his agent, Jimmy Sexton.

Of course, Tim.

Coach McDaniels was on the line, but he didn't seem at all in a hurry to get down to business. He made small talk and asked Tim if he was enjoying the night. *Oh, and by the way, we're going to trade up and take you.*

The electrifying news swept through the living room just as an ESPN camera cut away to the joyful scene of Tim hugging his family and friends. Then Team Tebow brought out the Broncos hats, and Tim, wearing an ear-to-ear grin, slipped one on.

At 10:09 p.m., in the midst of the pandemonium, Commissioner Goodell's official announcement came that Tim Tebow was a first-round draft choice of the Denver Broncos.

The proclamation sent shock waves through Radio City Music Hall and caused Mel Kiper Jr. to blanche like he'd just swallowed a dose of cod liver oil.

"I just think I showed them [the Broncos] I was willing to do whatever it took," Tim told ESPN. "I want to thank everyone in the organization. Over the last few weeks, we really hit it off. I was hoping and praying that was where I could play."

Tim said his private workout three days earlier with the Denver coaching staff raised his hopes that Denver would be the team that would take him. "It was awesome," he said of his day in Denver. "It was a day full of ball. We talked ball, watched film. We watched so much stuff . . . . It was the best day I've had. I enjoyed it. Their coaches are awesome. It was great. Their coaches are just like the coaches I have at Florida. I'm just excited to be a Bronco."

The Denver media reported that the Broncos knocked the NFL on its insignia ears by selecting Tim, and headlines around the country called Denver's drafting of Tim "surprising" and "shocking."

There was electricity in the rarefied Colorado air, but there were also some interesting dynamics regarding the pick. The Centennial State is really the tale of two cities: Denver, the state capital, and Colorado Springs, 60 miles to the south, along the Front Range corridor. Denver (and nearby Boulder) is uniformly more liberal, while Colorado Springs, which is home to dozens of Christian ministries, including Focus on the Family, is more conservative.

Would Tim be a polarizing figure in such an environment?

"Tim Tebow is a lightning rod," said Bill McCartney, the former University of Colorado football coach and founder of the Promise Keepers men's ministry. But, he added, "There is an anointing on Tim and his family. He's one of those guys who comes along who has God's handprints all over him." McCartney predicted that Tim, who's heavily involved in philanthropic efforts through his Tim Tebow Foundation, would make a difference for Denver's poor and oppressed.

Perhaps that's why *Denver Post* columnist Woody Paige—a regular panelist on the ESPN sports-talk program *Around the Horn* who is not known for any conservative views—preached tolerance shortly after Tim was drafted. The headline on his sympathetic column: IT'S NOT FAIR TO RIP TEBOW FOR HIS FAITH.

Maybe the Mile High City took Paige's column to heart. It was about to start on an improbable journey with Tim Tebow—and declare its love.

ROOKIE YEAR

Being an NFL rookie quarterback is a tough gig.

From their first snap, first-year signal callers discover that the pro game is played at a much faster pace than in college. They are pitted against more athletic defenses, and they must perform under a new spotlight. Because NFL players are paid for their services, home-field fans feel freer to vent their displeasure after an interception or a three-and-out series. The local media, often friendly boosters in college towns, delight in carving up pro players like a Thanksgiving turkey—proving the adage that the pen is mightier than the sword.

It generally takes a few seasons for a young quarterback to mature and feel comfortable in the National Football League. That's why Drew Brees caddied for Doug Flutie during his rookie year with the San Diego Chargers in 2001, playing in just one game. When Philip Rivers was drafted behind Brees in 2004, he threw only three passes as a third-string rookie.

Those who *do* play a lot during their first season in the pros take their lumps while adapting to a faster and tougher professional game. For nearly every hotshot collegian entering the league, it's *normal* to struggle in the rookie season. Learning an NFL offense is like learning a new language, and with speedy 250-pound linebackers shooting through the gaps, it's easy to see why rookie quarterbacks are often overwhelmed when they line up behind center.

Looking at today's ranks of premier quarterbacks, only one held his own in his first year of pro ball:

> **Peyton Manning,** playing with the Indianapolis Colts, set five different NFL rookie records, including most touchdown passes in a season, but he also threw a league-high 28 interceptions for a team that struggled to a 3–13 record.

Tom Brady, drafted almost as an afterthought by the New England Patriots in the sixth round, started the 2000 season as the fourth-string quarterback. He threw just three passes his rookie year, completing one.

Michael Vick, the No. 1 draft choice in 2001, was brought along slowly by Atlanta Falcons head coach Dan Reeves. He played in eight games, starting two, while experiencing marginal success for a team that finished 7–9.

Aaron Rodgers arrived in Green Bay in 2005 where Brett Favre was only in his 15th season. Rodgers saw limited action in three games.

Ben Roethlisberger, thrust into a starting role early due to injuries, turned in the best season ever for a rookie QB in 2004, going 13–0 as a starter and leading the Pittsburgh Steelers to the AFC Championship game.

Tim arrived in Denver supremely happy that he'd been picked in the first round by the Broncos. The local media swooned over the Florida quarterback, even admitting they were seduced by his charismatic charm and his aw-shucks, Jack Armstrong, all-American attitude. Many fans warmed to the idea that Tim could take hold of the franchise like Hall of Famer John Elway did in the 1980s and 1990s.

If Tim had worked hard in the months leading up the NFL draft, he doubled down during training camp. Tim told reporters he had a saying on his bedroom wall at home: "Hard work beats talent when talent doesn't work hard."

His presence drew a record 3,100 fans to the first day of training camp, and Tim worked his way past Brady Quinn on the depth chart to establish himself as the No. 2 quarterback behind starter Kyle Orton. In the middle of summer camp, Tim showed that he wasn't a prima donna by readily submitting to a ridiculous "Friar Tuck" haircut—a humongous bald spot on top of his dome surrounded by a ring of hair. Looking like he stepped out of a Robin Hood and Sheriff of Nottingham movie, the monk haircut was part of a rookie hazing ceremony. Tim said he went along with the gag to build team chemistry.

For most of the 2010 season, as the team kept losing and losing, the Broncos' team chemistry wasn't good. Sure, head coach Josh McDaniels—who made it no secret that Tim was his pet project—featured him in the team's "Wild Horse" packages on third-and-short and goal-line situations early in the season, but Tim was kept on the shortest leash possible. He didn't throw his first pass until the middle of the November—a mini three-yard touchdown toss.

By then, the Bronco season was already in tatters, but the worst was yet to come. During the last week of October, the Broncos had flown to London, England, to play the San Francisco 49ers as part of the NFL's "International Series" outreach. Steve Scarnecchia, the team's director of video operations, taped the 49ers' walkthrough practice at Wembley Stadium—and was caught doing so. The practice is strictly forbidden.

The media dubbed it "Spygate II" because what transpired was reminiscent of the New England Patriots' Spygate scandal of 2007–08. Since McDaniels was a Patriots assistant coach at the time and a Bill Belichick acolyte . . . well, you can connect the dots.

McDaniels was fired in early December for his role in Spygate II as well as the Broncos' 3–9 belly flop. With the disastrous season going nowhere and starting quarterback Kyle Orton out with injured ribs, diehard Broncos fans—and the Denver media—clamored for something to cheer about. *Give Tebow the rock!*

With three games left on the schedule, interim head coach Eric Studesville decided it really was Tebow Time, naming Tim the starter for a road game against the Oakland Raiders.

With Silver and Black fans screaming "Tebow Bust! Tebow Bust!", Tim electrified his teammates by galloping up the gut for a 40-yard touchdown—and endeared himself to his fans when he admitted afterward that he was supposed to hand the ball to running back Correll Buckhalter. In other words, he scored on a busted play.

Although Denver lost to Oakland, Tim infused energy into the Broncos players, showing leadership and determination. He also had the dirtiest Denver uniform when the clock ran out.

The following game, against the Houston Texans, became the first installment of the Tebow legend in Denver. Playing before a boisterous sellout crowd with only 5,717 no-shows, the Broncos fell behind 17–0 at halftime—which was par for their season. A Tebow interception in the end zone didn't help their cause.

Then, after intermission, something special happened. Tim unleashed a 50-yard bomb to receiver Jabar Gaffney on the opening drive of the second half that led to a touchdown. The next two drives resulted in a field goal and another touchdown. With the Bronco defense suddenly developing a spine, Denver was down just 23–17 with 7:42 remaining.

A clutch third-and-10 dump-off pass netted 22 yards. Then Tim lasered a 15-yard strike, followed by an 11-yard scramble. Down at the 6 yard line, Tim took the ball in the shotgun, shook off a sack, and had the football sense to pivot to his left where there was plenty of green grass and no white Houston uniforms in the vicinity. Tim won the footrace to the pylon, and Denver's comeback was complete, 24–23.

If you can't chuck it, then tuck it.

Bronco supporters rejoiced that their team had snapped a five-game losing streak, and some fans believed a star was born that afternoon against Houston. Speculation ran rampant about whether Tim was a modern-day Moses who would lead the Broncos out of the wilderness and into the Promised Land of the NFL playoffs.

Tim's three-game audition probably raised as many questions as answers about his future as an NFL quarterback. He certainly proved that he belonged behind center and could lead his team down the field, seemingly by force of will. But being an NFL quarterback was a lot more than a seven-step drop and flinging the ball down the field, as Tim was learning.

Bronco legend John Elway, who was named executive vice president of football operations following the disastrous 2010 season, said Tim needed to work on the fundamentals of being a pocket passer and anticipating throws. "We all agree on one thing," Elway said. "Tim Tebow is a darn good football player. What we have to make him is a darn good quarterback, and that is what we have to figure out."

TELLING HIS STORY

On May 31, 2011, I (Mike Yorkey) flew with my wife, Nicole, to her native county of Switzerland. Our routing that day took us from San Diego to Washington, D.C.'s Dulles Airport to Geneva. We were traveling to attend the wedding of Nicole's goddaughter, Seraina.

I was on a mission as soon as I stepped off the plane in Washington—find a copy of *Through My Eyes*, Tim's autobiography written with collaborator Nathan Whitaker. May 31 was the day the book went on sale. Hey, I didn't mind paying full freight in the airport bookstore because *Through My Eyes* was an enjoyable read that made the hours pass quickly as our red-eye flight crossed the Atlantic. I would have liked a little less football and a little more personal stuff—like why sexual purity was important to him—but *Through My Eyes* was a fine, worthwhile book.

The public agreed with me. *Through My Eyes* became the No. 1 bestselling Christian book in 2011, with around 400,000 copies sold. With the NFL lockout in full swing, Tim had time to make the promotional rounds in New York, giving numerous print and TV interviews. The 23-year-old QB quipped, "Most people wait until they're at least 24 to put out an autobiography." Tim also participated in massive book signings in his home state of Florida, where long lines formed hours before his arrival. He cheerfully signed hundreds of books in two-hour appearances—which had to put some stress on his throwing arm.

Meanwhile, pro football fans everywhere were stressed about whether there would even be a 2011 season. Tim was not allowed any contact with his coaches or to step on the grounds of the Bronco training facility in Denver, where he could have met with new head coach John Fox, worked on his mechanics, and learned coverages during the off-season.

When the lockout finally ended and the players got into training camp, it soon became evident there was a new pecking order on the depth chart: Tim had lost his starting quarterback position to Kyle Orton and was fighting Brady Quinn for the backup job. There were even rumors that the Broncos were going to wash their hands of Tim by releasing him.

Taking note of the situation, ESPN columnist Rick Reilly wrote that Tim was a "nice kid, sincere as a first kiss, but he's not ready yet, might never be ready. Somebody alert the Filipino missionaries. If he doesn't improve, he might be among them sooner than we thought."

Tim kept plugging away and working hard, but it was hard to gain experience when he was getting crumbs—a few fourth-quarter snaps in preseason games against the other team's third string. When the season started, Orton was firmly entrenched as the starter.

The Broncos split their first two games at home, losing to Oakland but bouncing back to beat the playoff-bound Cincinnati Bengals. A close road loss to the Tennessee Titans and a blowout by the Green Bay Packers had the natives getting restless. Employees at Multiline International Imports, which has a large digital sign adjoining Interstate 25, the main north-south corridor in Denver, decided to express their frustration with the team's tailspin by printing the following message on their billboard:

BRONCOS FANS TO JOHN FOX: PLAY TEBOW!

Talk about a quarterback controversy. Denver fans chanted "Tebow! Tebow!" after each three-and-out by the inept offense, and the pressure intensified on Coach Fox to yank Orton and give Tim a chance. The boo birds were really giving it to the coaching staff when the Broncos fell behind 23–10 against the San Diego Chargers in Denver. Those catcalls turned to cheers, however, when Coach Fox benched Orton in favor of Tim in the second half. After a scoreless third quarter, the Broncos were way behind, 26–10, but then the fourth-quarter magic started: Tim scrambling for a 12-yard touchdown . . . Tim throwing a 28-yard touchdown pass . . . Tim driving his team in the last minute. Only a batted-down "Hail Mary" pass in the end zone preserved the Chargers' 29–24 victory.

"He makes plays, you can't deny that," said relieved Chargers' linebacker, Takeo Spikes. "People can talk about the way he throws the ball, people can talk about his release. But at the end of the day, this league is about *What have you done for me lately?* And if you can come in and make plays that another can't, then you'll play a long time."

The Broncos were now 1–4. Coach Fox noticed the spark in his players when Tim was under center. Should he dump Orton and turn the team over to Tebow? Their next game was in Miami against the Dolphins.

With a bye week coming up, he had some time to think about it.

THE MIRACLE IN MIAMI

NFL teams aren't supposed to win games in which they've been shut out for 55 minutes and struggled to put together a first down, let alone a decent drive. The Broncos were down 15–0 in Miami, and Tim was either overthrowing or short-hopping his frustrated receivers. If he had been a baseball pitcher, he was throw-it-to-the-backstop wild.

The Dolphins, thinking they had the game well in hand, put their defense in "prevent" mode with 5:23 left. Denver was eating up time when, out of nowhere, Tim hit Matt Willis on a crossing pattern for a 42-yard gain that took the Broncos down to the 12-yard line. Three plays later, Tim found Demaryius Thomas in the corner of the end zone. Now the score was 15–7, with only 2:44 remaining.

An onside kick bounced Denver's way, and here's where things got interesting: both sides knew the stakes—if Denver scored a touchdown, the Broncos would be a two-point conversion from tying the game.

Tim led Denver steadily down the field, the tension rising with each play. The hometown crowd—who chanted "Tebow sucks!" in the first half—had changed their tune. Now they were screaming "Tebow! Tebow!" because many had seen him play so well in the clutch at Florida—and wanted to witness something special in Miami. The biggest play of the drive was a diving catch by Daniel Fells—good for 28 yards to the 3-yard line—with less than half a minute to play. On second down, Tim passed to Fells again for the touchdown. A two-point conversion would push the game into overtime.

Was there any doubt that Tim wanted the ball in his hands on the biggest play of the game? From the shotgun, he took the snap, saw a big hole to the right, and darted into the end zone untouched.

Miami won the overtime coin toss and elected to take the ball. But Broncos linebacker D.J. Williams soon stripped the ball from Dolphins quarterback Matt Moore. Three plays later, Matt Prater nailed a 51-yard field goal, and the jubilant Broncos players sprinted onto the field with their helmets held high. White-shirted Denver coaches jumped into each other's arms and bear-hugged. Everyone in the organization was celebrating on the sidelines like they had just won the Super Bowl on a final play.

Except for Tim. In the midst of the pandemonium, he dropped his right knee to the ground and started praying, worshipping the Lord of the Universe. Then he pointed his finger to the heavens.

We can't get into Tim's mind to know exactly what he communicated to God in those few moments, but I would imagine he was thanking the Lord for what had just happened.

Tim's moment was witnessed by millions watching on TV— and tens of millions more who would later see the clip of Tim genuflecting, offering a prayer of thanksgiving, then pointing to the sky in worship.

Among those watching the amazing comeback was Jared Kleinstein, a 24-year-old Denver native living in New York City. A half-dozen Denver expats were watching the game at Sidebar on East 15th when Jared noticed Tim taking a knee in prayer while his teammates jumped up and down. To commemorate the moment, Jared asked his friends to step outside the establishment, where he took a picture of them hunched down on one knee, their fists against their foreheads. Then, as young people do these days, he posted the photo on Facebook.

The "likes" poured in by the hundreds, which got him thinking. The following day, he created a "tebowing" blog on tumblr.

com, then two days later purchased the *tebowing* domain name from GoDaddy.com and created a website.

Don't get the wrong idea: Kleinstein wasn't mocking Tim's act of supplication. In fact, on his splash page, he defined *tebowing* as a verb meaning to "get down on a knee and start praying, even if everyone else around is doing something completely different." Visitors to tebowing.com were invited to submit photos of others striking a tebowing pose.

How long did it take for the tebowing phenomenon to go viral? A day or two. Once the national news media got hold of the story, it seemed everyone was either tebowing or talking about it. Or submitting their random acts of tebowing to tebowing.com. There were pictures of

- an entire aisle of a 737 jet filled with passengers on one knee
- a bridal party—four groomsmen and four bridesmaids—tebowing while the just-married couple were locked in a kiss
- a college-aged tourist striking the pose with the Roman Colosseum in the background
- soldiers in Afghanistan tebowing in their camos
- the man himself—Tim Tebow—smiling next to a young Broncos fan who's tebowing on him

It's pretty cool how tebowing took on a life of its own, how people had fun with it without ridiculing Tim or his Christian faith.

The best part of the story: Jared Kleinstein is Jewish.

THE MILE HIGH MESSIAH

What happened in Miami made those who follow the NFL closely sit up and take notice: no team since the AFL-NFL merger in 1970 had ever won a game after trailing by 15 points or more with less than three minutes to play. Everyone, it seemed, was talking about the game. If Tim could snatch a victory like that from the jaws of defeat, the feeling was that he could do anything—like make the Broncos a winner again.

But here is where the Tim Tebow bus took a detour. In the very next game, a home contest against the hot Detroit Lions, Tim suffered through a humiliating afternoon. There were eight three-and-outs. A miserable 8-for-25 passing. An interception returned 100 yards for a coast-to-coast touchdown. Seven sacks. And at least two instances of on-the-field "tebowing" by Detroit players who *were* mocking the prayer pose.

The humbled Broncos stood at 2–5, and the question thrown at Coach Fox was whether Tim would remain Denver's starting quarterback. I remember watching that game, feeling Tim looked overwhelmed by a massive pass rush that gave him very little time to find a receiver. Once again the social media chatter exploded in volume: *Tim Tebow is not an NFL quarterback. The pro game is too fast for him. He can't make the progressions.*

Coach Fox stayed the course, and it's good that he did—because that allowed Tebow fans to experience a wondrous six-game tear in which the Broncos won incredibly close games, often in the last series or in overtime. Most of the games were decided by a single touchdown or a field goal. Here's a recap:

- Against the Oakland Raiders—in the Black Hole—Denver fell behind 17–7 at the half, but Tim and the Broncos found their mojo and came roaring back. It wasn't until wide receiver Eddie Royal returned a punt 85 yards with six minutes to go in the game that Denver put their nose in front of their conference rival. Using the read-option like he was a magician, Tim either tucked the ball into the belly of running back Willis McGahee or kept it himself, punching out chunks of yards to keep the chains moving in the Broncos' 38–24 victory. Tim threw fewer times—only 21 attempts—but connected for two touchdowns. He was sacked only once after taking 13 in his first two games. Denver's record: 3–5.

- Tim threw even *fewer* times against Kansas City in Game 2 of the streak—only eight passes, with only two completions. But one of his passes—a beautiful deep ball that streaking Eric Decker caught over his shoulder—resulted in a 56-yard, fourth-quarter touchdown that was a dagger to the Chiefs' heart. The lightning strike put the Broncos ahead by 10 points in what would turn out to be a 17–10 victory. Denver's record: 4–5.

- The Broncos had just three days to prepare for

their Thursday night game against the New York Jets in Denver. With a national audience watching on the NFL Network, Tim and the Broncos were backed up on the 5-yard line, down 13–10 late in the fourth quarter. Tim had struggled much of the game to find his rhythm. But with the game on the line, it was like Tim stepped out of a phone booth wearing a blue-and-orange Superman outfit. Running the read-option, spread offense to perfection, Tim led Denver down the field with his feet and his arm. Facing a third-and-four on the 20-yard line, the Jets threw an all-out blitz at Tim, who slipped off the left side and churned his legs toward the end zone for the game-winner. Final score: Denver 17, New York 13. Football pundits started calling him the "Mile High Messiah," and they had a point: Tim was taking a few measly fish and loaves of bread—his uneven play—and feeding the 5,000 in miraculous fashion with incredible last-minute comebacks. Denver's record: 5–5, exceeding their win total of 2010.

- Trailing 13–10 with just over five minutes to go in San Diego, Tim confidently marched the Broncos downfield for the tying field goal. Though it looked for awhile like neither team would score in overtime, resulting in a rare tie, Tim pushed Denver close enough for Matt Prater's 37-yard, game-winning kick with just 29 seconds left. Final score: Denver 16, San Diego 13. Denver's record: 6–5, one game behind Oakland.

• A road game in Minneapolis was Tim's next test. Denver started off slowly—what else is new?—but in the second half, the Broncos opened up the playbook. After intermission in the Metrodome, Tim showed he could sling with the best of them, completing six of nine passes for 173 yards and two touchdowns. He also earned a two-point conversion in the fourth quarter when he rolled to his right and found the goal line to tie the game at 29. Shades of Miami.

The wide-open second half felt like a shootout, but Tim and the Broncos still found themselves down by a field goal with three minutes to go. A 40-yard pass play got Denver within field goal range, and Matt Prater punched through a 46-yarder to knot the game again at 32. Then, with only 1:33 remaining, Tim watched Minnesota's rookie quarterback, Christian Ponder, make a horrible sideline pass that was intercepted deep in Viking territory. Tim ran the clock down before Mr. Automatic won it with a chip-shot field goal as time expired.

Denver record: 7–5, now tied for first with the Raiders, who'd lost.

- The beat went on in Chicago, in the NFC's Black and Blue division. After a half of bruising football—and a rare scoreless tie—da Bears took a 10–0 lead early in the fourth quarter. But Tim started the comeback at the 4:34 mark, engineering a snappy seven-play drive that ended with a 10-yard touchdown pass to Demaryius Thomas. But with 2:08 to go, the Broncos were out of timeouts.

  Unlike the Miami game, an onside kick didn't go Denver's way. It looked like Chicago would simply run the ball three times and punt; Denver might get the ball deep in its own territory with about 20 seconds to play. But Chicago running back Marion Barber made a mental mistake, allowing linebacker D.J. Williams to push him out of bounds. That meant an extra 40 seconds or so for Denver, which took a punt at 1:06 to start a final drive from their own 20, and advanced—on Tebow passes to three different receivers—39 yards to the Chicago 41. Matt Prater's longshot 59-yard field goal attempt had enough leg to pass over the crossbar, forcing overtime. Of course.

  Of course, the Bears' Marion Barber fumbled

on the first possession of OT, with Chicago on Denver's 34-yard line, well within range of a game-winning field goal. Of course, Tim authored a heady, nine-play drive to *Chicago's* 34-yard line. Of course, Prater rocketed a 51-yard kick through the uprights for Tim's *sixth* game-winning drive in either the fourth quarter or overtime in his eleven starts.

Denver record: 8–5 after six straight wins, now first in the AFC West as Oakland lost again.

PATH TO THE PLAYOFFS

The Broncos were in the driver's seat. They controlled their own destiny. Win out, and they would ride a whole lot of momentum into the NFL playoffs.

One team they would expect to see in the postseason was New England, led by Tom Brady, considered by many the best quarterback in the game. And next on the regular-season schedule was the Patriots, in the Mile High City.

Rather untypically, Tim played great early to lead Denver to a 16–7 lead in the second quarter. But then it was *whoosh*. New England reeled off 27 unanswered points in annihilating the Broncos 41–23. The six-game streak was history.

Okay, no one was expecting this game in the W column anyway. Buffalo, which had lost seven in a row, was coming up—so you'd have to think things were looking good.

Think again. The Bills throttled the Broncos, 40–14. Now it looked like the Broncos *had* to win their final regular season game against Kansas City to advance to the playoffs. And coming to Denver was none other than former Bronco starter Kyle Orton, waived a month earlier and picked up by the division rival Chiefs.

You can figure Orton had this game circled on his calendar.

The former Bronco quarterback didn't play spectacularly, but the Chiefs defense thwarted Tim and his offense the entire game, holding Denver to a single field goal in a 7–3 loss. But there was good news from Oakland, where the San Diego Chargers played spoiler with a 38–26 victory. Denver, Oakland, and San Diego each finished with 8–8 records, but Denver won the tiebreaker because of their better play against common opponents (5–5 for Denver; 4–6 for Oakland and San Diego).

Though the Broncos backed into the playoffs, they were a division winner—and would have home field advantage against Pittsburgh. The Steelers, who had finished just behind New England with a sterling 12–4 record, were heavily favored.

THE FOOTRACE TO THE END ZONE

If you like drama, you got nearly four hours of excitement in early January 2012.

The storyline going into the opening-weekend matchup was that the Steelers would steamroll the slumping Broncos because their "Steel Curtain" defense was arguably the toughest in the NFL. Besides, Tim's confidence had to be shot after losing the last three games of the regular season. Only the game's location—in Denver—would keep it from being a complete blowout.

But Pittsburgh had some issues, as well. Ben Roethlisberger, the sturdy-in-the-pocket passer, had suffered a high ankle sprain several weeks earlier and was far from 100 percent. Big Ben's howitzer arm still made him a dangerous threat, though.

In the lead-up to the big game, John Elway—the former Denver great—told a *Denver Post* columnist that Tim needed to "put everything behind him, go through his progressions, and pull the trigger."

Yes, sir.

Tim responded to the directive with one of his best passing games ever—and Denver's 20-point explosion in the second quarter was a thing of beauty. In addition to a pair of Matt Prater field goals, Tim lofted a handsome 30-yard pass to a well-covered Eddie Royal in the end zone and swiveled his hips on an eight-yard touchdown run of his own.

But you can never count Big Ben out—and by the force of his will and supreme talent, Roethlisberger brought the Steelers back from a two-touchdown deficit to force overtime. Denver won the toss . . . and everyone knows what happened next.

Following a touchback, on the first play of overtime, Tim strode to the line of scrimmage. The Steelers were showing a run-heavy front with nine men in the box, leaving a gaping hole in the middle. Then cornerback Ike Taylor crept up to the line, where Demaryius Thomas had lined up split wide left.

Tim faked a handoff, then whistled a clean pass to Thomas, running a post pattern. The Denver wideout straight-armed Taylor and turned up the sideline with nothing but green real estate ahead. Turning on the afterburners, Thomas outran safety Ryan Mundy to the end zone.

Watching the play develop, Tim took off after Thomas, hoofing it to the end zone to celebrate with his delirious teammates.

"When I saw him scoring, first of all, I just thought, 'Thank you, Lord,'" Tim said. "Then I was running pretty fast, chasing him—like I can catch up to DT. Then I just jumped into the stands. First time I've done that. That was fun."

Tim's version of the Lambeau Leap—throwing his exhilarated body into the stands—had some fearing we'd never see him again. But he survived, and even had a spiritual moment amidst the hoopla. "Then I got on a knee and thanked the Lord again," Tim said, "and tried to celebrate with my teammates and the fans."

The 80-yard pass-and-catch was the longest scoring play in NFL overtime history. And it was the shortest overtime ever as well—only 11 seconds. Accolades poured in, and Tim was the toast of the NFL for the next week.

What I loved was that even some sports commentators caught the amazing coincidence that Tim threw for 316 yards, completing ten throws for an average of 31.6 yards per completion.

Guess what happened next? John 3:16 was the most popular Google search the following Monday.

THE END OF THE LINE
The top-seeded New England Patriots, who had smoked Denver just a month earlier, were waiting patiently after a first-round bye. They had plenty of motivation: much was made of the fact that the Bill Belichick-coached team had lost three consecutive play-off games, dating back to the 2008 Super Bowl XLII heartbreaker that ruined their supposed-to-be-first-ever 19–0 season.

In a highly anticipated Saturday night game, Tim and the Denver Broncos were taken out of the game early as Tom Brady threw *five* first-half touchdown passes. The Patriots coasted in the second half to an easy 45–10 victory. Tim wasn't much of a factor as a consistent pass rush either swallowed him up or caused him to throw away too many balls.

The magical mystery ride was over—but what a fascinating season of football. As they say sometimes, *You can't make this stuff up*.

That's certainly true of Tim Tebow's career. Considering the path he traveled—languishing on the sidelines in training camp, playing sketchy stretches of football, then conjuring up one amazing comeback after another—it makes you wonder if the Lord was having a little fun with football fans in America. But there was one more surprise lurking in the off-season.

Tim stayed busy with a series of appearances and speaking engagements. He attended Cartoon Network's Hall of Game Awards in Santa Monica, California, where he walked the green carpet with the likes of NBA icon Shaquille O'Neal, soccer star David Beckham, and a bevy of pro athletes from other sports.

Asked on the green carpet what he thought of Jeremy Lin, the Asian-American, outspokenly Christian, overnight sensation with the New York Knicks, Tim replied, "I really like him. I respect him a whole lot. I've had the pleasure to really get to know him over the last few weeks. What a great guy he is. I just wish him the best of luck. How he handles himself and how he carries himself, I think he's a great role model. And I'm proud of him."

Tim was also approached to be on ABC's hit show *The Bachelor*. Personally, I couldn't see how hot tub hookups and Tim's stand for premarital purity would be a good match for the program . . . and Tim came through as I figured: "Haha rumors can be crazy!" he typed on his Twitter account. "Even though I've watched the show before, I'm definitely not gonna be on the Bachelor."

Then he had a "dinner date" with country music star Taylor

Swift, who is certainly a cutie and just as famous as Mr. Tebow. But don't make too much of the tabloid fodder. Yes, the two dined at Toscanova Italian Restaurant in Los Angeles' Century City, but they were with William Morris agents—they're both represented by WME—so there's no way we can know why they were meeting or what they were discussing. Seems like they would make a nice couple, though . . .

And then there was a speaking engagement in Las Vegas, where Tim spoke about faith and football to 20,000 one weekend at Canyon Ridge Christian Church. During a Q&A time, when senior pastor Kevin Odor asked him about "tebowing," Tim showed him how to properly strike the prayerful pose on the church stage as the standing-room-only crowd howled.

"One of the reasons I get on a knee is because that's a form of humbling yourself," Tim explained. "I want to humble myself before the Lord and say thank You for this opportunity. Thank You for letting me play the game I love."

HIS LIFE TURNS UPSIDE DOWN

Following the 2011 season, the Indianapolis Colts had a big—and expensive—decision to make regarding their quarterback, Peyton Manning, widely viewed as one of the best signal callers in NFL history for his pinpoint passing and uncanny ability to read coverages. The team's most popular player, a Super Bowl winner, and four-time MVP, Manning had played his entire 14-year career in Indianapolis. He was the face of the Colts franchise. Well-liked. A pro's pro.

But Manning, sidelined by a series of neck surgeries, didn't play a down in the entire 2011 season. Without Old Reliable playing pitch and catch with his receivers, Indianapolis' record plummeted to 2–14, the worst in the NFL. The only good thing to come from the disastrous season was a guaranteed first pick in the 2012 NFL draft.

The Colts management had to decide whether to pick up the remaining four years on Manning's five-year, $90 million contract. If they did, that would mean paying an option bonus of $28 million on March 11, 2012. If the team released Manning, however, they could use that money to sign a new quarterback with their No. 1 draft pick—like Stanford University star Andrew Luck.

And so, with tears and fanfare, the Colts bid good-bye to Peyton Manning. All parties agreed it was a business decision: after all, Manning was turning 36 years old, had a creaky neck, and was due a ton of bonus money.

A dozen NFL teams inquired about being stops on the Peyton Manning Road Show. But it soon became apparent that only three were in serious contention—the Tennessee Titans, the San Francisco 49ers, and the Denver Broncos.

The news that the Broncos were interested in Manning—with John Elway leading the pursuit with the single-mindedness of a fourth-quarter drive—sent shock waves through the sporting universe. What about Tim Tebow? Hadn't he shown true grit with all those amazing late-game comebacks and leading the Broncos to a playoff win? Wasn't he responsible for changing the Broncos' culture of losing?

Sure he was. But since this was John Elway's rodeo, we'll never really know what the boss was thinking. We can figure that Manning felt very comfortable being wooed by Elway—they were kindred spirits, equals in the pantheon of great NFL quarterbacks. Elway probably said that he understood Manning's situation since he—Elway—had played quarterback at the same age. Elway had performed well, too, in his final act, winning Super Bowl rings when he was 37 and 38. Manning ultimately said yes to the Broncos, signing a $96 million, five-year contract.

Which meant Tim had to go. There was no way the Broncos organization or the coaching staff wanted the distraction that Tim would add to the mix, so Denver placed No. 15 on the trading block.

The New York Jets and the Jacksonville Jaguars stepped up with offers. The Jets had missed the playoffs in 2011, and fans and media seeking someone to blame cast their eyes on Mark Sanchez, the third-year quarterback who played poorly at times. Tim would give the Jets another option.

Jacksonville—Tim's hometown—certainly wanted to bring their favorite son back to Florida. Owner Shahid Khan, who had just completed his purchase of the Jaguars in January 2012, saw the value in having a guy like Tim Tebow on his team. Since the Jaguars had had attendance problems, Tim would fill up Ever-Bank Field and certainly give football fans in Florida something to talk about again. The Jags had a promising quarterback in Blaine Gabbert—but he hadn't set the world on fire in 2011.

In the end, Tim had a certain amount of say-so about the team he would play for. Exactly how much, we'll probably never know—but it was clear that Tim wanted to become a Jet, though he knew he was joining the team in a backup role. Perhaps he was thinking, deep down, that he could beat out Sanchez as the starting QB. And even if he didn't, he might push Sanchez to play better. Tim would do whatever he could to help the Jets win, whether that was running the Wildcat offense (where the guy taking the hike in short-yardage situations is expected to run the ball) or lining up at H-back to give the defense something else to think about.

But make no mistake about it—Tim has been and always will be a quarterback. That dream did not die when the Broncos showed him the door, and it won't die now that he wears a Jets uniform. And that's why the 2012 season will be such fun to watch. If Sanchez doesn't play up to par and the Jets lose a few games, it's a lock that frustrated fans at MetLife Stadium will chant "Tebow! Tebow!" just like they did in Denver.

So it's back to the future. Tim is starting over with a new team. He'd tell you that he's in New York for a reason, and it's all part of God's plan.

But who could have predicted this turn of events, especially after that magical 2011 season? But that's football—and Tim has always said the game comes in third on his list of priorities, after faith and family.

Just imagine, though, if he does get a chance—and makes the most of the opportunity. If the Jets pile up wins, they'll be talking about "Timsanity" in Gotham, much like Jeremy Lin touched off "Linsanity" during the strike-shortened NBA season.

So isn't it interesting that two of the most celebrated Christian athletes today find themselves in the center of the media universe, playing before an audience that literally numbers in the millions?

Let's pray that Tim will be remain humble and strong, stay free from injury, and continue to be a bold witness for Christ in the Big Apple. We can thank God that Tim has his football helmet screwed on straight, that he's a godly young man seeking to use his physical gifts for the glory of God.

Because this is a young man playing with purpose.

2.

JEREMY LIN:
WELCOME TO THE SHOW

He's been called "Lincredible," a balm of "Liniment" for the NBA, and the architect of "Linsanity." In early 2012, he was one of the most talked-about athletes on the planet.

Of course, we're talking about Jeremy Lin, the twenty-three-year-old Asian American point guard for the New York Knicks who's moved from anonymity to stardom—even pop icon status—faster than an outlet pass off a clean rebound.

In early February 2012, he was the last man coming off the Knicks' bench during garbage time; by Valentine's Day, his dribble drive through five Los Angeles Lakers graced the cover of *Sports Illustrated*, basketball pundits on ESPN SportsCenter had run out of superlatives to describe him, and his No. 17 Knicks jersey was the NBA's top seller—telling touch points of stardom reminiscent of another professional athlete who had recently seized the public's imagination: Tim Tebow.

Think about it: the professional version of Tebowmania dominated the national conversation in the late fall and early winter months of 2011, continuing into the NFL playoffs. *Everyone* talked about Tebow's quick slant pass to Demaryius Thomas on the first play of overtime and the thrilling footrace to the end zone. The mighty Pittsburgh Steelers were slain, and the legend of Tim Tebow was writ even larger.

And then, barely a month later, Jeremy Lin leaped into our living rooms. In one short week—in just a handful of games in a consolidated, lockout-shortened season—Jeremy progressed from anonymous benchwarmer to the toast of the Big Apple as the Knicks' leading scorer, playmaker, and spiritual leader.

West of the Hudson River, he galvanized our attention in a fragmented media universe. The reason why is simple: everyone loves an underdog story, and Jeremy's improbable journey has all the ingredients of a Hollywood fairy tale.

I watched all this develop with great interest since I had been following Jeremy Lin for more than a year. I had interviewed him twice after he finished his rookie season with the Golden State Warriors, and was enraptured by how this son of Taiwanese immigrants overcame preconceived ideas of who can and can't play basketball at the highest levels of the game.

I shared those thoughts in an earlier version of this book, *Playing with Purpose: Inside the Lives and Faith of Top NBA Stars*, which released in November 2011. We chose to put Jeremy's picture on the cover because we believed in him—his "upside" as they like to say in sportspeak. Quite frankly, though, we were taking a chance with Jeremy. Nobody knew what the future portended.

The jury was out on whether he'd stick with the NBA.

During his rookie season with the Golden State Warriors, Jeremy played in nearly as many games (20) for the club's D-League team, the Reno Bighorns, as he did with the Warriors (29). When he was part of the parent club, he rode the Golden State bench. Many nights, "DNP" appeared next to his name in the box score. When he did see action, he averaged 9.8 minutes and scored just 2.6 points per game for a sub-.500 team that failed to make the playoffs.

Nobody was saying that Jeremy was the next Jerry West, but I was fine with that. The fact that Jeremy even made it onto an NBA roster was noteworthy for several reasons:

1. At 6 feet, 3 inches, he wasn't tall for a game dominated by humongous athletes who could have played Goliath's team back in the day.

2. He came from an Ivy League school, Harvard University, which last sent a player to the NBA in 1953—the year before the league adopted a 24-second shot clock.

3. He was the first American-born player of Chinese or Taiwanese descent to play in the NBA.

These against-the-grain characteristics caused us to put Jeremy on the cover of *Playing with Purpose*, but none of us knew about the breathtaking odyssey awaiting him in 2012. We'll get to that, but first you need to read about his remarkable backstory: where Jeremy came from, how he was raised, and how this undrafted prospect beat the odds to play in the NBA.

WHERE IT ALL BEGAN

There are plenty of entry points for Jeremy's story, but a good place to start would be by painting a picture of China in the late 1940s, when civil war ripped apart the world's most populous country. Chinese Nationalist forces led by General Chiang Kai-shek fought the People's Liberation Army—led by Chinese Communist Party leader Mao Zedong—for control of China, which, at that time, was a feudal society where a small elite class lived well and hundreds of millions barely survived. In 1949, after three years of bloody conflict, the Communist forces won, and Chiang Kai-shek and approximately two million Nationalist Chinese fled for their lives to the island of Taiwan off the coast of mainland China.

Among those refugees were Jeremy's grandparents on his mother's side. Shirley Lin ("Shirley" is actually an anglicized version of her Chinese first name) was born to a mother who was one of Taiwan's first prominent female physicians. One time during the 1970s, a contingent of American doctors visited Taiwan to study the advances Taiwanese physicians were making in health care. As Shirley's mother made contacts with those in the American medical community, the seed was planted to immigrate to the United States, where the family could pursue a better life. In 1978, just after Shirley graduated from high school in Taiwan, she and the family moved to the United States.

Shirley worked hard learning English and later enrolled at Old Dominion University, a college in Norfolk, Virginia. Her major was computer science, a discipline with a bright future. Many felt the computer revolution would explode in the 1980s. A newfangled invention called the PC, or personal computer, was starting to find its way into American homes.

There weren't too many Asians (or second-generation Asian Americans, for that matter) at Old Dominion, and those who spoke Mandarin could be counted on two hands. The dozen or so Chinese-speaking students formed a small Asian support group for fun and fellowship, and one of those who joined was a graduate student from Taiwan—a handsome young man named Gie-Ming Lin, who'd come to the United States to work on his doctorate in computer engineering. His ancestors had lived in Taiwan since the nineteenth century, long before Communist oppression began on the mainland in the late 1940s and early 1950s.

Sharing the same cultural background and a common language brought Gie-Ming and Shirley together, and they began dating. It wasn't long before their love blossomed. When Gie-Ming told her that his plan was to finish his doctorate at Purdue University in West Lafayette, Indiana, they decided to move together to Purdue, where Shirley would continue her undergraduate classes in computer science while Gie-Ming worked on his PhD.

Don't get the idea that these two foreign-born students had plenty of time to linger over coffees at the student union, attend a concert at the Elliott Hall of Music, or go sledding down Slayter Hill after the first snowfall of winter. Gie-Ming and Shirley's parents didn't have the financial resources to contribute to their education, so they both had to work to pay their own tuition and living expenses. Shirley took shifts waitressing and bartending, while Gie-Ming moonlighted in his chosen field of computer engineering.

While at Purdue, Shirley was introduced to a Christian fellowship group, and she heard the Gospel presented for the first time. Curious about who Jesus was, she began exploring and learning about the Lord of the Universe and how He came to this earth to die for her sins. She fell in love with Christ and got saved. When she told Gie-Ming what she had done, he investigated the

Gospel and became a Christian as well. They soon plugged into a Chinese-speaking church and began their walk with Christ.

Gie-Ming and Shirley married while they were still in school. They liked living in the United States and became two of the many millions of immigrants chasing the American dream.

They certainly weren't afraid to work hard—or live frugally. Early on, Gie-Ming and Shirley would go fishing on the weekend at a nearby reservoir. Behind the dam was a lake teeming with bluegill, shad, crappie, and huge bass. Gie-Ming, who loved fishing and was quite good at it, would catch his limit and then bring home his haul in a galvanized bucket. They ate some of the fish that night and tossed the rest into the freezer.

And that's how the young couple would feed themselves all week long—from the fish Gie-Ming caught on weekends.

One evening, Gie-Ming flipped on the television to relax, and he came across a basketball game. The Lakers were playing the Celtics during one of their great 1980s NBA Finals battles, and the sight of Bird and Magic doing wondrous things on the Boston Garden parquet floor mesmerized Gie-Ming. He was smitten by the athleticism of these larger-than-life figures who made the basketball court look small. Gie-Ming started watching NBA basketball every chance he had, but that wasn't often since his studies and part-time work took up much of his free time.

Wait! Wasn't there a new technology arriving in people's homes back then? Yes, it was called the VHS recorder, and this then-state-of-the-art electromechanical device could record television broadcasts on cassettes that contained magnetic tape. Suddenly, the images and sound of TV shows and sporting events could be played back at a more convenient time—or replayed over and over for the viewer's enjoyment. The advent of the VHS tape in the 1980s revolutionized the way Gie-Ming—and millions of Americans—watched TV.

Gie-Ming started taping NBA games, and he loved watching Kareem's sky hook, Dr. J's gravity-defying dunks, and Magic leading the fast break and handling the ball like it was on the end of a string. It wasn't long before Gie-Ming was a certifiable basketball junkie. He studied those tapes with the same fervor as when he studied for his PhD. He couldn't tell friends *why* he loved basketball, but he just did.

Gie-Ming also started playing a bit of basketball himself. He taught himself how to dribble and how to shoot by practicing jump shot after jump shot at a nearby playground. He was too shy to join a basketball league, but he could be coaxed into playing the occasional pickup game. He loved breaking a sweat on the basketball court, and playing the game became his favorite form of exercise.

When Gie-Ming and Shirley completed their schooling at Purdue, they moved to Los Angeles, where Gie-Ming worked for a company that designed microchips. Shirley jumped on the mommy track and gave birth to their first child, a son they named Joshua. Two years later, on August 23, 1988, ten years to the day after Kobe Bryant entered the world in Philadelphia, Jeremy Shu-How Lin was born.

A WESTWARD MOVE

A job offer moved the Lin family to Florida for two years, but then Silicon Valley lured Jeremy's parents, Gie-Ming and Shirley, to Northern California in the early 1990s. Gie-Ming's expertise became computer chip design, while Shirley—who had given birth to her third son, Joseph—returned to work in her specialty: quality control, which meant making sure new computer programs were bug-free when they were released.

The Lins settled in Palo Alto, a community of sixty thousand residents that bordered Stanford University. Gie-Ming, who wanted to introduce his favorite game—basketball—to his three sons, signed up for a family membership at the local YMCA. (You can be sure that James Naismith would have been very pleased.) When firstborn Joshua was five years old, Gie-Ming introduced him to the fundamentals of basketball by using the passing, dribbling, and shooting drills he'd studied on his VHS tapes. Jeremy received the same instruction when he started kindergarten, and so would Joseph when he reached that age.

When Jeremy entered first grade, his parents signed him up for a youth basketball league. But at that young age, Jeremy wasn't very interested in the action around him. He was like those kids in T-ball who lie down on the outfield grass and watch the clouds pass by instead of what the next batter is going to do. Most of the time, Jeremy stood at half-court and sucked his thumb while the ball went up and down the floor. Since he couldn't be bothered to try harder, his mom stopped coming to his games.

As Jeremy grew and matured, he eventually became more interested in basketball, especially after he grew big enough to launch an effective shot toward the rim and watch it swish through the net. As shot after shot poured through the hoop, he was hooked. He asked his mother if she would come back and watch him play, but she wanted to know if he was actually going to try before she committed to returning to his games.

"You watch," he promised. "I'm going to play, and I'm going to score."

He scored all right. Sometimes Jeremy scored the maximum amount of points one player was allowed to under biddy basketball rules.

For the rest of Jeremy's elementary school years, his parents regularly took him and his brothers to the gym to practice or play in pickup games. They also enrolled him in youth soccer, but basketball was the game he wanted to play.

As the demands of schoolwork grew, Jeremy and his brothers would do their homework after school, wait for their father to come home for dinner, and then everyone would head over to the Y at eight o'clock for ninety minutes of shooting and pickup games. Gie-Ming continued to stress the fundamentals because he wanted the game's basic moves to become second nature to Jeremy.

As Jeremy improved, he couldn't get enough hoops action. On many nights, he and his family practiced and played right up until the time they closed the doors at the Palo Alto Family YMCA at 9:45 p.m.

While basketball turned out to be a fun family sport for the Lins, they weren't going to sacrifice academics or church on the altar of basketball. Academics were important to Gie-Ming and Shirley because they had seen firsthand how education could give them a better life. Church was even more important because they knew what a relationship with Christ meant to them and to the spiritual well-being of their sons.

Wherever they lived, the Lins gravitated toward a Chinese Christian church. When they moved to Palo Alto, they found a church they immediately liked: the Chinese Church in Christ in nearby Mountain View. This place of worship was really two churches in one. There were two services every Sunday at 11 a.m.—one in Mandarin and the other in English—in separate fellowship halls. Usually two hundred or so attended the Mandarin-speaking service, while around a hundred attended the worship service presented in English.

The strong demand for a church service in Mandarin was reflective of the demographics of the San Francisco Bay Area, home to the nation's highest concentration of Asian Americans. At one time, the US Census revealed that 27 percent of the people living in Palo Alto were Asian Americans—racially identifying themselves as Chinese American, Filipino American, Korean American, Japanese American, or Vietnamese American. There was a large Taiwanese American community in nearby Cupertino (24 percent of the population), while other bedroom communities like Millbrae, Foster City, Piedmont, and Albany had Asian populations of 10 percent or greater.

Stephen Chen, pastor of the Chinese Church in Christ, remembers the first time he met Jeremy a little more than ten years ago, when Chen was the youth counselor. "Jeremy was around thirteen when I first ran into him," he said. "We were having a church cleaning day, and he was running around with his friends and being rambunctious. I remember scolding him, saying, 'Hey, we're trying to clean things up, and you're making things more messy.' "

Feeling chastised, Jeremy went home and told his parents he didn't want to go to that church anymore because the youth guy had been so mean to him. His parents didn't take his side, however, and the incident soon blew over.

Stephen Chen, looking for things to do with the youth in the church, discovered that Jeremy and his older brother Josh were avid basketball players. Josh was starting to play high school basketball, and Jeremy was living and breathing the game in middle school.

"I hadn't played a lick of basketball before that time," Stephen said. "But I wanted to connect with the Lin brothers, so I asked them if we could do a little exchange: I would teach them about the Bible and they would teach me how to play basketball."

Josh and Jeremy readily accepted. After youth group was over, they'd go to a nearby basketball court, where the Lin brothers taught Stephen how to do a layup, properly shoot the ball, and box out on rebounds. Then they would get the youth group together, choose up sides, and play basketball games.

"Jeremy would pass me the ball, even when the game was on the line," Stephen said. "He wasn't afraid that I'd lose the game for him. If we did lose, his older brother would get upset, but Jeremy would even console his brother. Even at that young age, Jeremy was hospitable, eager to get along with different types of people. He was also a natural leader, and kids listened to him."

Before entering high school, Jeremy wanted to get baptized as a public statement that he believed in Jesus Christ as his Lord and Savior. Stephen was pleased to hear of that desire. The Chinese Church in Christ had a baptismal inside the church sanctuary, and Jeremy was dunked during a Sunday morning service. Not long after that, Stephen asked him if he'd become part of the youth ministry's leadership team.

Jeremy was willing. The church had been renting out a local high school gym on Sunday evenings so the kids in the youth group could play basketball and invite their friends to join them. "Jeremy would always be the one who would ask other kids to come out and play basketball with us," Stephen said. "And they would come. Jeremy wanted everyone to feel at home. That was just another way how he extended kindness to others."

The gym had two full courts across the main court. Many dads saw how much fun their kids were having, so they would play, too—fathers on one court and their sons on the other. Moms would visit with each other during the games of roundball.

All this basketball playing—after school, on weekends, and on Sunday nights—helped Jeremy to become quite a player, even though he was a shrimp on the court. As he entered his freshman year of high school, Jeremy topped out at 5 feet, 3 inches tall and weighed 125 pounds. Jeremy had set his sights on playing high school basketball, but he knew that if he didn't grow a lot in the next couple of years, he wasn't going to get a chance to play, no matter how talented he was.

One day, Jeremy told Stephen, "I want to be at least six feet tall."

Stephen looked at Jeremy. He knew that Asians were stereotyped as a short people, and there was some truth to that. The average male height in the United States is 5 feet, 10 inches, while in China, the average male height is 5 feet, 7 inches. Unfortunately for Jeremy, his parents weren't tall either. Both stood 5 feet, 6 inches, so he didn't have a great gene pool working for him.

"So how are you going to become six feet tall?" Stephen asked.

"I'm going to drink milk every day," young Jeremy replied.

For the next few years, Shirley was constantly running to the local supermarket to buy milk by the gallon. He drank the dairy product like it was . . . water. Jeremy had a glass of milk with his breakfast cereal, drank milk at lunch, and always had a couple more glasses of milk with dinner.

"I drank so much milk because I was obsessed with my height," Jeremy said. "I'd wake up in the morning and measure myself every day because I heard that you're always taller in the morning, at least when you're growing. I wanted to see if I had grown overnight."

Jeremy's great wish was to be taller than his older brother, Josh, who was in the midst of a growth spurt that would take him to 5 feet, 10 inches during high school. Desperate to will his body to grow taller, Jeremy even climbed on monkey bars at school and let himself hang upside down, thinking that would expand his spinal column and make him taller.

Jeremy understood that he couldn't "force" his body to grow, but he also believed that to be competitive in the game of basketball, he had to grow to at least six feet tall.

MIRACLE-GRO
Jeremy enrolled at Palo Alto High School, where he made a big impression on his freshman basketball coach—even though he was one of the smallest players on the team. Years of playing in youth basketball leagues at the Y had honed his skills. His freshman coach stood up at the team's end-of-the-season banquet and declared, "Jeremy has a better skill set than anyone I've seen at his age."

And then something miraculous happened.

Jeremy grew.

And grew.

And grew.

By Jeremy's junior year, he had sprouted *nine inches* to reach the magic number—six feet of height. But he wasn't done. Jeremy would go on to add two more inches by his senior year and another inch or inch-and-a-half in college to reach his present height, which is a tad over 6 feet, 3 inches. He also added bulk: his body filled out to a solid 200 pounds.

Not only did Jeremy grow like a beanstalk during his freshman and sophomore years, but he also showed Palo Alto High opponents that he could run the offense, shoot lights-out, and make the player he was guarding work extra hard. His position was point guard, which is perhaps the most specialized role in basketball. The point guard is expected to lead the team's half-court offense, run the fast break, make the right pass at the right time, work the pick-and-roll, and penetrate the defense, which creates open teammates when he gets double-teamed.

When Jeremy dribbled the ball into the front court, he played like a quarterback who approached the line of scrimmage and scanned the defense to determine its vulnerabilities as well as its capabilities. Jeremy's mind quickly determined how an opponent's defense was set up and where the weak spots were. His quickness and mobility were assets.

During his sophomore season, Jeremy was not only good enough to win the point guard starting role, but his fantastic play also earned him the first of three first-team All-Santa Clara Valley Athletic League awards. During his junior season, he was the driving force behind Palo Alto High, helping the team set a school record for victories by posting a 32–2 record.

It was during Jeremy's senior year that he was the motor that propelled his team to the Division II California state championship. Going into the championship game, Palo Alto was a huge underdog against perennial powerhouse Mater Dei, a Catholic high school from Santa Ana in Southern California. No team had won more state basketball titles than Mater Dei, and the Monarchs, who had a 32–2 record, came into the game ranked among the nation's top teams.

Talk about a David-versus-Goliath matchup. Mater Dei was loaded with Division I recruits and had eight players 6 feet, 7 inches or taller, while Palo Alto had no one over 6 feet, 6 inches. Playing at Arco Arena, home of the Sacramento Kings, Jeremy was all over the court and personally engineered the plucky and undersized Palo Alto team to a two-point lead with two minutes to play. Could the Vikings hang on?

Jeremy brought the offense up the floor, trying to eat up as much clock as possible. Suddenly, there were just seconds left on the 35-second shot clock. Jeremy was above the top of the key when he launched a rainbow toward the rim to beat the shot clock buzzer. The ball banked in, giving Palo Alto a five-point lead.

Mater Dei wasn't finished yet, and neither was Jeremy. The Monarchs cut the lead to two points with 30 seconds to go, and then Jeremy dribbled the ball into the front court. Mater Dei didn't want to foul him because the Monarchs knew he was an excellent free throw shooter, so they waited for him to dish off to a teammate. Jeremy, however, sensed an opening and drove to the basket in a flash, taking on Mater Dei's star player, 6-foot, 8-inch Taylor King, in the paint. Jeremy went up and over King for a layup that gave him a total of 17 points in the game and iced the state championship in the 51–47 win.

You'd think that with all the college scouts in the stands for a state championship game, Jeremy would have to go into the Federal Witness Protection Program just to get a moment's respite. But the recruiting interest had been underwhelming all season long and stayed that way after the win over Mater Dei. It wasn't like Jeremy played for a tumbleweed-strewn high school in the middle of the Nevada desert. He was part of a respected program at Palo Alto High, and his coach, Peter Diepenbrock, was well-known to college coaches.

And Jeremy was highly regarded in Northern California high school basketball circles. He was named first-team All-State and Northern California's Division II Scholar Athlete of the Year. The *San Francisco Chronicle* newspaper named him Boys Player of the Year, as did the *San Jose Mercury News* and *Palo Alto Daily News*.

Despite all the great ink and the bushel basket of post-season awards, despite sending out a DVD of highlights a friend at church had prepared, and despite Coach Diepenbrock's lobbying efforts with college coaches, Jeremy did not receive *any* scholarship offers to play at a Division I school. That MIA list included Stanford University, which was located literally across the street from Palo Alto High. (A wide boulevard named El Camino Real separates the two schools.)

It's perplexing why Stanford didn't offer Jeremy a scholarship. After all, Jeremy checked off a lot of boxes for the Cardinal:

- great high school basketball résumé
- local product
- strong academic record
- Asian-American

Regarding the last bullet point, almost 20 percent of the undergrad Stanford student body was Asian-American, and, as you read earlier, the school was located in a part of the country with a strong Asian population. But the Stanford basketball program took a pass. Some Stanford boosters interceded for Jeremy, telling the coaches that they had to give this Lin kid a look. But the best response the family received was that Jeremy could always try to make the team as a walk-on.

The Lins' eyes turned across the bay toward Berkeley, but the University of California coaching staff said the same thing: *You can try to walk on, but no guarantees.* During one recruiting visit, a Cal coach called Jeremy "Ron."

The disrespect continued at Jeremy's dream school—UCLA, where Josh was enrolled. Jeremy would have loved to have played for the storied Bruin program, and he was the kind of upstanding young man legendary Bruin coach John Wooden would have loved to recruit back in the 1960s and 1970s. But the message from UCLA coaches was the same: *You'll have to make the team as a walk-on.*

Jeremy knew that few walk-ons—non-scholarship players invited to try out for the team—ever stick on the Division I basketball roster. He would never say it himself, but some basketball observers thought the fact that Jeremy *was* Asian-American cost him a Division I scholarship. Recruiters couldn't look past his ethnicity, couldn't imagine an Asian-looking kid having the game to compete against the very best players in the country. For whatever reason, they couldn't picture him playing basketball at the Pac-10 level.

RUNNING UP AGAINST A WALL

Jeremy had run into a "system" that blocked his path like two Shaqs in the paint. College coaches, who are the decision makers, look for something quantifiable in a high school player—like how tall he is or how high he can jump or how many points per game he scores. Jeremy's greatest strengths didn't show up in a box score. His game was running the show, leading the offense, and setting up teammates. He had an incredible feel for the game, a Magic-like peripheral vision, and a take-charge attitude that coaches love to see in their point guards.

"He knew exactly what needed to be done at every point in the basketball game," said his high school coach, Peter Diepenbrock. "He was able to exert his will on basketball games in ways you would not expect. It was just hard to quantify his fearlessness."

The problem likely stemmed from the fact that major college coaches had never recruited a standout Asian player before, so they didn't know what to do with Jeremy. Asian American gym rats like him were a novelty in college basketball; only one out of every two hundred Division I basketball players came from Asian American households. In many coaches' minds, college basketball stars had a different skin complexion or looked different than Jeremy.

The family had some options, however, thanks to Gie-Ming's and Shirley's insistence that their sons study and perform just as well in the classroom as they did on the basketball court. Jeremy carried a 4.2 grade-point average (in the grade-point system, an A is worth 4 points, but AP or Advanced Placement classes were weighted heavier because of their difficulty) at Palo Alto High, where he had scored a perfect 800 on his SAT II Math 2C during his *freshman* year. Jeremy's parents felt that if Pac-10 and other Division I teams didn't want their son, then maybe he could play for a top-ranked academic college—like Harvard.

The Lins looked east—toward the eight Ivy League schools, which are the most selective (and therefore elite) universities in the country. Harvard and Brown each stepped up; both coaches said they'd guarantee him a roster spot. Each made the case that they *really* wanted him to play for their basketball programs.

In the Lin family, there was no discussion. If Harvard—the assumed No. 1 school in the country in nearly everyone's eyes—wanted him, then he was going to play basketball for Harvard, even if that meant his parents would pay for his schooling out of their own pockets. Harvard, like Yale, Princeton, Columbia, and the rest of the Ivy League schools, didn't offer athletic scholarships.

This was no small consideration for Jeremy's parents. In round numbers, a year of undergraduate studies at Harvard costs fifty thousand dollars, which covers tuition, room and board, books, fees, and the like. The Lins were already shelling out for Josh's education at UCLA.

"The tuition is nuts," Jeremy said. "My parents did everything they could to get me through school. I received some financial aid from Harvard and took some loans out."

It turned out to be a great investment on the academic as well as the athletic side.

DEALING WITH THE YAHOOS

Harvard basketball dates back to 1900, when John Kirkland Clark, a Harvard Law School student, introduced the game to the school. Basketball at Harvard, and at other colleges around the country, changed during the next century, and one telling example is the student section. You don't have to be studying to become a rocket scientist to know that college basketball crowds can be brutal.

So it should come as no surprise that the sight of a prominent, all-over-the-floor Asian American basketball player personally *beating* their team would prompt a few immature—and likely drunk—members of student sections to taunt Jeremy during his four-year playing career at Harvard.

Some yelled really stupid (and racist) stuff, like "Hey, sweet and sour pork" or "wonton soup" from the stands. "Go back to China" and "The orchestra is on the other side of campus" were some of the other dim-witted taunts. One time at Georgetown, Jeremy heard terribly unkind remarks aimed in his direction, including the racial slurs "chink" and "slant eyes."

Jeremy just showed God's grace and gave his tormenters the other cheek. But he also played harder. Granted, the taunts bothered him at first, but he decided to let his game speak for itself. In the process, he helped make Harvard relevant again in college basketball and revived a dormant program.

During his junior and senior years, he was the only NCAA Division I men's basketball player who ranked in the top 10 in his conference for scoring, rebounding, assists, steals, blocked shots, field goal percentage, free throw percentage, and three-point shooting percentage.

Was there anything missing? Well, he was co-leader of a campus Bible study group, so maybe there was a "souls saved" category that didn't get counted.

Many college-age Christians lose interest in their faith, even live prodigal lives when they go off to college. Jeremy, though, grew spiritually because he connected with the Harvard-Radcliffe Asian American Christian Fellowship (HRAACF). Although his involvement with the group was limited by the demands of classwork and playing basketball, he met regularly with Adrian Tam, an HRAACF campus staffer. Adrian became a spiritual mentor to Jeremy, as they studied the Bible together and read books like *Too Busy Not to Pray*. "He loved his roommates, spending lots of intense one-on-one time with them, leading investigative Bible studies with them, and just plain hanging out with them," Adrian said.

What Tam remembers most about Jeremy, from their very first meeting, was his humility. "Even though he was more accomplished, smarter, and just plain bigger than I was, he always treated me with respect and honor," Tam says. "He was real with me, earnestly desiring to follow God in all things. He had a quiet ambition—not only to be the best basketball player he could be, but also to be the best Christ-follower he could be."

That quiet ambition was fully displayed on the basketball court, where Jeremy was a hit, pure and simple. He was such an exciting player that Harvard fans wore crimson red T-shirts with the words "Welcome to the Jeremy Lin Show" silkscreened across the front. He achieved such notoriety that Santa Clara University, which is located fifteen miles from Palo Alto, invited the Harvard team to the West Coast for a "homecoming" game during Jeremy's senior year and sold out its 4,700-seat arena.

The East Coast media heard of the Jeremy Lin Show and sent reporters from New York and Boston to check him out. Some of the more memorable quotes:

- "Jeremy Lin is probably one of the best players in the country you don't know about" (ESPN's Rece Davis).
- "He is a joy to watch. He's smooth, smart, unselfish, and sees the floor like no one else on it sees" (*Boston Herald* columnist Len Megliola).
- "Keep an eye on Harvard's Jeremy Lin. The fact that

he's an Asian-American guard playing at Harvard has probably kept him off the NBA radar too long. But as scouts are hunting everywhere for point guards, more and more are coming back and acknowledging that Lin is a legit prospect" (ESPN NBA draft analyst Chad Ford).

Jeremy's stock rose during his senior year when Harvard played then No. 12-ranked University of Connecticut, a traditional college basketball powerhouse, on the road. He dissected and bisected UConn for 30 points and nine rebounds and threw a scare into one of the top teams in the country. Harvard lost 79–73.

When Jeremy's playing career at Harvard was over, he had high hopes that an NBA team would draft him and give him a clean shot at making the roster. But then . . . God had another plan because the way Jeremy made it to the NBA only could have happened in God's economy. In other words, it was a miracle.

Let's review what happened.

After pre-draft workouts with eight teams, including his hometown Golden State Warriors, Jeremy was passed over through two rounds and sixty players chosen in the 2010 NBA draft. Playing at an Ivy League school probably had a lot to do with that—the last Harvard player to wear an NBA jersey was Ed Smith, who played all of eleven games in his one-season career back in 1953–54. The conventional wisdom among pro scouts was that Harvard players never pan out in the NBA.

After the draft, Dallas general manager Donnie Nelson invited Jeremy to play on the Mavericks' Summer League team. NBA Summer League games are played at frenetic pace, and they can be a bit sloppy, but for rookies or other non-roster players like Jeremy, summer league provides a fleeting chance—perhaps a *last* chance—to pit their skills against NBA-level players and make an impression. The eight-day summer league season was held in Las Vegas in July 2010.

Jeremy wasn't a starter for the Maverick Summer League team, not by a long shot. He sat behind an electrifying point guard named Rodrigue Beaubois, whom Dallas coaches were appraising for a roster spot. In the first four summer league games, Jeremy was a spot substitute who averaged just 17 minutes and eight points a game.

In summer league's final game, Jeremy's team was playing the Washington Wizards Summer League team, which featured John Wall, the No. 1 overall draft pick in the 2010 NBA draft.

Jeremy's teammate, Rodrigue Beaubois, twisted an ankle and had a poor outing in the first half. When Jeremy took his place, he outplayed, outhustled, outdrove, and outshined John Wall while leading his team to a big comeback—drawing oohs and ahs from the crowd with several fearless drives to the rim.

After that single half of brilliant play, several NBA teams looked at Jeremy in a new light. The Mavericks, the Los Angeles Lakers, and the Golden State Warriors all saw something in the kid. They thought that with the right seasoning, he could develop into an NBA player. Their thinking was that Jeremy could play a season in the NBA's Development League—known as D-League—and see where that took him.

And then Joe Lacob entered the picture.

Who is Joe Lacob?

During the summer of 2010, Lacob was in the midst of purchasing the Golden State Warriors with Peter Guber, the former chairman of Sony Pictures. Together, they put a $450 million tender to buy the team.

So how did this affect Jeremy?

Well, it turns out that Joe Lacob had coached his son's youth basketball team, which played against Jeremy when he was a pipsqueak. This fascinating interview between Lacob and *San Jose Mercury News* columnist Tim Kawakami explains things:

Let's just confirm that you made the call to sign Jeremy Lin.

Lacob: It was my call.

Why Lin?

Lacob: Well, that's a special situation.

Your son played with Lin? Against Lin?

Lacob: There were probably three guys that were pretty much the best point guards in high school in this area at that time, and Jeremy Lin was probably the best of them. And my son, Kirk, was right there with him. I've watched them play against each other, and I've coached against him since he was this high.

So I know him from [the time he was] a little kid. Also at Palo Alto I watched him win the state championship over a superior team, and he dominated Mater Dei. And he has heart, he has a lot of talent, he's athletic, which a lot of people don't understand. He's pretty long.

He has a game that translates to the NBA. He can drive, he's a slasher. He needs to shoot better, obviously. He needs to be a better outside shooter.

It's funny, people don't know his game. They say, oh, he's a shooter but he doesn't have these other skills. No, that's not true, it's the opposite.

Jeremy Lin, I think, can play. He didn't sign because he's Asian-American. That was a nice feature, like anything else. And I think it's great for that community and for the Warriors. But he got signed because he can play.

And that's how Jeremy Lin got his chance to play in the NBA. Two weeks after summer league, he signed a two-year contract with the Warriors, and the news of his signing sent a shockwave through the San Francisco Bay Area—especially the Asian-American community. Then, through hustle and grit in training camp, he won a spot on the Warriors roster.

Undrafted, given up, and forgotten, Jeremy had somehow beaten the incredible odds to put on an NBA jersey.

Even better, his hometown team wanted him—and so did the hometown fans.

HIS ROOKIE YEAR

Jeremy made his debut in Golden State's second game of the 2010-11 season—on "Asian Heritage Night"—before a crowd of 17,408 fans that exploded with cheers when he was inserted into the game with two-and-a-half minutes to go. Jeremy had the honor of dribbling out the final seconds of a hometown victory over the Los Angeles Clippers.

Jeremy Lin had made history. Not only did he become the first Chinese/Taiwanese American basketball player in the NBA, but he was the first American-born player of Chinese descent to step onto an NBA court.

His parents had some advice for him when the season started. "They said, 'Be smart. There are going to be girls throwing themselves at you, so be smart.' Typical parent stuff," Jeremy said. "They also reminded me to make sure that I took care of my relationship with God first."

"So was it difficult or easy being a Christian in the NBA?" I asked.

"I don't want to say it was easy, but it wasn't as bad as I thought it would be. It helped that I had a couple of teammates who were strong Christians—Stephen Curry and Reggie Williams. We would go to chapel together before the games, and we would occasionally have Christian conversations, so that was definitely helpful. I had a lot of accountability in terms of a small group at home. And I was at home playing for the Warriors, so I went to my home church whenever I could. I had my pastor, Stephen Chen, and then I had my small group."

After signing with the Warriors, Jeremy got his own place in Hayward, located roughly midway between his parents' home in Palo Alto and the Oracle Arena in Oakland, where the Warriors play.

Having his family nearby made the transition into the pros a lot easier, Jeremy said, but the difficult part was not having any type of rhythm.

"You know, church is really tough to attend, and the schedule is so crazy. I had to listen to sermons on my computer on a lot of Sundays. The sermons would not always be from my home church but from a variety of places. My dad burned a bunch of sermons for me onto a CD, so I would carry a little case of all the sermons. Devotionals were a big part of my walk this year—just quiet times in my hotel rooms."

I asked Jeremy about those stretches in hotel rooms, since there's a lot of downtime in the NBA during long road trips that can stretch from five to eight days.

"Yeah, I had more spare time this year and more time to spend with God this year than I have ever had," he said. "That was one of the parts that made it easier versus in college, where you wake up, go to class, practice, then do your homework and go to sleep. I had a lot more free time, since I was no longer in school."

"And what about the temptations?" I asked. "I imagine one of the difficulties about playing in the NBA is all the women hanging around the hotel rooms and all the people trying to talk to you and that type of thing."

"Yes, I think that's definitely true, but it wasn't really an issue for me because I didn't go out very much. And then there were guys on my team that I hung out with, and we had a different lifestyle, so it wasn't a huge issue. But it's definitely out there if you want it, but I chose to take it out of play. Once you take a stand for something at the beginning, everybody respects that and they don't bother you about it."

Jeremy wore No. 7 while at Golden State—the biblical number that denotes completeness or perfection—and local fans loved cheering for their native son. But all the attention created an intense spotlight that followed him everywhere, and it became apparent that he was and would be a work in progress as a basketball player.

In late December 2010, the Warriors reassigned Jeremy—who had been averaging 17 minutes a game—to their D-League affiliate, the Reno Bighorns. It was hard for him not to see the move as a demotion.

"It was a shock because I did not realize how different the two leagues were," he said. "It was also humbling because the locker rooms, facilities, attendance at games, the travel—it was all very different. Playing in Reno gave me a whole new perspective on everything. In the NBA, it was easy to complain about this or about that, but after being in D-League, I gained a greater sense of gratitude."

The Warriors coaching staff sent him down to give him playing time, and for the rest of the season, he bounced back and forth between Reno and Oakland. By the end of his rookie season, he had played in only twenty-nine games for a struggling Golden State team that finished 36–46.

So how did he take all those difficulties?

"It was really hard," he confessed. "People don't believe me when I say my rookie season was the toughest year of my life, but it was. I had a lot of long nights and struggles. I had to really learn how to submit my will to God and learn to trust Him while going through difficult situations that I thought were maybe unfair at times or things that I had wished would have gone in a different way.

"What I learned was to lean on God in those situations, and to make my relationship more intimate by spending more time with Him every day. I did a lot of reading and I did a lot of praying. More praying than I had ever done. I just learned a ton."

Jeremy had signed a two-year contract with Golden State, so there was every expectation that the team would bring him along, give him more playing time, and help him become the best player he could be.

Funny how things worked out.

THE LOCKOUT

The 2011 NBA lockout was the fourth in the league's history and nearly cost the NBA the 2011–12 season. As it was, the 161-day work stoppage began on July 1, 2011, and ended on December 8, 2011. The lockout delayed the start of the regular season from November 1 to Christmas Day, and reduced the regular season from eighty-two to sixty-six games.

During the lockout, Jeremy could not step inside the Warriors' gleaming training facility in downtown Oakland. Nor was he allowed any contact with the coaches, trainers, or staff. It was up to Jeremy to stay in shape, but he didn't lack in motivation. He worked harder than ever to be ready when the NBA started up again.

His schedule was Navy SEAL Team 6 material:

- 10–11 a.m.: agility training
- 11–noon: weight training
- 1–2: shooting work with a private coach
- 2–4 individual work

He posted YouTube videos of his maniacal workouts on the court and in the weight room while keeping an eye on the latest news of the contract negotiations. As each "deadline" passed without an agreement, both sides inched closer to the unthinkable—losing the entire season.

At the eleventh hour, the two sides reached an agreement on November 25, 2011. NBA commissioner David Stern announced that the first practice would be Friday, December 9, with the official season beginning on Christmas Day.

Jeremy arrived at the Oakland facility for the first day of practice and suited up. He had just met his new coach, Mark Jackson, who had never seen him play. Undoubtedly, Jeremy felt mounting pressure to prove himself all over again.

He was loosening up when he was told that general manager Larry Riley wanted to see him. The Warriors hadn't even started their lay-up drills.

If you've seen the Brad Pitt movie *Moneyball*, you know it's never good news when the GM asks to see you. This occasion was no exception.

Jeremy, the Warriors organization has decided to put you on waivers. We think you'll clear the waiver wire so that we'll get you back.

No matter how much perfume Riley sprayed into the air, the pronouncement stunk. Jeremy was being let go, cut from the team, categorically released. For all he knew, his short-lived NBA career was over.

This is where the "business" side of professional basketball can snap a player's dream in a heartbeat. What happened is that the Golden State management made a calculated decision to go after Los Angeles Clipper center DeAndre Jordan, a restricted free agent, to shore up a big hole in their low court. But to make Jordan an offer he couldn't refuse, the Warriors had to create room under their salary cap. That meant moving a few pieces around the chess board: cut Jeremy loose, use their amnesty clause on veteran guard Charlie Bell, and delay the signing of two rookies they liked—Klay Thompson and Jeremy Tyler. Then, under salary cap rules, the team would have enough money to bring in the center they desperately needed.

Once Jordan was signed, sealed, and delivered, the Warriors could bring back Jeremy—if no other team claimed him.

On the same day—December 9—something important to Jeremy's story was happening in New York. The Knicks waived veteran point guard Chauncey Billups and signed center Tyson Chandler, leaving the team out of cap space and without a true point guard.

Three days later, the Houston Rockets picked up Jeremy, so he *couldn't* go back to his childhood team. To add insult to injury, Clippers owner Donald Sterling—a notorious skinflint—matched

Golden State's overly generous four-year, $43 million offer for De-Andre Jordan, which meant the bruising center was staying in Los Angeles.

Talk about collateral damage. Golden State's gamble had blown up in their faces, and Jeremy was starting all over with a new team in Houston.

Jeremy arrived in Space City to discover he'd have to take a number and wait his turn to make an impression on the coaches. The Rockets were overstocked with point guards, and Jeremy had a hard time getting reps in practice. In two preseason games with the Rockets, he got on the floor for only eight minutes in each.

"At the time, I was thinking if this doesn't work out, I maybe needed to take a break from basketball," Jeremy told Marcus Thompson II with the *Silicon Valley Mercury News*. "I put in four months of training. I felt like I worked harder than anyone else. And now I was fighting for my chance to practice. I was questioning everything."

Then, on Christmas Eve, Jeremy woke up to find a lump of coal under his tree: he was being waived—let go—by Houston. This time GM Daryl Morey was the bearer of bad news, and he didn't salve the wound by saying that he hoped Jeremy would be back. His explanation was that the Rockets needed cap room to sign Haitian center Samuel Dalembert.

Merry Christmas, kid. Best of luck to you.

This could have been the end of the line. Yet Jeremy knew that faith was assurance of things hoped for, the conviction of things not yet seen (Hebrews 11:1), and this latest zigzag was not the time to doubt that God was still in control. It was the time to double down on his commitment to the Lord.

"As he headed back to the Bay Area, he gave up trying to control everything," Thompson wrote. "He gave up worrying. Or at least he tried like crazy."

The day after Christmas, Jeremy woke up at his parents' place and did a devotional before heading to the gym to stay in shape. During his shootaround, each time anxiety about the future crept in, he whispered Romans 8:28 to himself:

> *And we know that in all things, God works for the good*
> *of those who love him, who have been called according*
> *to his purpose.*

Something good was about to happen, he was sure of it. But Jeremy had no idea that more trials were ahead of him.

NEW YORK, NEW YORK

The New York Knicks had a guard problem.

When the lockout was over, the club signed thirty-two-year-old Baron Davis to be their point guard, even though he had a back injury that would keep him out until the end of February. Until Davis could join the team, the Knicks would forge ahead with veteran guards Mike Bibby and Toney Douglas at point and Iman Shumpert as a shooting guard. Bill Walker (six feet, six inches) and Landry Fields (six feet, seven inches) were small forwards who could play in the backcourt, too.

Then in the Christmas Day season opener against the Boston Celtics, Iman Shumpert got tangled up in the paint and injured his right knee. After the game, the team medical staff called the injury a sprained medial collateral ligament and said Shumpert would need two to four weeks to heal.

The Knicks were down to two guards.

The front office searched the waiver wire for a body—and Jeremy Lin was available. On December 27, the team claimed Jeremy, prompting Knick head coach Mike D'Antoni to say, "Yeah, we picked up Jeremy Lin off of waivers [as] a backup point [guard] in case. We've always liked him as a player, so we'll see where we go with it."

Reaction among the New York media was more muted. "The Knicks offense didn't get a huge boost Tuesday, but their collective GPA sure did," sniffed *New York Daily News* beat writer Sean Brennan, referring to the new Ivy Leaguer in their midst.

Jeremy didn't see it that way. He hit his Twitter account and sent out this message: "Thankful to God for the opportunity to be a New York Knick!! Time to find my winter coats from college lol!"

He was back in the NBA, but his contract wasn't guaranteed. He could be cut any day, so there was no reason to shop for a Fifth Avenue penthouse.

Fortunately, by this time his big brother Josh was living in the Big Apple, attending New York University as a dental student. Josh had married and set up housekeeping in a one-bedroom apartment in the Lower East Side, so if Jeremy didn't mind sleeping on the couch . . .

At Madison Square Garden, Jeremy was parked at the end of the bench like there was a wheel clamp strapped to his Nikes. D'Antoni rarely called his number, which was No. 17. His favorite, No. 7, wasn't available because the team's marquee player, Carmelo Anthony, wore it. We can surmise that Jeremy added a 1 before the 7—1 being the numeral that symbolizes unity and primacy, as

God is one, although in three persons. (At least that's *my* interpretation for Jeremy wearing No. 17.)

From December 28 to January 16, Jeremy played sixteen minutes in twelve games, scoring a total of nine points. I didn't see his name pop up very often in the box scores, but I was thankful he was still in the NBA. He was, after all, still on the cover of *Playing with Purpose*, though driving to the hoop in a navy blue Golden State jersey.

The Knicks were losing more than they were winning. And there was no way Jeremy could get into the offensive flow at the end of the game when the outcome had been decided and the play was chaotic and unrehearsed. He couldn't learn D'Antoni's system because there were very few practice days in the contracted season.

On January 17, Jeremy was demoted to D-League—the Erie BayHawks, the Knicks' developmental team affiliate.

Not again!

"I had no opportunity to prove myself," he said. "There was definitely a little bit of 'What's going on?' in my prayers. My flesh was constantly pulling at me. Whine. Complain. Whine. Complain. But the other side of me was thinking, *My God is all powerful . . . why do I even doubt God?* At the same time, it's a growing process."

And at least he'd get to play ball. In his BayHawks debut against the Maine Red Claws on January 20, Jeremy laid down a triple double: 28 points, 12 assists, and 11 rebounds. He played forty-five of the forty-eight minutes and repeatedly beat defenders with an extremely quick first step.

The Knicks scouts were impressed, as they should have been. Jeremy was immediately recalled to New York, where the season was going nowhere fast. Throughout the rest of January and early February, losses piled up like snowdrifts. Six losses in a row. Win a game. Three losses in a row.

Mike Bibby and Toney Douglas were playing horribly. Baron Davis was still out. Iman Shumpert showed little aptitude for the point guard position. Then Carmelo Anthony, the team's leading scorer, suffered a groin injury in mid-January and looked to be out for six weeks. There was no clear ball handler or offensive catalyst on the Knicks team. Jeremy was still the forgotten man on the bench.

On Saturday, February 4, at halftime of a home game against the New Jersey Nets, the injured star Carmelo Anthony— dressed in street clothes—pulled Coach D'Antoni aside in the locker room. He suggested that he play Jeremy more. See what the kid could do. What was there to lose? The Knicks had been beaten in five of their previous six games and were on a 2–11 losing jag.

Jeremy played like he was back with the Erie BayHawks—aggressive, like he belonged in the NBA. D'Antoni left him in, and Jeremy grabbed the reins of leadership. He scored 25 points, snared five rebounds, and dished out seven assists—all career highs—leading the Knicks to a 99–92 victory.

D'Antoni liked what he saw—a real point guard running the offensive show. "You're starting Monday night," he told the second-year player.

Linsanity was about to be unleashed on an unsuspecting public.

THE MIRACLE NEAR 34TH STREET

On the morning of Jeremy's first NBA start against the Utah Jazz on Monday, February 6, the Knicks webmaster made some changes to the team's website: the smiling face of youthful Jeremy Lin greeted eyeballs on the splash page. The marketing department sent out an e-blast with "Lisanity!" in the subject line.

The Knicks were shorthanded without Amar'e Stoudemire, who was granted bereavement leave after his older brother Hazell was killed in a car crash in Florida. Carmelo Anthony tried to play but had to leave the game after six minutes because of a strained right groin.

Time to step up.

Jeremy set the tempo again with dazzling dribbling and sweet drives to the basket. A nifty midair hand change for a reverse layup prompted the Knicks home crowd to chant "MVP! MVP!" They were obviously still in a celebratory mood after cheering their beloved New York Giants to a come-from-behind victory over the New England Patriots a day before in Super Bowl XLVI.

Jeremy scored a career-high 28 points, showing that his 25-point performance against the New Jersey Nets was no fluke. The fact that Jeremy orchestrated a win against a decent team attracted some notice around the league. But this was going to be a busy week for the Knicks. On Wednesday, they had a quick road trip to play the Washington Wizards, then a return home to host the Kobe-led Lakers on Friday night, followed by *another* road trip to Minnesota to play the T-Wolves on Saturday night.

Awaiting Jeremy in the nation's capitol was John Wall. Remember him? He was the No. 1 pick in the 2010 draft—and Jeremy's foil in the final game of Summer League, the game where

Jeremy played flawlessly and earned a roster spot with the Golden State Warriors.

On this evening, Jeremy was guarded closely by Wall when he employed a crossover dribble and blew past his defender like his sneakers were nailed to the floor. The lane opened up like the parting of the Red Sea. Instead of kissing the ball off the glass with a lay-in, Jeremy elevated and slammed a one-handed dunk that electrified the home crowd.

"I think they messed up their coverage," Jeremy said after the game.

Chalk up Jeremy's first double-double: 23 points and 10 assists in a 107–93 victory.

A tsunami was building. It wouldn't crest yet—that would happen two days later when Kobe and the Lakers came to the Garden. But for now, "the fluke no longer looks so flukey," wrote Howard Beck in the *New York Times*. "The aberration is not fading away. Jeremy Lin is not regressing to the mean, what that mean is supposed to be."

Surely he'd be put in his place by the great Kobe Bryant. Surely the thirty-three-year-old star had taken notice of the hoopla and would show this young buck a thing or two. Surely Jeremy wasn't still sleeping on his brother's couch.

Actually, he wasn't. Now he was sleeping on the couch of his teammate Landry Fields. The night before his breakout game against the New Jersey Nets, Jeremy found himself homeless. The comfy sofa where he laid his head at his brother's pad in the Lower East Side was reserved for friends who were coming over for a party.

Landry heard about Jeremy's plight and said he could crash

at his place in White Plains, New York, which was close to the Knicks' training facility. Landry had a nice large brown couch in the living room. A flat-screen TV, refrigerator, and bathroom were steps away. What more did a bachelor need?

There was no way that Jeremy or Landry were going to change a winning routine. Jeremy was sleeping on that couch whether he wanted to or not.

A date loomed with Kobe Bryant—the player he shared a birthday with—in the heart of downtown Manhattan. It's hard to describe how the American and global media apparatus had trained its lens on Madison Square Garden that evening, but they had. A galaxy of celebrities was on hand, including filmmaker and Knicks superfan Spike Lee, actor Ben Stiller, erstwhile wrestler and actor Dwayne "The Rock" Johnson, and New York Giants receiving hero Justin Tuck.

A lot—really a lot—was riding on the sinewy shoulders of Jeremy Shu-How Lin. He had everything to gain and much to lose, which is why you have to love what he did that night. All the pressure, all the hype, all the microphones, all the cameras examining every muscle twitch—and he didn't flinch.

I mean, laying down 38 points on Kobe and the Lakers was ridiculous. He made everything, including scoring nine of the team's first 13 points to help the Knicks build a large lead. Analysts like to call that "making a statement." He nailed short jumpers, put a deft spin move on Derek Fischer to beat him to the hoop, and flung in a three-pointer from the left baseline. Kobe nearly matched him, scoring 24 of his 34 points in the second half—but Bryant left the Garden on the wrong side of a 92–85 Knicks victory.

There was a telling moment when the torch of popularity may have been passed. Derek Fisher had been manning him, but on this possession, Kobe and Jeremy were running down the court together. Kobe reached out and put his hand on Jeremy's body. This was a subtle yet effective way for Kobe to establish defensive dominance and put Jeremy in a subservient position.

Jeremy, without hesitation, quickly but firmly pushed the hand away, as if to say, *There's a new sheriff in town.*

Jeremy proved he was no one-week wonder in outplaying Kobe Bryant and the Lakers team. He was being called the "Taiwanese Tebow" for the way he impacted his teammates and lifted their games—and for the forthright and earnest way he spoke about his faith afterward.

The hype surrounding Jeremy would only grow. He was legit. He had four straight games with at least 20 points and seven assists. In the history of the NBA—since the 1976 NBA/ABA merger—no player had scored more points in his first four starts.

More importantly, he had embraced the challenge of beating one of the league's top franchises in his first nationally televised game.

A LIFE OF ITS OWN

The Knicks had a tall order following the Lakers win: hop on the team plane and fly to Minneapolis for a road game the following night. Prior to tipoff, Jeremy and his new "roommate" Landry Fields enacted a rather unique pregame ritual that they first tried out against the Washington Wizards four days earlier.

Facing each other in front of the Knicks' bench, Jeremy pretended to flip through an imaginary book that Landry was holding in their hands. Then the pair pretended to take off their reading glasses, which they placed into imaginary pocket protectors. The routine ended with both players simultaneously pointing to the sky.

Okay, so it's not as dramatic as LeBron James throwing talcum powder into the air, but it was pretty cute. More than a few bloggers figured it was some sort of nerdy, bookwork *faux* handshake involving a Harvard grad with a former Stanford student-athlete. Actually, there was a lot more significance than that.

Landry Fields said that after Jeremy's first start, they had to come up with something since everyone was talking about the Harvard/Stanford connection between the two. "So we wanted to go out there and do something that was lighthearted and not too serious," he said.

The book is not a college textbook, Landry said, but God's Word. "It's a Bible because at the end of the day, that's what we're playing for. And that's why we point up toward the sky at the end."

The Jeremy Lin Show, meanwhile, played well off Broadway. Jeremy scored 20 points, reaching the 20-point plateau for the fifth time in a row, and his free throw with 4.9 seconds left (after missing the first) gave the Knicks a 99–98 lead and capped a furious fourth-quarter 12–4 comeback.

Jeremy and the Knicks team knew they stole one in Minnesota. After starting off hot in the first half with 15 points, the man guarding him, Ricky Rubio, showed why he was the league leader in steals. He forced Jeremy into making multiple turnovers, and Rubio even swatted away one of his lay-up attempts.

And just like there are no ugly babies, there's no such thing as an ugly win. The Knicks had now captured their fifth in a row without Carmelo Anthony and Amar'e Stoudemire, who was burying his brother in Florida.

From my home in Southern California, I was doing my best to keep up with Linsanity. The Knicks, I noticed, were finally getting a breather—two glorious days—before their next game in Toronto against the Raptors.

The game wasn't on any of my 500 channels, so I did the next best thing: I turned to *NBA Gametime Live*.

"Here's what's going on in Toronto," host Ernie Johnson said, then showed a clip of Jeremy driving into the maw of the Raptor defense. Jeremy was met there by Raptor Amir Johnson. A collision ensued, and on the continuation, Jeremy double-pumped a feathery four-footer into the hole. Three-point play!

Jeremy's fearless drive to the rack capped a 17-point rally to tie the game. A minute and five seconds was left to play.

Great, I thought. *I'm just in time to see a thrilling ending.*

"We cannot take you live to that game because of contractual restrictions," Ernie said, as if he was reading my mind. "But we will keep you up to speed. It's eighty-seven a piece in Toronto."

Ernie attempted to make small talk with analysts Greg Anthony and Chris Webber, but Anthony stared off into the distance, no doubt watching the live feed on an off-camera monitor.

Ten or fifteen seconds passed when Ernie interrupted the patter to announce an update from Toronto that they *could* show. The visual is still imprinted on my brain: Jeremy, yo-yoing the ball above the top of the key, letting the clock run down. The crowd of twenty thousand on its feet. A quick feint, and Jeremy pulls up for a beyond-the-arc, high-flying rainbow that sails cleanly through the net to give the Knicks a 90–87 lead with .05 seconds to go.

"Are you kidding me?" EJ exclaimed. "Are you kidding me? This story gets crazier and crazier every night the Knicks play."

He had done it again.

LOOKING AHEAD

What has Jeremy Lin wrought?

Who knows? But that's the beauty of sport. You never know the outcome.

As this edition of *Playing with Purpose* goes to press, Jeremy's story has taken on a life of its own. People genuinely *like* him, and well they should. They understand that stories like this happen so rarely. They recognize that Jeremy's an uncommon young man with uncommon leadership skills and extraordinary athletic gifts.

It's all happened so fast, arriving at the busy intersection where sport, religion, fame, and pop culture meet.

Pray for Jeremy Lin as he looks both ways and crosses the street.

Pray that he continues to hold the Lord's hand.

3.

LUKE RIDNOUR:
HEIR TO PISTOL PETE

Luke Ridnour was in fourth grade when his schoolteacher announced a big assignment she wanted Luke and his classmates to complete in two weeks.

The task?

Write a three-page paper on a person of their choosing.

Luke shifted eagerly in his seat. He knew exactly whom he wanted to write about.

When school let out, Luke gathered his backpack and sprinted from the rear of Blaine Primary School, past the green tennis courts, to the Blaine High gymnasium. The elementary school, middle school, and high school were located on the same campus, so the distance was only a hundred yards. Luke knew his father—a PE teacher and the high school's head basketball coach—would be in his office preparing for practice.

The Ridnour family lived in Blaine, Washington, a small town of four thousand situated in the very northwest corner of the continental United States. The border town is the terminus point for Interstate 5, the West Coast highway that links the Canadian border with the boundary of Mexico, 1,381 miles to the south. Blaine's colorful past dates back to the Fraser River gold rush of 1858, which brought an influx of eager prospectors into the region.

When Luke bounced into Rob Ridnour's office that afternoon, he told his dad about the assignment he had received that day.

"Who are you going to write about?" his father asked.

"Pistol Pete."

Of course, Rob thought.

Ten-year-old Luke knew about Pistol Pete because he and the family had recently watched *The Pistol: The Birth of a Legend*, a video that had been released a few months earlier. The slice-of-life movie told the story about Pete Maravich's eighth grade year when he played on the varsity basketball team at Daniel High School in Central, South Carolina, despite being too young to attend the school.

Set in 1961, the film recounted how Pete's teammates ostracized him because of his young age and because of his unworldly talent for shooting and whipping behind-the-back passes. *The Pistol* also explored the supportive father-son relationship between Pete and his father, Press Maravich, who was a former pro player and Clemson University coach.

"Well, you'll have to do some research on Pistol Pete before you write your paper," said Luke's father, who knew the entire Maravich story. Rob was a middle-schooler in the late 1960s, when Pete's sleight-of-hand artistry left crowds gasping and sportswriters crooning about the new sensation from Louisiana State University. (You'll read a lot more about Pete Maravich in the last chapter.)

Over the next couple of weeks, Luke read Maravich's

autobiography *Heir to a Dream* and also watched *Pistol Pete's Homework Basketball* training videos, which mesmerized him. Luke had been dribbling a basketball since age three and was a very skilled player for his age, but Pete could make the basketball do things he'd never seen before. Pete's effortless demonstration of ball-handling prowess captivated Luke's young imagination.

Luke emulated everything Pistol Pete did on the *Homework Basketball* videos—from ball-handling exercises like the Square V dribble, the crossover dribble, and the through-the-legs dribble, to positioning his wrist properly so as to impart backspin and thus more control on the jump shot. Luke even taught himself to twirl the ball on his right index finger like a spinning top.

Since Pete had said he took a basketball everywhere with him when he was a youngster, Luke started doing the same thing. He started carrying a basketball into Blaine Primary School and dribbling in the hallway on his way to class, though he sometimes got into trouble for being disruptive. After the final bell, he would dribble from the elementary school to his father's office inside the gym, where he'd hang out for a bit before leaving to shoot baskets with the high school players.

"I emulated everything I saw Pete do because I wanted to handle the basketball just like he did," Luke said. "I tried dribbling from a car while my dad drove down the street, and I dribbled on a railroad rail, but that was pretty difficult."

Luke even slept with his basketball, just like Pete.

There was another reason Rob Ridnour and his wife, Muriel, supported Luke's desire to write a paper on Pete Maravich. You see, Pistol was very outspoken about the transformation he had experienced after accepting Jesus Christ as his Lord and Savior following his retirement from pro basketball. That part of Pete's story was the focal point of *Heir to a Dream*, which was published a few months prior to his death from a sudden heart attack at age forty.

Rob and Muriel had Luke listen to a "Focus on the Family" broadcast in which Dr. James Dobson talked about the dramatic morning when Maravich collapsed and died after playing in a pickup basketball game with the Focus on the Family radio host and members of his staff. "I learned that Pistol Pete, toward the end of his life, was sold out for Jesus," Luke said. "That was the big thing that stands out in my memory, more than the basketball stuff. Yes, Pete was passionate about basketball, but when he found Jesus, that became his main passion."

Luke's parents were familiar with Dr. Dobson because they listened to Christian radio programs like "Focus on the Family" on Praise 106.5 FM while riding in the car. In addition, they raised Luke and his older sister, Heather, in the Christian faith and took them to church every Sunday morning and Wednesday night.

A COMMITMENT TO THE GAME

While working on his Pistol Pete paper, Luke saw the commitment Pete had made to the game at a young age—and he was inspired to do the same. Beginning in the fifth grade, he would get up at five every morning, rain or shine, to start his training regimen.

Blaine, since it lies so far north, can be a chilly, damp place in winter. The average highs in December and January are barely above 40 degrees, and it's not unusual for the lows to dip into the 20s. Rain is a constant. That never stopped Luke from his workouts, though. "He would religiously get up and do those drills *every* morning," Rob said. "Rain, snow . . . it didn't matter. He was out there every day from the fifth grade through his senior year of high school, even in winter and the pre-dawn darkness."

One Saturday, Luke had set a goal of making fifteen hundred free throws. Even though there was a driving snowstorm in Blaine that day, Luke stayed outside, his numb fingers stiff from the freezing cold, until he made his fifteen hundred free throws.

Rob had installed a basketball rim in the backyard patio, and that's where Luke practiced every morning before school. He began his training with a jump rope routine to warm up, and then he'd move into the "Maravich drills" he'd seen in the videos or that his father used in his summer basketball camps.

On one occasion, Luke asked his father how he could increase his quickness. "Now we're talking about a fifth-grader asking that question, which shows you how determined he was to improve every facet of his game," Rob said. "I told him boxers always had good body balance, good footwork, and improved quickness from jumping rope. So he decided to try rope jumping, and Luke became very good at it. I think jumping all that rope really helped his career. He's always had good feet and good body balance."

All that hard work—day after day, week after week—helped Luke make big leaps in his game. While he was still in elementary school, he would get the local parents clapping and cheering at his father's games at Blaine High when he put on dribbling demonstrations during halftime. Luke, whose specialty was simultaneously dribbling two balls at the same time, could dribble circles around anyone.

After seeing his halftime shows, friends of Luke's parents lavished praise on him, and some started calling him "Cool Hand

Luke"—after the famous 1960s film starring Paul Newman.

By the sixth grade, Luke had outgrown his middle school competition in Whatcom County, so his parents had him try out for an elite travel team from Seattle. When he was accepted, it necessitated some huge sacrifices on his parents' part. They had to drive Luke 220 miles roundtrip to the big city three times a week for practices and games.

COURT HUSTLER

When Luke Ridnour was in middle school, he'd often challenge the high school players on his father's team to three-point shooting contests before they started practice. The stakes: a bottle of Gatorade from the vending machine.

It wasn't long before the upperclassmen discovered that shooting treys against Luke was a losing bet.

So one time Luke said he'd shoot his three-pointers left-handed. This time he got some takers.

Big mistake.

They all had to pay up.

Luke was one of the youngest kids on the Seattle travel team—and the only white player. His black teammates called him "Casper," but that didn't bother Luke—in fact, he had fun with it. His team played in numerous AAU tournaments up and down the West Coast, which necessitated expensive road trips but also boosted Luke's basketball experience and abilities. His Central Area Youth Association (CAYA) team qualified for a national tournament in Lexington, Kentucky, and played in Florida.

All that tournament experience helped Luke make great strides in his game, and that was a big help when he started playing for his father during his freshman year of high school. Luke would become a dominant high school player and would help guide the Blaine Borderites (don't you love that mascot name?) to the Washington Class 2A state championship during his junior season. The grateful townspeople threw a huge parade down H Street for their favorite son and favorite team.

As Luke headed into his senior year, everyone could see that the 6-foot, 2-inch point guard was an awesome talent. All the 5 a.m. workouts, all the after-dinner shooting in the Blaine High gym, and all the out-of-state competition paid off as college scholarship offers began rolling in. College coaches could see he was a natural in the way he created separation with the dribble, pumped the perfect pass to his teammates, displayed his silky stroke at the free-throw line, and showed leadership on the floor.

Luke was the prototypical point guard the top-flight college basketball programs desired. Kentucky and Utah wanted him. So did Gonzaga University, an up-and-coming program in Spokane, located in the eastern part of Washington. In the Pac-10, the University of Washington was waiting to roll out the purple carpet in Seattle. Further south, Oregon and Oregon State both wanted Luke, but he couldn't visit both schools because he only had one recruiting trip left. The NCAA limits high school players to five out-of-town recruiting trips.

Luke flipped a coin to see which Oregon school he would visit. The University of Oregon won, and during his weekend visit in Eugene, he called his parents to tell him how much fun he was having.

Luke liked what he saw during his recruiting trip. I'm sure McArthur Court—the field house known as "The Pit" because of the way the crazy fans sit in bleachers almost directly on top of the players and shake the building from its wooden rafters to its hardwood floor—made a huge impression on him. Built in 1926, Mac Court's electric atmosphere was the consummate stage for college basketball.

Luke committed to Oregon before the start of his senior year, but he didn't put his game into cruise control. The way he played during his final season made him the talk of high school basketball in the state of Washington. Luke and his teammates at Blaine High netted another state championship, and McDonald's and *Parade* magazine named Luke a high school All-American.

During his four seasons of high school varsity basketball, Luke led the Blaine Borderites to a 97–11 record.

GO, DUCKS, GO!
Eugene, Oregon's second-largest city, is a college town, pure and simple. Humorist Dave Barry once said that Eugene is "approximately 278 billion miles from anything," but that's not really true. Eugene is a happening place—and the birthplace of Nike—that evokes a retro vibe that comes from a high concentration of hippies and vegetarian restaurants. While the Emerald City promotes its natural beauty and recreational opportunities—with a focus on the arts, alternative lifestyles, and a live-and-let-live culture—at the end of the day, Eugene is a small city that revolves around the twenty-three thousand students attending the University of Oregon.

Sure, Eugene is also a liberal enclave, where protests against "Big Oil" are clothing optional and people pass the tofu pâté around a campfire of hemp. But once you get beyond the red flannel shirts and the Birkenstocks, people are people. Not many are Christians, though. Eugene is the least-churched city in the least-churched state in the country. No one would ever confuse the Willamette Valley with the Bible Belt.

Yet Luke will tell you that it was a divine appointment for him to play his college career in Eugene for the Oregon Ducks, and much of the reason is because he met an ex-Marine who mentored him during this three-year career at the school.

That ex-Marine was Keith Jenkins, pastor of Jubilee World Outreach church, which grew from a congregation of seventeen persons in 1996 to nearly a thousand while Luke was in Eugene.

"Pastor Keith," as the Oregon athletes called him, was a volunteer chaplain for the University of Oregon sports teams who forged deep bonds with Duck athletes. In Luke, Pastor Keith saw a young man from the uppermost corner of Washington who needed a place of refuge, a Christian community he could plug into.

It helped that Luke's coach at Oregon, Ernie Kent, encouraged his players to foster relationships with their team chaplain. Luke didn't have to be asked twice. He and Pastor Keith met for Bible studies, and those times of reading God's Word deepened Luke's faith immeasurably. Sure, he had believed in Jesus since he started playing biddy basketball, but the things Pastor Keith taught him about God kicked things up a notch. "Really, when I started reading the Word with my chaplain, everything changed—the way I thought, the way I acted, and my attitude," Luke said. "It was like I was being washed by the Word."

Luke had a frustrating freshman year at Oregon, averaging seven points a game and shooting 33 percent from the field for a Duck team that was expected to do better. Oregon won half its games, finishing 14–14, but posted a dismal 5–13 record in the Pac-10 Conference. Still, Luke attracted notice for his play and was voted to the Pac-10 All-Freshman team.

Luke, who wanted to have a better sophomore year, went back to work during the off-season. It was hard to keep him out of Mac Court. Thanks to his father, Luke was used to having his own key to the gym, but at Mac Court, he had to be more creative. He made his way in during off hours by sticking athletic tape over the strike plate of one of the broad doors leading to the locker room so it wouldn't lock.

During Luke's sophomore season, the Duck basketball program won a lot of games because of him and *another* Luke on the team—Luke Jackson, a left-handed 6-foot, 7-inch small forward with a sweet jump shot and athletic in-the-paint moves. The two collaborated on a rip-and-run style that often saw Luke Ridnour accept an outlet pass, run the floor on the fast break, and hit the streaking Luke Jackson for a layin or dunk. Coach Ernie Kent preached up-tempo basketball—the equivalent of a no-huddle, two-minute offense in football—and that was the two Lukes' kind of game. Defenses chased Luke & Luke all game long.

As the Ducks piled up wins during the 2001–02 season, sportswriters began proclaiming Luke Ridnour the best point guard in the country—someone who could play in the NBA. Glowing stories about Luke called him an "old school" player who could have stepped off the set of the movie *Hoosiers*, the 1986 film about a small-town Indiana high school basketball team that won the state championship in 1952, at a time when all high schools in Indiana, regardless of size, competed in one state championship tournament. Sportswriters compared him to Jimmy Chitwood, the shy, reserved player who made the last-second shot to win the title for Hickory High.

Luke also showed spiritual leadership on a team that included a half-dozen Christians—including Luke Jackson—by helping organize voluntary pregame chapels and by asking the entire team to recite the the Lord's Prayer in the locker room before tipoff. These "kumbaya" moments translated to the court, too: the Ducks were ranked in the top five in the country for eleven different offensive categories during the 2001–02 season, including No. 1 in points per possession and true shooting percentage.

These Ducks liked to pass the ball around, and most of the assists came from Luke Ridnour, who showed an uncanny ability to penetrate and dish as well as work the pick-and-roll with his teammate and friend, Luke Jackson. Coach Kent summed up his point guard's contribution this way: "He gives himself up for his teammates."

The Luke & Luke Show helped the Ducks capture their first Pac-10 championship since 1945 and advance to the Elite Eight in the NCAA Tournament. Their title dreams ended with a loss to the No. 1 overall seed Kansas, however.

Back to sneaking into Mac Court through one of the taped-up back doors during the off-season.

ONE MORE COLLEGE SEASON . . . THEN ON TO THE NBA

The fall before his junior year at Oregon, Luke was named to *Playboy* magazine's preseason All-American team. As far as Luke was concerned, however, that was a nonstarter. He politely turned down *Playboy*, saying, "My mom wouldn't be too happy about it, and I didn't feel I should do it. It's a great accomplishment and all that, but it was a beliefs thing for me."

Interesting how God honored that stand. Not too long after Luke passed on *Playboy*, Nike announced it was commissioning a 50-by-170-foot billboard of Luke as a candidate for the Wooden Award, one of college basketball's top individual honors. The seventeen-story portrait of Luke, with ball on hip, was erected on a skyscraper near New York City's Times Square.

Luke didn't win the Wooden Award during his junior year at Oregon, but he cemented his status as one of the elite players in college basketball. He won plenty of other awards, including Pac-10 Conference Player of the Year after averaging 19.7 points a game.

The iron was hot, and it was time to strike and turn pro, although the Mac Court fans chanted "One more year!" so loudly during Luke's last home game that play had to be stopped as he walked off the court.

Luke made himself available for the 2003 NBA draft, and lo and behold, his hometown team, the Seattle SuperSonics, took him as the fourteenth pick. In many ways, it was a dream come true for Luke and his family: he would be playing NBA basketball within driving distance of his hometown of Blaine, meaning his parents could come to a lot of his games. Also, the Sonics needed a talented point guard prospect to replace aging Gary Payton, who was traded to Milwaukee.

Prior to his rookie season, Luke underwent surgery on his abdomen and groin, which forced him to miss nearly the entire slate of preseason games. Once he was healthy, he played in spurts—sometimes ten minutes a night, sometime twenty-five. His rookie season was marked by ups and downs, which were reflected in the team's season. Seattle floundered and missed the playoffs with a 37–45 record.

Luke had a breakout season during his second year in the league. He won a starting position in training camp, and with Luke quarterbacking the offense from his point-guard position and sharpshooter Ray Allen scoring from the shooting guard slot, the Sonics turned things around. Seattle was the surprise of the NBA early in the 2004–05 season, winning 23 of its first 29 games. The Sonics climbed to the heady heights of 40–16 in early March before slumping the last six weeks of the season. After finishing 52–30, their quest for a championship was dashed with a loss to the San Antonio Spurs in the second round of the NBA playoffs.

SETTLING IN AND SETTLING DOWN

Luke's sophomore season showed that he belonged in the NBA, and since then, he has settled into a good pro basketball career. Off the court, he also decided to settle down, too. In August 2005, he married Kate Reome, whom he had been dating for three years.

Luke and Kate first met during the state basketball tournament in his senior year of high school. They had both been asked to appear at a Rotary Club luncheon honoring the best high school basketball players in the state. Luke represented Blaine High, while Kate was invited on behalf of Lakeside High in Spokane.

Luke and Kate sat next to each other at the luncheon. Kate knew about Luke because all the girls on her team had a crush on this cute boy with tight blond curls. Kate wasn't completely impressed, though, because she thought Luke looked like a slacker. He was dressed in his standard uniform—faded T-shirt, beige cargo shorts, and backward hat—while everyone else, including herself, had dressed nicely for the occasion.

Luke went off to the University of Oregon, while Kate had another year of high school before moving on to Central Washington University in Ellensburg, where she had earned a scholarship to play volleyball. You would think that would be the last time Luke and Kate would ever see each other. But you'd be wrong.

Luke and Kate's opportunity to "reconnect" started when she visited a guy friend who happened to be an acquaintance of the Ridnours. She needed to get this fellow's e-mail address—as well as the e-mails of any of their common friends—because she had lost her contact list.

As her friend scrolled through his smartphone, his voice raised an octave. "Oh, here's Luke's e-mail! Do you remember him?"

Sure, she remembered Luke Ridnour. He was practically famous in Washington sports circles. But she didn't think it was a good idea to send Luke a "Hi, howya doing?" e-mail out of the blue; after all, it had been two years since their one meeting at the Rotary luncheon. She thought that if she e-mailed him, he'd probably think she was some eighth-grade teenybopper.

Kate changed her mind, though, and sent Luke a friendly e-mail reminding him of how they sat at the same table at the Rotary luncheon. The e-mail went out during March Madness in 2002, the year the Ducks were in the national championship hunt.

To her everlasting surprise, Luke quickly responded and said, "Of course I remember you."

As they got to know each other through phone calls and e-mail messages, Luke learned that he and Kate were in sync spiritually. Back in high school, she had become interested in Christianity while attending Young Life events. Then several of her girlfriends invited her to a Wednesday night service. That night, the speaker said if anyone at the service hadn't made a decision to accept Jesus into their life, that would be a great time to do it. Kate knew she didn't understand everything about Christianity, but something in her heart prompted her to move forward and start down the road of life . . . with Jesus Christ holding her hand every step of the way.

Luke and Kate's long-distance relationship grew slowly. After three years, their love blossomed. When she walked down the aisle in a wedding dress, on the arm of her father, she was ready to marry a young man she was crazy in love with.

Here's how Kate described her courtship to Jill Ewert, editor of *Sharing the Victory* magazine:

You must have made a big impression on him then.

Kate Ridnour: You know, I guess so. He told me later on that after we met at that Rotary Club, he went home and tried to get my phone number from my high school. I kidded him that he was a stalker.

But I look back on that day when I went over to my friend's place to get those e-mail addresses. It was such a God thing because it was windy out. I was like, *I don't want to go anywhere.* But then I decided to go see this guy so that I could keep in touch with friends. Funny how things panned out.

You can see how you almost didn't go, right?

Kate: Oh, yeah! Looking back you can see how it was just scripted, you know? God was like, *Okay, go here. Go there. Okay, e-mail. Talk. Now you're together.*

It's funny. It's almost a boring story because we weren't high school sweethearts. But it's neat because I did know him before he was in the league. I knew him before he was the big Luke Ridnour from the Seattle SuperSonics. I knew the little, scrawny white guy.

Is that how you still think about him?

Kate: Oh, no! He's so much bigger. He's strong and manly! But you know, he is just a boy. There are things that he does and in how he acts. He's just a boy in a big man's world.

Believe me, Kate was not in any way putting down her husband. For the longest time, Luke was content to drive around an old beat-up truck, but his sensible wife pointed out to him that he was being pennywise but pound foolish—if the truck broke down when he was on his way to practice and he was late, the fine would be five thousand dollars.

The couple lived in a waterfront home on Lake Washington that Luke had purchased after the Sonics drafted him. Following their marriage, they settled into the NBA lifestyle—but not the lifestyle many associate with professional basketball players. Luke was a devoted husband who had no interest in straying. Being separated from Kate during long road trips wasn't easy for him, so Luke took advantage of advances in modern technology. He and Kate got into Skype, a software application that allows users to make voice calls over the Internet and to see each other via webcams on their computers. As soon as he arrived at the team hotel—as long as it wasn't late at night or in the wee hours—Luke would call his wife for a chat.

I asked Luke how he handled it when the team bus pulled

up to the player hotel at 3 a.m., following a plane flight, and he saw all sorts of women hanging out in the lobby. Since he always walked straight to his room without passing Go or collecting two hundred dollars, as they say, how did he protect himself from temptation?

By wearing the full armor of God, he told me.

Luke says that Ephesians 6:11—"Put on the full armor of God, so that you can take your stand against the devil's schemes"—is a reminder that Satan will always try to come at him but that the Lord always prevails in the lives of those who "armor up."

BENDS IN THE ROAD

Three years into their marriage, life threw Luke and Kate a pair of curves—on the same day. They weren't *bad* curves . . . just new bends in the road for them to navigate.

The 2007–08 season, Luke's fifth in the league, was filled with turmoil for the SuperSonics. The team had been sold in 2006 to a group of investors from Oklahoma City that included Clay Bennett. The handwriting was on the wall: Bennett threatened to move the team to Oklahoma if a deal for a new lease at KeyArena couldn't be worked out between the franchise and the city of Seattle. The Sonics were looking like a lame duck team to their fans.

Then, in August 2008, a blockbuster trade involving three teams and six players was announced, and it included Luke, who was being shipped to the Milwaukee Bucks.

Trades happen in the NBA.

On the same day Luke heard that he would be playing for Milwaukee, he and Kate learned she was pregnant with their first child. That was a double-barrel blast of family news.

Kate always liked the name Trey, but after Luke got *traded*, she started playing around with that verb and came up with "Tradon"—pronounced TRAY-don.

"I think it's a pretty unique name," Luke said.

Tradon Lukas Ridnour was born on April 13, 2009.

Luke played two seasons with the Bucks, averaging 10.9 points, 4.9 assists, and 2.2 rebounds per game. He became a free agent after the 2009–10 season and signed a four-year, $16 million contract with the Minnesota Timberwolves.

Luke's veteran presence on the floor was an asset, but the T-wolves fell on hard times during the 2010–11 season, compiling the NBA's worst record at 17–65. As the losses piled up like snowdrifts, Kate learned she was expecting again. Ultrasounds revealed that the Ridnours would become parents of twin boys in early February 2011.

When Beckett and Kyson Ridnour were born, Luke and Kate were stunned to learn that Kyson suffered from life-threatening complications in the esophageal area. Though Kyson's condition has made for difficult times in the Ridnour household, Luke and Kate hold fast to their faith in God.

And they're praying for a miracle.

"I don't want to get into the details of what's going on, but Kate and I believe that one day there will be an amazing testimony that we'll be able to share with thousands and thousands of people about the miracle that God has done," Luke said.

Luke and Kate have received emotional support from friends and from the pastor of their home church in Seattle, who flew into Minneapolis to pray and lay hands on Kyson. (The Ridnours maintain a permanent home near Seattle during the off-season.)

Their home church, Eastridge Church in Issaquah, sent out prayer chain updates regarding the family's difficult situation.

"It's been a tough go for the family," said Rob, "an emotional time for Luke, but he's holding on to his faith and praying for God's healing."

It hasn't been easy, but Luke says he has an extreme amount of peace about what will happen with Kyson as family perseveres through this tough time.

"We believe miracles still happen."

2012 update: Kyson continues to make progress as his father contributes to the Timberwolves' cause, but the family is still in the thick of things.

4.

STEPHEN CURRY, NENÊ, REGGIE WILLIAMS, NICK COLLISON, KEVIN DURANT, GREIVIS VASQUEZ: THEY'RE PLAYING WITH PURPOSE IN THE NBA, TOO

STEPHEN CURRY
GOLDEN STATE WARRIORS

Twenty-three-year-old Stephen Curry has some impressive genes working for him.

Stephen, the son of former NBA sharpshooter Dell Curry and former Virginia Tech volleyball standout Sonya Curry, is coming off a strong second season with the Golden State Warriors. As the team's point guard, he averaged 18.6 points and 5.8 assists in 34 minutes a game during the 2010–11 season—although it remains to be seen how much of a load he will carry in the upcoming year.

Stephen became a Christian in fifth grade, when he responded to an altar call at Central Church of God in Charlotte, North Carolina. His parents thought it was important that he attend a Christian high school, so he played prep ball at Charlotte Christian School, where he scored more than fourteen hundred points to become the school's all-time leading scorer.

Stephen's father played for Virginia Tech back in the day, so he naturally wanted to follow in his father's footsteps. But when the Hokies didn't offer him a scholarship, he chose a school close to home—Davidson College in Davidson, North Carolina—that played a Division I schedule and occasionally qualified to play in the NCAA tournament.

One time before a preseason practice heading into his freshman season at Davidson, Stephen opened a cardboard box containing a new pair of sneakers. He then took a Sharpie pen with silver ink and wrote "Romans 8:28" on each toe as a reminder of his mother's favorite verse. That became something he did with all his basketball shoes.

It was during Stephen's sophomore year at Davidson that he first attracted national attention. During the 2008 NCAA tournament, he led tiny Davidson all the way to the Elite Eight. The Wildcats registered upset victories over Gonzaga, Georgetown, and Wisconsin before the Kansas Jayhawks, the eventual national champions, ended their Cinderella run with a 58–57 win in front of seventy thousand fans at Ford Field in Detroit.

During the 2008 March Madness tournament, Stephen averaged 34 points a game (including 30 in the *second half* against Gonzaga), prompting reporters to ask him about the meaning behind a different silver inscription on his sneakers that read: "I can do all things." Was he exhibiting the "look at me" mentality that's often seen today, or was it a simple case of an overblown ego?

"Oh, that," Stephen replied. "That's Philippians 4:13: 'I can do all things through him who strengthens me,'" he told reporters. "It's always been one of my favorite Bible verses [because it helps me] realize that what I do on the floor isn't a measure of my own strength. Having that there keeps me focused on the game, a constant reminder of who I'm playing for."

Stephen upped his scoring production during his junior year to 28.6 points per game—the best in the nation. As a consensus All-American getting a lot of ink, he decided to skip his senior season and turn pro. The Golden State Warriors took him with the seventh pick in the first round of the 2009 NBA draft.

Stephen had a good rookie season in 2009–10, and he finished second in the Rookie of the Year voting. He then backed up his solid first year with an outstanding second season with the Warriors. His future is bright as he plays to bring glory to God through basketball.

Keep an eye on Stephen, just like his headmaster at Charlotte Christian School, Dr. Leo Orsino, has been doing for the last half-dozen years. It turns out that Dr. Orsino is a blogger, and he had this to say about his former student:

On behalf of the faculty, staff, and Board of Trustees, we want to congratulate Stephen Curry and his family. We are extremely proud of him and blessed by his character and accomplishments.

Can you imagine being on national television? Can you imagine handling all of the pressure both on and off the court? Everyone who knows Stephen is not surprised by his success of Christ-honoring character. We experienced the same "humble superstar spirit" both on and off the court while he was a student at Charlotte Christian School. There is no doubt that there is something very special about Stephen Curry. We already know what makes him special. He loves Jesus Christ and knows the Truth of God.

NENÊ
DENVER NUGGETS

Nenê (the circumflex is often dropped in favor of an unaccented "e" when printed in the United States) is the legal name of Maybyner Rodney Hilário, the power forward/center for the Denver Nuggets.

Nenê, a native of Brazil, is the latest in a long line of Brazilian sports stars who have changed their legal names to a single word. Think Pelé, Ronaldo, Kaká, and Ronaldinho.

These one-word names have cropped up over the years because Brazilian full names tend to be rather long (for example, Pelé, the great soccer star of the 1960s and '70s, was christened Edson Arantes do Nascimento, which is a handful to pronounce). But the greater reason is because Brazilians value individuality and flair on the field, so going to a one-word moniker fosters a more intimate, romantic relationship with the fans. And probably more media attention as well, which is the name of the game when it comes to "branding" yourself and getting endorsement deals.

Enter Nenê, a 6-foot, 11-inch, 250-pound powerhouse with the Denver Nuggets since the 2002–03 season. Such a massive man taking the name Nenê—which means *baby* in Portuguese, the official language of Brazil—is filled with irony. Nenê is the only player in the NBA to go with only one name, and that makes him truly unique among professional basketball players.

Nenê's a late bloomer in the game of basketball. After playing soccer for most of his childhood and learning that sport was probably not in his future professionally, he took up basketball at the relatively late age of fourteen. He improved quickly, though, and turned pro at age sixteen, playing for a Brazilian team known as

Vasco da Gama. He got his big break after an NBA pre-draft camp in 2002, when the New York Knicks drafted him but promptly traded him to Denver.

Moving to the United States at the age of nineteen presented challenges for Nenê. Not only did he have a lot to learn about playing in the NBA, but he also had to learn a new language, adjust to the different foods here in the States (no *frango com quiabo*, or chicken with okra), and live in a cold city (the Mile High city of Denver). He has adapted well, and he now speaks fantastic English and connects with fans. On the court, he has performed admirably for the Nuggets, showing that he is a player who can dominate the offensive end of the court. His critics, however, say he lacks aggression and is soft on defense.

Nenê said he is seriously thinking of retiring by 2016 to work in ministry at his church in Brazil, known as God Is the Answer.

"I have like a deal for my pastor," he told one interviewer. "I want to get involved with the church right here in Brazil. If my financial situation is stable, why am I going to [want to] have more money? I'm not crazy for money. I think the best I can do is with the church . . . I can help with things with my testimony."

Nenê will be thirty-three at the start of the 2015–16 season, and athletes are notorious for changing their minds about retirement (and who can blame them since jobs that pay several million dollars—even tens of millions of dollars—come to few individuals who inhabit this planet). But Nenê has shown that his heart is in the right place as he looks at his future beyond the boundaries of the basketball court.

Perhaps facing his mortality several years ago helped him see things in a different light.

In early 2008, Nenê took a leave of absence from the Nuggets after he learned why he hadn't been feeling well: at the age of twenty-four, he had testicular cancer. Several other high-profile athletes have dealt with this serious, life-threatening disease, including bicyclist Lance Armstrong, ice skater Scott Hamilton, and baseball player/ESPN commentator John Kruk.

In January 2008, Nenê submitted to surgery to have his right testicle and a malignant tumor removed. "It was scary, but I believe in God," Nenê told the *Denver Post* when he went public with his story in the spring of 2008. "And now I'm a survivor."

So far, it looks like Nenê's doctors detected and treated the cancer early enough. And with the departure of Carmelo Anthony to the New York Knicks during the 2010–11 season, the Denver Nuggets are looking to Nenê to hold down the fort until a better cast is assembled around him.

But the Denver front office had better work quickly.

There's a church in Brazil waiting for Nenê to arrive and lend a hand in ministry.

REGGIE WILLIAMS
GOLDEN STATE WARRIORS

You'd think that leading the NCAA in scoring for two consecutive seasons would make a player a lock to play in the NBA.

But things didn't happen that way for Reggie Williams, the shooting guard from Virginia Military Institute (or VMI) who quarterbacked a run-and-gun offense that regularly scored more than 100 points per game—not an easy task in a 40-minute game.

When Reggie wasn't selected in the 2008 NBA draft, he kept a great attitude. He didn't lash out in anger or complain but said that being passed over "definitely made me humble myself." Sure that God had a different plan for his life, Reggie took his game overseas—like Anthony Parker did—and played for a French team in Dijon, France.

Reggie put enough *moutarde* on his jump shot in Dijon to earn a spot the following season with the Sioux Falls Skyforce of the NBA Development League—the Triple A level of professional basketball. This was actually something of a step back for Reggie. He didn't have a car in frigid South Dakota and was paid a scant $19,000 for the season, but the way he saw it, playing in Sioux Falls was his best chance to get a shot in the NBA. He played great in Sioux Falls and, finally, the phone rang. The Golden State Warriors were on the line, and they offered Reggie a ten-day "take-a-look" contract toward the end of the 2009–10 season.

Reggie showed enough moxie and game that Golden State signed him for the 2010–11 season. Reggie joined Jeremy Lin as another rookie guard trying to make an impression with the Warriors. He also got a salary bump to $762,195 for the season.

Even though he and Jeremy came from different backgrounds and college experiences, they were brothers in Christ. The pair fell in with each other for morale and support.

In Reggie's first outing of the 2010–11 season, he turned a few heads when he scored 10 points, dished out five assists, and grabbed five rebounds in twenty minutes of playing time against the Miami Heat, who would later lose to the Dallas Mavericks in the 2011 NBA Finals.

Reggie had a knack for making buckets, whether he was taking awkward but athletic shots ten to fifteen feet from the basket, or drilling spot-up jumpers from beyond the three-point line. He found ways to score within the flow of the game, showing that he's the type of player who can "quietly" score 20 points in a game.

Reggie didn't receive consistent minutes during his rookie season, so his stats were up and down. But he nailed his three-points shots with Korver-like accuracy, making 42 percent of his tries beyond the arc. He scored more than 20 points in five games, but there were also plenty of games in which he scored just two or three points.

Finally, we have this anecdote to share about Reggie:

When Reggie mentioned to the media that he was looking for a church to attend, Pastor Ryan Nash of Union Baptist Church in nearby Oakland went to a Facebook page dedicated to Reggie (but not Reggie's personal page) to personally invite him to drop by. "Please feel free to come by anytime, no pressure to join," the pastor wrote. "I just want to offer a place where you could worship. Please forgive this form of communication as I had no other way to reach you."

When Reggie put himself out there and told reporters covering the Warriors that he was looking for a church, he sent a signal about who he was and what was important to him.

And that's cool to see from an NBA player.

NICK COLLISON
OKLAHOMA CITY THUNDER

Maybe Nick Collison should change his name to Nick *Collision*.

The 6-foot, 10-inch power forward with the Oklahoma City Thunder is known for planting his feet in the lane and letting the LeBrons and the Carmelos of the league plow into him so that he can draw the offensive foul.

It's called "taking a charge."

Charges taken is not an official NBA statistic, but if it were, Nick would probably rank among the league leaders. What he does is the spiritual equivalent of giving his body up for his teammates—something the apostle Paul wrote about: "No, I strike a blow to my body and make it my slave so that after I have preached to others, I myself will not be disqualified for the prize" (1 Corinthians 9:27).

Here's how Nick "strikes a blow" to his body. When a bulky and well-built behemoth charges toward the rim—only to find Nick blocking his path—what happens next isn't pretty. The crash usually sends both players to the floor—and it's almost always Nick who gets the worst of it. Even a collision with a diminutive point guard can hurt since he's coming at full speed and often sticks his pointy knees into Nick's chest.

Those who follow Oklahoma City closely say Nick takes three times as many charging fouls as anyone on the Thunder roster. "It's a good play for our defense," he said. "It's better than a blocked shot because you get the ball back, and you get a foul on someone on the other team. On a block, you might get the ball back, and you might not. And you don't draw a foul."

Nick is also one of the league's most underrated defenders—a "glue-guy" who usually takes on the other team's best forward. His top-notch defensive skills are why he's paid in the $11 million a year range—which is close to All-Star numbers. A native Iowan who helped Kansas University reach two consecutive Final Fours (2002 and 2003), Nick's been called the ultimate hard-hat player.

Nick and his wife, Robbie, have hosted several charity events in Oklahoma City, most notably an annual Passion for Fashion benefit for AIDS foundations in the area. He became interested in helping fight AIDS after traveling to Johannesburg, South Africa, with Basketball Without Borders, which partnered with Habitat for Humanity and the Sky Foundation, which helps people with the HIV virus.

While in Johannesburg, Nick and Robbie, a microbiology major in college, witnessed firsthand how AIDS has ravaged families in South Africa and left so many children orphaned. The visit to South Africa inspired them to organize a fashion show benefit and silent auction, which has become a big hit in Oklahoma City since the first one in 2009.

But don't ask Nick to walk down the runway in a smart suit.

"Luckily, I've got the excuse that they've got no clothes that fit me," he said. "There's no big-and-tall line [in the fashion world]. There's nothing for me to model."

Actually, Nick is modeling Christ to those attending the annual charity event on behalf of orphaned children.

KEVIN DURANT
OKLAHOMA CITY THUNDER

While Nick Collison is the blue-collar, in-the-trenches player every team needs, Kevin Durant, Nick's teammate with the Oklahoma City Thunder, is the go-to-guy at crunch time, the big-time player who understands the responsibility of being "the guy" to carry the team. As one of the NBA's rising stars, he accepts the spotlight and the accolades, but as a young Christian man of faith, he doesn't seek the fame and attention.

It's hard to escape fame and attention, though, when you're a two-time NBA scoring leader. His game is smooth and seamless, a mixture of grace, class, and force. He's the face of the Oklahoma City Thunder franchise.

"In short, Kevin Durant is endorsement gold right now because he's good, he's new, he's young, he's intelligent, he's humble, and he's the centerpiece of a rags-to-riches story that has made him a hero to the citizens of Oklahoma City," wrote Patrick Rishe in *Forbes* magazine.

During the 2010–11 playoffs, Kevin showed up at post-game news conferences wearing a Nike backpack that will be part of his KD III line that's coming out during the 2011–12 season. Eventually, the inevitable question came from the back: "Hey, Kevin, what's in your backpack?"

Well, I've got my iPad, my earphones, my phone chargers—and my Bible.

Actually, the Bible was a recent addition to his backpack, but more on that later.

Kevin was raised in a Maryland suburb of Washington, DC. His mother and grandmother cared for him and his older brother Tony after their father left the family when Kevin was eight months old. As Kevin was growing up, he was always the tallest person in his class, but his grandmother Barbara consoled him, saying that his height would be a blessing—just wait and see.

He didn't have to wait long.

Kevin was a phenomenal basketball player from a young age, and when he was in middle school he joined an AAU team. His AAU coach, Taras "Stink" Brown, laid down several rules, and Rule No. 1 was "no pickup games"—because his coach thought they engendered bad habits. Instead, Coach Brown gave Kevin a set of drills to perform. During his summer breaks, Kevin was often in the gym eight hours a day.

Kevin played his freshman and sophomore years at Montrose Christian High in Rockville, Maryland, where he was so good that his older teammates threatened to stop passing the ball to him because they didn't want Kevin to show them up. He later transferred to Oak Hill Academy in Mouth of Wilson, Virginia, where he played well enough to be named a McDonald's All-American. His shooting and driving skills were unmatched among prep players.

The University of Texas won the recruiting war for Kevin. As an eighteen-year-old freshman, Kevin controlled the flow of the game—and there was never a reason to call for a set play when he was on the floor. He posted twenty 30-point games, was named the Associated Press College Player of the Year, and won the Naismith and Wooden awards.

And promptly declared himself eligible for the 2007 NBA draft after one college season.

The Seattle SuperSonics (who would become the Oklahoma City Thunder) took Kevin with the second overall pick in the draft. He would become the NBA Rookie of the Year.

For a 6-foot, 9-inch player, Kevin has an usually long wingspan of 7 feet, 5 inches. Think about what impressive wingspan means to his game: With his arms outstretched on defense, he is eight inches *wider* than he is tall, which gives him the appearance of a windmill with four blades. As for the offensive side of the court, his long arms and quick first step make him a nearly unstoppable force. Whether he's pulling up for a jumper or slashing through the lane, he makes it look easy—as most scoring champions do.

Some people believe Kevin could break Kareem Abdul-Jabbar's all-time NBA scoring record of 38,387 points. Kevin has one advantage that could help him break Abdul-Jabbar's record. Kareem stayed at UCLA for four years, so the great center didn't turn pro until he was twenty-two years old. Kevin will be twenty-three years old at the start of his fifth NBA season, giving him a three-season leg up on Abdul-Jabbar.

Through his first four seasons, Kevin had a lifetime scoring average of 25.9 points per game, and he figures to up his point-per-game average in coming years. Since Abdul-Jabbar averaged 24.3 points per game over a twenty-year career, Kevin would have to . . . well, the mathematic permutations are numerous.

But back to how the black leather Bible with his name engraved on the front cover got into his Nike backpack.

Kevin's strong faith comes from how his mother and grandmother brought him up. He says he went to church a lot when he was young, but as year-round basketball took up so much time in his adolescence, he attended church less. When he arrived in the NBA, a Christian teammate named Kevin Ollie took him under his wing and helped him feel more comfortable about talking about his faith, about praying for others out loud, and about attending chapels before games. It has helped that there were a half-dozen players on the Thunder who took their faith seriously and were walking with the Lord.

Kevin comes across as a down-to-earth humble player, a guy you won't catch pounding his chest and getting in the grills of opponents. When he was asked how he appeared to stay humble while living and working in a world where it's easy to get caught up in the hype of fame and fortune that defines the NBA, Kevin said, "It's tough, man. I can't lie about that. But I always kind of pinch myself and say that any day this can be done. In the Bible, [it says] the Lord exalts humility, and that's one thing I try to be all the time. When I'm talking in front of people or when people tell me I'm great, I [remind myself that I] can always be better. I've just got to be thankful to the Lord for the gifts He's given me. My gift back to Him is to always be humble and to always try to work as hard as I can."

Kevin started toting his Bible around in March 2011 after making a commitment to read scripture passages at his locker before games. He told reporters that he wants to grow spiritually with the Lord, especially after a Thunder team chaplain stressed the difference reading the Bible each day can make in one's life.

"I'm keeping strong at it, just trying to make my walk with faith a little better," he said. "That's making me a better person, opening my eyes to things. I'm also maturing as a person. I'm just trying to grow."

Growing spiritually, growing into one of the elite basketball players in the world, Kevin Durant is someone to keep your eyes on—and pray for.

GREIVIS VASQUEZ
MEMPHIS GRIZZLIES

When Greivis Vasquez attends the NBA chapels before every game, he enjoys praying with opposing players because he enjoys being with other believers so much.

"I've got Jesus in my heart," he told Bill Sorrell, a Memphis-based sportswriter. "I put everything in his hands. I live out of grace."

Greivis grew up playing street basketball in the barrios of Caracas, Venezuela. He and his family lived in a downtrodden neighborhood known as El Coche, where the young boys would huddle up and watch basketball on televisions so small that they could barely make out the players running up and down the court.

Greivis was such a flashy dribbler that his friends called him *Callejero*, or street-baller. Seeing how big and tall Greivis was growing during adolescence, Venezuelan sports ministers plucked him out of the barrios and put him into the national development program.

As Greivis' skills progressed, his family made the tough decision to send him to the United States so he could further his basketball skills. They enrolled him at Montrose Christian Academy in Rockville, Maryland—a private high school known for its basketball prowess. "Your potential is God's gift to you," begins the program's motto. "How you choose to use your potential is your gift to God."

When Greivis arrived in the United States, he didn't know how to speak English or anything about a personal relationship with Jesus Christ. He quickly picked up English, and he was introduced to a personal relationship with Christ, which left Greivis a changed young man.

Greivis went on to play college ball at the University of Maryland, where the 6-foot, 6-inch point guard became the first-ever Atlantic Coast Conference player to score at least 2,000 points (2,171), ring up 750 assists (772), and grab 600 rebounds (647). In 2010, he won the Bob Cousy Award as the nation's best point guard.

The Memphis Grizzlies drafted Greivis in the first round of the 2010 NBA draft, and his rookie year went well for him. He received more and more minutes as the season wore on, especially in the playoffs, where Memphis went much further than anyone expected before losing to Oklahoma City and Greivis' former teammate from Montrose Christian High, Kevin Durant.

Greivis is the third Venezuelan to play in the NBA, but his countrymen—Carl Herrera and Oscar Torres—were journeymen players who didn't see much action during their short two-year careers. After Greivis' better-than-average rookie season, he has a strong shot at becoming the first impact player from his country. He's known for his instinctive nature on the court and ability to make things happen.

Maybe God has bigger plans for Greivis. In the interviews he's given, he certainly hasn't shown any reluctance to talk about being a Christian. It must help that there are other Christians on the Grizzlies team—like Xavier Henry, Ishmael Smith, and Rudy Gay, who recites Philippians 4:13 before every free throw: "I can do all things through him who strengthens me." Greivis has memorized scripture, too—the entire eighth chapter of Romans.

Asked how his Christian faith has helped him in the NBA, Greivis replied, "It helps me in every aspect of my life. I have a sense of peace because I know God has blessed me so much. I thank Jesus every day, no matter what happens, good or bad. My faith is what got me to where I am today."

Greivis is active on Twitter, where he routinely talks about his faith in Spanish or English—sometime in both languages—like the time he tapped out the following message: EASY WITH THAT BRO. JESUS ES UN CABALLO!" (*Caballo* means rider or horseman, but in this context, the phrase is Venezuelan slang meaning *He's a Big Guy*.)

Other tweets are more straightforward, like this one: "On my way to church. Thank you God for another day."

At last count, thirty-five thousand people following Greivis on Twitter.

Maybe a few of them went to church that Sunday after reading his tweet.

5.

CLAYTON KERSHAW: STANDING ON THE PRECIPICE OF GREATNESS

You are God's field.
1 CORINTHIANS 3:9

In the gloaming, the curious children came.

Their little heads bobbed up and down in the tall, weed-infested field like inquisitive prairie dogs. They came from their hillside village—a shantytown, really—where ramshackle homes populate the landscape and hope remains a street urchin.

In the distance, the sun was setting over this forgotten corner of the world, casting long shadows over the village. Shadows are nothing new in Zambia. Moral decay, poverty, and deadly disease have veiled this small, south-central African nation in spiritual darkness for many years. The bleakness, visitors say, is palpable.

Past the field, the children gathered on both sides of a skinny dirt road. Their clothes were tattered and their feet were dusty, but their smiles were radiant.

They came to marvel at the stranger.

"Musungu!" some of them exclaimed. Others didn't know what to say. They had never seen a white man before.

Standing 6 feet, 3 inches tall and weighing 215 pounds, the Texan towered over the children as he and another foreigner threw an odd, white spheroid with red stitches back and forth. Soon, the *musungu* handed a glove to one of the boys, backed up a few feet and played underhanded catch. He did the same for every child. The youngsters giggled with delight. No language barrier could conceal the fact that everyone was having the time of their lives.

But the *musungu* hadn't traveled across ten time zones to promote baseball. He had come to pierce the oppressive shadows with the light of Jesus Christ.

Five months later, on a beautiful Southern California morning, the screaming children came.

Their energetic legs churned as they sprinted across the manicured fields of Pasadena Memorial Park like excited puppies. Here, in the prosperous shadows of the City of Angels, hope and opportunity soar upward like the lush mountain peak of Mount Wilson to the north and the skyscrapers of Los Angeles to the south.

The children came to marvel at their sports hero.

"It's Clayton Kershaw!" they cried incredulously.

The children surrounded—accosted, really—Clayton, his wife, Ellen, and two of the Kershaws' childhood friends as the adults were coming back from breakfast. In a region known for its celebrity sightings, the kids had hit the jackpot. Lacking paper or baseball cards, several boys thrust out their arms for Clayton to autograph their flesh. One boy lifted his shirt.

"Whoa, whoa, whoa!" Clayton said, smiling as he stymied the impromptu tattoo session. Ellen got some paper from their car nearby, and he obliged every child.

Somewhere, between these two disparate fields of dreams, you can find Clayton Kershaw. The Los Angeles Dodgers' budding young superstar lives at the intersection of Christianity and Growing Fame. It's a tricky junction, with plenty of distracting, and often dangerous, traffic coming at him from all directions. Some terrible wrecks have happened there.

But Clayton seems different. He has a strong faith, a great support network of friends and loved ones, and a humility that is as striking as his vast career potential, which portends multiple Cy Young Awards.

Consider this: At the callow age of twenty-two, he became the staff ace on one of baseball's most historic franchises in America's second-most populous city, just a long fly ball away from the glitter of Hollywood. Yet when his sublime abilities are the subject of conversation, he squirms—seems even a bit repulsed.

How many professional athletes do you know like *that*?

"It's never about him," said longtime friend John Dickenson. "It's humility at its best."

THE NATURAL

Clayton didn't always live at this complicated intersection. Life used to be much different.

Born on March 19, 1988, Clayton grew up as an only child on

Shenandoah Drive in Highland Park, a posh northern suburb of Dallas known as "The Bubble" for its insular qualities. Highland Park is a white-collar town of forty-something professionals with a median household income hovering around $150,000—more than three times the national average. Houses are huge, crime is low, schools are great, and people are nice. It's Pleasantville.

The Kershaws were typical suburbanites. Clayton's dad wrote TV commercial jingles, and his mom was a graphic designer. The only reason they stuck out in Highland Park is because they didn't live in one of the town's ubiquitous mansions.

Fame? That was a foreign concept. Well, Clayton *was* the great-nephew of Clyde Tombaugh, the man who discovered Pluto. But Great-Uncle Clyde died before Clayton was born and, heck, poor Pluto's not even considered a planet anymore. So that probably doesn't count.

Young Clayton was always on the move. As a child, his favorite toy was a life-size Flintstones car with a hole for his feet to touch the floor, so he could scoot around just like Fred and Barney.

That *yabba-dabba-doo* energy was quickly parlayed into athletic prowess. Clayton learned to walk at seven months, and his first word was "ball." Before he lost all his baby teeth, he earned the nickname "The Brick Wall" for his soccer goaltending skills in a local select league.

Losing his baby fat was another matter. When he was in high school, Clayton stood about 5 feet, 10 inches tall, but his waistline housed a few too many burritos from Qdoba's, a local Mexican restaurant where he loved hanging out with his buddies.

"Growing up," Dickenson said, "he was always a chubby

puffball." It's nice to have pals, eh?

It also must be nice to have natural athleticism oozing from your pores. Clayton excelled at virtually any sport he played—basketball, football, tennis . . . you name it. Even Ping-Pong. His long arms and great hand-eye coordination meant his childhood buddies were no match for him. In fact, they still aren't.

"He's an amazing Ping-Pong player," Dickenson said. "If he could, he'd give up baseball to do that."

About the only sport Clayton isn't good at is golf. "We played golf the day before his wedding," said Josh Meredith, Clayton's best friend. "He hit one [drive] from the tee box that ricocheted off a tree and landed fifty yards from where he hit it. I laughed pretty hard at that."

By ninth grade, Clayton's athleticism had landed him on the varsity football and baseball teams at Highland Park High School, a rarity for a freshman. During the fall, he played center, snapping to a quarterback whose name you might recognize: Matthew Stafford, the Detroit Lions' number one overall draft pick of 2009.

But Clayton's true love was baseball. That spring, he earned the number two spot in the varsity rotation and soon became one of the most ballyhooed prep pitching prospects ever in Texas, which has produced its fair share of future stars (see "Ryan, Nolan," "Clemens, Roger," "Pettitte, Andy," et al.). With colleges banging down his door, Clayton signed with Texas A&M University, largely because that's where Ellen Melson, his girlfriend and future wife, was going.

Clayton's sublime senior season in high school had the whiff of legend, like a real-life pitching version of *The Natural*. Highland Park, like most of Texas, is batty for high school football, but on days Clayton pitched, the Scots' modestly sized baseball stadium became a hub of interest. Folks wanted to witness the tall, powerful lefty with the mid-90s fastball and sweeping curve do something amazing—which happened often.

Scouts, too, came out in droves. Like a conductor's baton cueing orchestral instruments, dozens of radar guns would pop into position behind home plate whenever Clayton started his windup.

The whole scene was surreal, especially for those who remembered Clayton's freshman physique.

"Early on, he was baby-faced, almost roly-poly," said Lew Kennedy, his former Highland Park coach. "Pretty soon, he lost all that baby fat and turned into a monster. At times, he was virtually untouchable. Batters were happy just to foul one off."

That's not hyperbole. Clayton's statistics as a senior prompt a double-take: In 64 innings, he posted a 13–0 record, 0.77 ERA and 139 strikeouts. No typo there.

Clayton appeared mortal in the Scots' regular-season finale after a strained oblique muscle sidelined him for several weeks. But when he returned to action against Justin Northwest High in the regional playoffs, he one-upped himself with the rarest of gems—a perfect game in which he struck out *all fifteen batters* in a five-inning, mercy-rule-shortened contest.

True to form, as his teammates celebrated around him, he calmly walked off the field with a satisfied smile. To each teammate who showered him with praise, he simply replied, "Thanks, man." Nothing more.

"He was so soft-spoken," Kennedy said. "Very humble. He was one of the guys. He didn't lord it over anybody. Everybody looked up to him."

After the season, the accolades came rolling in, none more prestigious than the Gatorade high school national baseball player of the year award. He entered the 2006 draft ranked as *Baseball America's* top prep pitching prospect and the sixth-best prospect overall.

The fun was just about to begin.

FAITH IN THE HEART OF TEXAS

On America's extra-large Bible Belt, Dallas is the big ol' shiny brass buckle. On any given Sunday, you can find a church as easily as a Cowboys jersey. Same for the Highland Park bubble. Everywhere you went, people called themselves Christians.

So Clayton did, too.

He grew up in a Bible-believing home, got confirmed at Highland Park United Methodist in sixth grade, and, because of the company he kept, thought his ticket to heaven was punched. Bad-da-bing.

But life in a fallen world isn't that easy, as Clayton quickly learned. When he was ten, his parents divorced and his dad moved out. It was an emotional hand grenade in his young life. To this day, he prefers not to discuss it publicly.

Clayton's mom, Marianne, sacrificed much for her son. Their house was a two-bedroom shoebox compared to some of the old-money mansions in Highland Park, but Clayton was never in want. Marianne began working from home so she could be there when Clayton returned from school, and they continued attending church.

Spiritually speaking, though, Clayton was on autopilot. Presented with a Bible trivia game, he could've fared well, but his faith was, well, trivial. Then the Holy Spirit began prodding him. He started considering deep spiritual questions that shook him out of cruise control: *Is the Bible really the inspired, inerrant Word of God? Was Jesus Christ really who He said He was? How can Christianity be true and all other religions false?*

By his senior year, Clayton understood his desperate need for a Savior. The deep, life-altering words of Ephesians 2:8–9 became truth to him: Salvation is by grace and faith alone, not by works. None of his upbringing, church attendance, or good deeds merited God's eternal favor. Only Jesus Christ could provide that.

"When you grow up in [Christianity], you assume it's the only way—'Oh, everybody is this,'" he said. "But when you get a little older and a little smarter, you hear about other religions and beliefs, and you start thinking, 'Why do I believe this?' That's when you make your faith personal."

Clayton already had a solid group of friends, so the transition to his new faith wasn't hard. Around age sixteen, he and seven other Christian buddies made an agreement: They didn't need alcohol to have a good time.

While other kids were sleeping off weekend benders on Sunday mornings, Clayton's crew was worshipping. One of his buddies, Robert Shannon, would drive through the neighborhoods and fill up his big Chevy Suburban with half a dozen guys. With Third Eye Blind cranking on the sound system, they'd all head to Park Cities Presbyterian Church in Dallas and then head out for lunch together. Holy rollers indeed.

"We all got very lucky with our group of friends," Meredith said. "It made it easy for us to live the right way at such a young age. A lot of people at our high school were doing their partying on weekends. All of us, we were doing our partying without the alcohol or whatever else was there."

PRINCESS ELLEN

Clayton spent plenty of time with the fellas in high school. But he always made time for someone else.

Life, it seems, has never been without Ellen, even though they didn't meet until their freshman year. Theirs is a true high school sweetheart story, with all the cute, funny, and awkward moments that usually accompany that sort of thing.

At the beginning, it was heavy on the awkward. In the Courtroom of Clumsy Teenage Love, Clayton was guilty as charged:

- Exhibit A: The first meeting

Before they started dating, Clayton and Ellen had never spoken to each other. Ellen, a short, pretty girl on the school's dance team, had no clue that Clayton played baseball. She just knew him as a "goofy kid" with "a ton of friends." One day, between school periods during their freshman year, Clayton stopped her in the hallway and mumbled something about going steady. She said yes.

And after that?

"We didn't speak for the first year of our relationship except at our locker and in large groups at lunch," Ellen said.

- Exhibit B: The first hangout away from school

"We played basketball at a park," Clayton recalled, laughing. "I tried to teach her how, and she wasn't too interested." It was the start of a good-natured yet unsuccessful attempt to turn Ellen into an athlete. Clayton hasn't given up yet.

"It still doesn't work out so well," Ellen admitted. "I've always been a dancer and he's always wanted me to be more athletic. One year, he bought me a pink baseball glove just to give me an incentive to help him throw over the summer." But aren't dancers athletic in their own right? "I don't know if he buys that," Ellen said with a chuckle. "I don't think he thinks it's a sport."

- Exhibit C: The first time he met his future in-laws

Imagine you are the loving parent of four children. You are trying to raise them well and instill proper values. Your second youngest, a girl, has an infectious smile and soft heart. Then, at the impressionable age of fourteen, she brings home a football player who has "55," his jersey number, shaved into the back of his head, thanks to a hazing ritual by his upperclassmen teammates. Now, ask yourself: What would *you* do?

"My parents were like, 'Who are you dating?' " Ellen said.

- Exhibit D: The first kiss

The epic moment happened at Caruth Park, a popular local hangout just north of Highland Park. Who better than Clayton's best buddy to provide the scoop? "The first time they kissed," Meredith said, "Ellen had some trouble breathing."

Ellen doesn't deny it, but she provides a bit of context: "Clayton and I were each other's first kiss," she said, laughing. "We were fourteen years old. Neither of us had experience." Fair enough.

Clayton and Ellen just seemed *right* together, despite the fact that they are polar opposites. She is 5 feet, 5 inches tall; he stands 6 feet, 3 inches. She likes watching girly TV shows; he likes video games and anything involving competition. She eats like a bird; he consumes like a hyena.

"Their No. 1 date spot was a Chili's [restaurant]," Dickenson recalled. "Ellen, she doesn't eat that much. She's tiny. She'd always get mac and cheese, and he'd get a huge platter. She'd eat two bites and he'd finish it. Even with his buddies, he'd wait for us to finish and then he's eyeing everybody's meals. The guy can eat."

The couple's memorable dating stories are as plentiful as

STANDING ON THE PRECIPICE OF GREATNESS

young Clayton's food intake. Once, early in the relationship, Ellen and some girlfriends were watching *The O.C.*, one of their favorite TV shows, at her house. Suddenly, Clayton and his buddies barged in, screaming and throwing a football around. They were wearing nothing but shorts and football shoulder pads. For whatever reason, Mr. and Mrs. Melson didn't install perimeter fencing that night.

Another time, the guys invaded the girls' *Friends*-watching party, turned off the TV, and pillaged their cake. Annoyed, the girls hatched a plan to lure the guys out of Shannon's house, where they often played "Halo" for entire days, to steal their Xbox.

On the day of The Great Video Game Heist, the girls drove into the neighborhood, parked the car down the street from Shannon's house and turned off the car. Ellen called Clayton's cell phone. "Clayton," she said, feigning excitement, "Jennifer Aniston is in Highland Park giving autographs!" Seconds later, the door flew open. Scientists are still investigating claims that this group of teenage boys broke the cheetah's land-speed record.

At the car, the guys practically dove feet-first through the windows, à la *Dukes of Hazzard*, fired the engine, and raced down the street, past Ellen and her giggling friends. The girls' plan seemed to be working perfectly . . . until they saw brake lights. Down the road, the guys' car was turning around. The jig was up.

The girls had made one crucial error: They didn't factor in one of Clayton's strangest abilities. As the boys were whizzing past, Clayton had recognized the plates on the girls' car. Somehow, he can remember the license plate numbers of friends' cars after only one glance.

"It's one of the weirdest things," Ellen said.

All things considered, Ellen didn't mind the failed plan. It was another chance to see "my Clayton," as she's fond of calling him.

The affection is a two-way street. Clayton has always been smitten with Ellen, too. Take, for instance, the alert on his cell phone. Whenever she calls, the screen reads: "Princess Ellen."

"When he wakes up every day, he just treats her like that—like his little Princess Ellen," Meredith said. "That's just the way it's always been."

In 2006, the Dodgers drafted Clayton out of high school and quickly shipped him to their Gulf Coast League rookie affiliate in Vero Beach, Florida. Ellen enrolled at Texas A&M. The distance was tough on the couple, but the time was "some of best years of our lives," Ellen said.

By 2009, Ellen was ready to tie the knot—but to stay sane, she convinced herself it might not happen soon. Clayton, meanwhile, was planning and scheming. He knew Christmastime was Ellen's favorite part of the year, not only for the holidays but because it was one of the few months when the couple was back together in Highland Park.

Clayton went all-out for the proposal. This is a man who gets ragged on by richly garbed teammates for rolling into the Dodgers' clubhouse every day in cargo shorts and a T-shirt. But he showed up to Ellen's house in a new suit—and a white limo. The couple ate in downtown Dallas at Wolfgang Puck's Five Sixty, a skyscraper restaurant that offers a stunning vista of the city from the fiftieth floor. He even shaved for the first time in years.

"That," Ellen said, "was a point of contention for years—his dadgum chinstrap [beard]."

After dinner, Clayton took Ellen to his new townhouse, which he had decked out as a winter wonderland, complete with music playing and rose petals strewn about the living room. There, he gave Ellen a box with a little Santa figurine holding a green velvet ring box before dropping to his knee and proposing.

After their heartbeats leveled off, they went to Ellen's parents' house for a prearranged engagement party. Not bad for the once-awkward freshman.

Clayton and Ellen were married on December 4, 2010, at Highland Park Presbyterian Church. At the reception, they picked a humdinger of a first dance. No slow jam for this couple. Instead, they performed a choreographed dance to Usher's hit, "DJ's Got Us Falling in Love Again." Ellen, it should be noted, achieved lieutenant status on the high school drill team. Clayton . . . well, he tried hard.

In front of five hundred people, Clayton sauntered onto the dance floor wearing shades and neon Nikes along with his tuxedo and tried to keep up with his bride. Those who witnessed their first dance will never forget it.

Someone uploaded the dance video to YouTube, and the Kershaws initially left it there so loved ones who weren't at the wedding could see it. By the time they removed the video a month later, however, it had attracted twelve thousand hits.

"Ellen was a dancer in high school, so she nailed it," Meredith said. "Clayton was lost."

"MIGHT AS WELL GO BY ZEUS"
It's not that Clayton is some sort of attention-allergic hermit. Clearly, the wedding dance antics prove otherwise. But he's never felt entirely comfortable with all the acclaim his

bestowed-by-heaven talents have invited. Hullabaloo has always been the obnoxious kid brother he can't shake.

When Los Angeles drafted Clayton seventh overall, the hype machine revved into action. Dodgers scouting director Logan White compared Clayton to Dave Righetti, a sixteen-year big leaguer who won the 1981 American League Rookie of the Year award, played in two All-Star games, and was once the best closer in baseball. Clayton had just turned eighteen.

Two weeks later, Clayton officially signed with the Dodgers for $2.3 million (no need to scavenge other people's mac and cheese anymore) and headed to Vero Beach, where he dazzled coaches and players. Still, he needed some seasoning. In 2007, he started with the Dodgers' Class A affiliate in Midland, Michigan —the Great Lakes Loons. Welcome to baseball's boondocks.

Clayton lived in a duplex—four players on one side and four on the other. The furniture in Clayton's unit consisted of two beanbags, a TV resting on a folding chair, and a card table with a few other chairs for dining. All the guys slept on air mattresses. Road trips consisted of twelve-hour bus rides and sharing hotel rooms with a half-dozen other guys.

"He loved it," Ellen said. "He had no other responsibility but to show up at the field and play baseball."

The decor was lacking those years, but Clayton's burgeoning legend wasn't. After another strong season, he entered 2008 with high hopes—he and every Dodgers fan on planet Earth.

During a spring training game against Boston, he struck out three-time All-Star Sean Casey on an 0–2 curveball so nasty that Hall of Fame broadcaster Vin Scully proclaimed it "Public Enemy No. 1." Two days later, Dodgers legend Sandy Koufax, whom some would call the greatest left-handed pitcher of all time, watched Clayton throw a bullpen session and predicted that he'd be called up to L.A. soon. As endorsements go, those are hard to beat.

After thirteen games at Double-A Jacksonville (Florida) to start the season, he had a 1.91 ERA. The hype machine's RPMs were redlining. A *Yahoo! Sports* article trumpeted his curveball as "probably the best in the world." The Dodgers could no longer justify keeping him in the minors.

On May 25, 2008, after only 48 minor league games, Clayton made his big league debut. Chavez Ravine was electric. The Dodgers beat St. Louis, 4–3, but Clayton got a no-decision despite a stellar effort: two earned runs on five hits and one walk with seven strikeouts in six innings.

The reviews were overwhelmingly positive. The following day, a *Yahoo! Sports* story said Clayton "might as well go by Zeus for all the mythology that accompanies him."

The dam of self-restraint had officially been breached. Praise flooded in from every direction.

"These guys don't come along often," Dodgers pitching coach Rick Honeycutt gushed in the same article. "There's been other guys—Doc Gooden comes to mind—who get it at this early an age."

Amidst towering expectations, the rest of the season didn't go as smoothly. Clayton finished 2008 with a pedestrian 5–5 record and 4.26 ERA in 22 games. The following year, he was even-steven again with an 8–8 record, although he pitched appreciably better, sporting a 2.79 ERA and 185 strikeouts.

Those who had been around baseball a long time saw nothing but upside. By 2010, the hype machine was running full-throttle again, spewing out hyperbole at a rapid-fire rate. "Ceiling? There is no ceiling," Honeycutt said of his then-twenty-one-year-old protégé in spring training.

No pressure, Clayton. Honest . . .

If he felt any pressure, he sure didn't show it—not with a 2.91 ERA and 212 strikeouts in his second full big league season. His 13–10 record would have been more impressive if the Dodgers, who finished a middling 80–82, would have scored more than 17 total runs in his 10 losses.

Clayton's standout year, at age twenty-two, elevated him into rarified air within one of baseball's most venerable franchises. For perspective, consider how some of the all-time Dodgers greats fared at the same tender age:

- Among the Dodgers' Hall of Famers, Dazzy Vance went 11–14 for the Superior Brickmakers in the old Nebraska State League (1913). In his second year with the Dodgers, Don Sutton had a losing record (11–15) and finished with an ERA barely under 4.00 (1967). And even Koufax was mortal at age 22, finishing his fourth year with the Dodgers with a .500 record and a 4.48 ERA (1958).

- Orel Hershiser was still three years away from cracking the Dodgers' rotation with a lackluster 4.68 ERA at Double-A San Antonio (1981).

- Future 27-game winner Don Newcombe was still trying to make it out of Triple-A Montreal (1948).

Did we mention that Koufax didn't have a sub-3.00 ERA until his eighth season, at age twenty-six? Clayton has had *three* such seasons by age twenty-three.

No pressure, Clayton. We're just sayin' . . .

Before the 2011 season, Honeycutt went so far as to compare the excitement buildup around Clayton to "Fernandomania," the hysteria that surrounded Fernando Valenzuela, the pudgy, look-to-the-sky Mexican sensation who won the National League Cy Young and Rookie of the Year awards and led the Dodgers to a World Series title in 1981—at age twenty.

"I was there when Fernando [played in L.A.]," said Honeycutt, a Valenzuela teammate from 1983 to 1987. "It's getting to be kind of like that hype. The fans are putting their hopes and dreams on this guy [Clayton] leading the team back to greatness and the World Series."

In February 2011, Dodgers manager Don Mattingly officially named Clayton the team's Opening Day starter. The move made Clayton, at twenty-three, the Dodgers' youngest such pitcher since, well, Valenzuela in 1983.

Clayton opened the season by throwing seven shutout innings in a 2–1 win over San Francisco, the defending World Series champion. The pitcher he outdueled? None other than Tim Lincecum, the two-time Cy Young Award winner.

If only the rest of the season had been so rosy. Clayton's season-opening gem was barely in the books when at least two men attacked and severely beat a Giants fan, Bryan Stow, in the Dodger Stadium parking lot, sending him into a coma.

The vicious assault only underscored the chaos plaguing the franchise in recent years under Dodgers owner Frank McCourt. Among the tabloid fodder:

- A bitter divorce court battle between McCourt and his ex-wife, Jamie, over control of the team that dragged through the 2011 season.

- The revelation from court documents that the Mc-Courts had borrowed more than $100 million from Dodgers-related business to fund a profligate lifestyle.
- Major League Baseball's assumption of team control in April 2011 and its ensuing rejection of a new, multi-billion-dollar TV deal between FOX and the Dodgers, forcing the troubled franchise to file for bankruptcy protection in August.
- McCourt's agreement on November 1, 2011, to sell the team, Dodger Stadium, and the surrounding parking lots in cooperation with Major League Baseball through a court-supervised process.

In the midst of the mayhem, Clayton was magnificent. He won the National League's "Triple Crown" of pitching with a 21–5 record, a major league-best 2.28 ERA, and league-leading 248 strikeouts to earn his first All-Star appearance and win the NL Cy Young Award. He even claimed his first Gold Glove Award for good measure.

(Note to the curator of the sizable Dodgers pitching pantheon: Time to create another wing. Clayton became the franchise's first Cy Young recipient since closer Eric Gagne in 2003 and the first Dodgers starter to win the award since Hershiser in 1988.)

Clayton's twentieth win, which came in a dominant 2–1 victory over the rival Giants in his penultimate start of 2011, made him the first Dodgers pitcher to go 5–0 against the Giants in a season since Vic Lombardi in 1946. And four of those victories came against none other than Lincecum.

Dodger fans love a Giant slayer.

Then there's this telling nugget: Only one lefty in Dodgers

history has recorded more strikeouts in a season—Koufax.

"There's no reason to really set limits on him as far as how much better he's going to get," Mattingly said, "because he's still young and he works awful hard."

No pressure, Clayton . . . aww, who are we kidding?

"FOR HIS GLORY"

How do you respond when fans, media, former All-Stars, and front-office cognoscenti are all tripping over themselves to adequately describe your abilities? Clayton simply shrugs it off.

"I've got a really, really, really long way to go," he said.

This is not false modesty. This is Spirit-led Clayton modesty. And it sticks out like a sore thumb in Tinseltown, where the twin gods of fame and riches are worshipped religiously.

Clayton is so *un*-Hollywood. The red carpets, velvet ropes, glittering marquees, screaming fans, and insatiable paparazzi of his six-month home are foreign to him. He's one of the best pitchers in the world, yet he and Ellen still get a touristy kick out of the area's palm tree-lined roads, the Hollywood Walk of Fame, and the mansions of Beverly Hills.

"I have my own version of celebrity stars tour," Ellen said. "I could be a certified stalker if I took people over there anymore."

Clayton has shot the breeze with Koufax, learned to bunt from Maury Wills, and achieved rapid renown in starry-eyed L.A. Yet you'd never know his day job if you saw him strolling hand-in-hand with Ellen in Malibu. At heart, he is just a big kid from Texas with a Lone Star lilt and a wide, toothy smile.

He honestly doesn't understand what all the fuss is about. Like the crush of autograph seekers leaning over the railing after games. Or the trash bags filled with fan mail that started piling up in 2010.

"He couldn't even get his head around it," Ellen said.

Those closest to him say he's the most humble person they know. C.S. Lewis once said, "Humility is not thinking less of yourself, but thinking of yourself less." It's a vertical-relationship thing, and Clayton seems to get it.

"Clayton doesn't lie about his abilities," Dodgers chaplain Brandon Cash explained. "He knows how good he is. But he realizes that no matter how good of a baseball player he is, it doesn't mean anything when he'll stand before God."

Said Clayton, "You have to understand what this platform is for."

Never was Clayton's humility more on display than during the 2010–11 offseason. Less than a month after getting married, as their loved ones were clinking glasses and singing *Auld Lang Syne* in the States, Clayton and Ellen were half a world away, toiling in a bleak, oppressed land. With sweat-soaked shirts clinging to their backs, they rang in the New Year in Zambia.

The trip marked Ellen's fifth visit, and Clayton's first, to the small, south-central African nation. Ellen had tried to prepare Clayton for what to expect, but no prior warning can fully assuage the culture shock.

Disease, destitution, hunger, moral neglect, and religious syncretism are like gloomy shrouds veiling the country in darkness. Zambia is one of the poorest nations in the world. Many people live on a dollar a day. Homes are often plastic tarps or tents with earthen floors. Affluence means your one-room home is made of cinder blocks or concrete and features an outdoor stovetop to cook on. Dishes and babies are washed in the same tub. A child's wardrobe is what he's wearing. Trash and raw sewage are everywhere.

So, too, are the orphans. Thanks to a widespread HIV/AIDS epidemic, nearly 47 percent of Zambia's population is zero-to-fourteen years old, and the median age is 16.5 years, according to 2011 US government figures. It's a place where kids are raising kids—where unmarried mothers abandon their children, like an endangered ship purging jetsam, to seek a different life in another province.

"It's an overwhelming task because you can't get to every kid," Clayton said. "It's hard. Some people don't go because you think, 'It's just one person.' But one kid you do help is one life affected."

The Kershaws affected plenty. During a nine-day missions trip with a non-profit organization called Arise Africa, Clayton, Ellen, and other Christians visited various "compounds," or slums, on the outskirts of Lusaka, the capital city.

The group delivered two thousand pounds of supplies to two schools that double as orphanages, constructed a four-room building for one of them, hosted a Bible camp for two hundred children, and cared for impoverished families. Clayton also got to meet twenty young orphan girls Ellen has spiritually invested in over the years.

To stay in baseball shape, Clayton ran and threw each day. The local children flocked to him, and he played catch with them every night. Using his God-given talents, he reached across a broad cultural chasm to shine the light of Christ. It was Matthew 19:14 in action.

"He has a heart of gold," said Alissa Hollimon, a college friend of Ellen's who started Arise Africa. "He jumped right in to whatever we were doing. I think he liked seeing Ellen in her element."

The trip said much about Clayton's priorities. Pitchers of his caliber don't just happen. It takes an extraordinary amount of work, especially in the offseason. Winters are also crucial down-time for athletes consumed by their profession from February through September.

Clayton could have just supported Ellen's passion project from a distance, by cutting a check and keeping his golden arm comfortably within American borders. Instead, he chose to travel to an ignored back alley of the world and open compassionate arms to those enslaved in darkness. For such a quiet man, this spoke volumes.

"He's characterized by humility," Cash said.

It's a humility that seeks to serve others wherever he is. Despite being one of the youngest players on the roster, he is the Dodgers' Baseball Chapel representative—the guy Cash looks to for getting guys in Sunday morning chapels and midweek Bible studies. He does charity work in greater L.A. through the team, and he speaks to the Fellowship of Christian Athletes group at his old high school each offseason.

Most of all, he and Ellen are looking forward to continuing their work in Zambia each offseason. Inspired by their trip, the couple started Kershaw's Challenge, an effort to raise $70,000 to build an orphanage outside Lusaka called Hope's Home, named after an eleven-year-old, HIV-positive orphan they met. Before the 2011 season, Clayton pledged to donate a hundred dollars for every strikeout he threw, which resulted in a $24,800 donation based upon his career-high 248 punch-outs.

Think God was at work there?

THE PARABLE OF THE TALENTS

Yes, the children will continue to come. They will travel across fields of indigence and affluence, through the forsaken slums of Africa and the shiny turnstiles of Chavez Ravine, all to see the meek wunderkind. Heck, plenty of adults will come, too. People are always attracted to greatness, and that's the precipice upon which Clayton stands.

This, of course, creates a lot of racket. The quiet, lanky Texan is still getting used to all the attention. His immense gifts, for some, might be the object of regular worship on *SportsCenter*, but he sees them through the lens of Jesus' parable in Matthew 25.

"I think it's for His glory, to make people aware that it's not something where I was lucky to throw baseball," Clayton said. "In Matthew, it says God gives everyone at least one talent. One guy hides his talent and gives it back, and God says, 'Cursed are you.' He doesn't want us to hide our talents; He wants us to put them in the spotlight and glorify Him.

"That's a pretty cool thing."

6.

ALBERT PUJOLS:
A HOME RUN HITTER WITH
A HEART FOR OTHERS

Every time St. Louis Cardinals All-Star Albert Pujols steps into the batter's box, the crowd buzzes in anticipation. They know something amazing *might* happen.

Albert has a lifetime batting average over .325, so the odds are pretty good that something remarkable *will* happen. No player in the history of baseball has amassed the kind of statistics Albert has put together during his first eleven years in the sport.

Not Babe Ruth.

Not Joe DiMaggio.

Not Ted Williams.

Not Barry Bonds.

Nobody.

And on this fall afternoon in 2010, Albert was about to give the crowd a treat.

The slugger walked confidently into the box and took his iconic stance. Feet wide apart. Hands held high. Legs crouched like a linebacker ready to explode into a tackle. When the ball left the pitcher's hand, one thing was certain—that piece of cowhide was about to get whacked.

That's because Albert doesn't hit a ball; he punishes it.

As the ball neared the plate, Albert's powerful swing was already in motion. His hands ripped through the hitting zone and sent a towering home run well over the left field fence.

The crowd leaped to its feet cheering. Albert's teammates emptied out of their dugout. Even the opposing players spilled onto the field to embrace Albert at home plate.

After all, this wasn't a major league contest at St. Louis' Busch Stadium. This was an exhibition softball game at a baseball field the Pujols Family Foundation helped build in Albert's hometown of Santo Domingo in the Dominican Republic.

Everybody was excited to be there and to see Albert do what he does better than anyone else: swing a bat. They also knew they had nearly missed the opportunity of watching their hometown hero in action. That's because a hurricane had skirted the country the previous day, leaving the field a muddy mess. A grounds crew had worked feverishly to get the field ready, even using gasoline to burn off the puddles. With the water semi-evaporated, the game went on as planned and Albert provided the memorable moment.

Every year, Albert returns to his home country to help the people in his old *batey*, what the shantytown neighborhoods are called in the Dominican Republic. The Pujols Foundation works year-round to provide the people there with medical care, food, clothing, and other necessities. It has even given new mattresses to families whose kids had doubled or tripled up on worn, lumpy beds.

Conditions in the batey aren't great, but some things are much better than when Albert was growing up in the D.R. in the 1980s. For one thing, he didn't have a nice baseball field to play on back then.

Albert developed his love of the sport using a stick for a bat, a milk carton for a glove, and a lime as a ball.

Today, though, children in Batey Aleman can play on a field where Albert's and several other players' pictures are painted on the outfield wall. The kids practice on Tuesdays and Thursdays and play games against each other on Saturdays all day long.

"That was me twenty-five years ago. I was one of those little boys with no hope and just a dream," Albert said in a *60 Minutes* interview in 2011 as he watched some kids he had been helping in his old neighborhood. "This is not so I can be looked at as 'Mr. Nice Guy.' I don't care less about that."

Albert helps out in the D.R. for one reason: He feels God has called him to give back. And Albert wants to honor God in every area of his life.

"Believe it or not, baseball is not the chief ambition of my life," Albert writes on his foundation's website. "Becoming a great baseball player is important to me, but it is not my primary focus because I know the Hall of Fame is not my ultimate, final destination. My life's goal is to bring glory to Jesus."

That's saying a lot, considering those words are coming from the best player in baseball during the first decade of the twenty-first century.

From the time Albert broke into the majors in 2001, he's put up monster numbers and been recognized for his talent. He won the National League Rookie of the Year his first season. From 2001 to 2010, he won three Most Valuable Player awards, six Silver Sluggers (given to the best offensive player at each position in both leagues), two Gold Gloves, and was named to nine All-Star games.

Between the 2001 and 2010 seasons, he became the only player in major league history to hit better than .300, hammer more than 30 home runs, and drive in at least 100 RBIs every season during his first ten years in the big leagues. No player had posted similar numbers in his first *two* years in the league, let alone ten. Unfortunately, that streak ended in 2011 when he came within a whisker—a home run?—of doing it for the eleventh season in a row when he batted .299 and had 99 RBIs to go along with his 37 home runs.

No matter. Albert's body of work would be phenomenal for any player, but it's especially impressive for someone who was selected 402nd in the Major League Baseball draft.

401 MOTIVATIONS

Coming out of high school, Albert wasn't on many professional scouts' radars. He'd lived in the United States for just a few years after his family emigrated from the Dominican Republic in 1996.

He ended up settling in Independence, Missouri, because his uncle already lived there. Not many Spanish speakers lived in Independence, but the town did have baseball. And on the diamond, there was no language barrier for Albert to overcome.

Baseball had always been a constant for Albert, even when nothing much else remained the same.

He was born José Alberto Pujols Alcántara on January 16, 1980. His mom and dad divorced three months later. His father, Bienvenido, had played baseball and was known as a good pitcher. Despite the divorce, Bienvenido stayed involved in Albert's life and was there for him and his mother.

But nobody was a bigger part of his life than his grandmother, America. (Yes, that's her real name.) She took on a lot of the duties raising Albert. His ten aunts and uncles were also around to provide guidance and a helping hand.

By United States standards, Albert grew up dirt poor. But he never saw it that way. He says he didn't feel poor because he ate breakfast, lunch, and dinner every day. Many of the kids around him were fortunate if they got just *one* meal. In his mind, *those* were the poor kids.

Living in the batey, Albert spent most of his time playing baseball. Before he was a teenager, he realized that his skills were ahead of those of his peers and that he might have the ability to make it to the big leagues.

"Growing up in the Dominican Republic, that's pretty much all I did is play baseball," Albert said. "That's pretty much everybody's dream, to play professional baseball."

When Albert moved to Missouri at age sixteen, one of the first things he did was walk into Fort Osage High School and say through an interpreter that he wanted to play baseball.

In his first season, Albert played shortstop and helped the Indians win the Class 4A state championship. His hitting totals were especially impressive: a .471 batting average with 11 home runs and 32 RBIs. *USA Today* recognized him as "honorable mention" in its All-USA baseball rankings.

Albert stayed hot in summer ball. Playing 60 games for an American Legion team, he blasted 29 home runs and had 119 RBIs.

The seventeen-year-old returned to Fort Osage in the fall and asked if he could repeat his junior year. Although he had cousins at the school who could translate for him, he struggled to pick

A HOME RUN HITTER WITH A HEART FOR OTHERS

up English. Albert really wanted to master the language and earn his high school diploma. The school and the Missouri State High School Activities Association agreed, giving Albert an extra year of high school eligibility.

During the 1998 season, Albert was a force for the Indians, hitting .660. The problem was, he couldn't sneak up on teams anymore. Everybody knew who he was and didn't want to give him a good pitch to hit. Albert drew a record-setting 26 walks that season, 18 of them intentional.

In the summer Albert's stature grew even more as he broke his own home run record by bashing 35 round-trippers, including one that caught the attention of *Independence Examiner* writer Dick Puhr, who described one of Albert's grand slams as a "blast down the left-field line [that] was higher than the light standards and sailed, not only over the fence, but the railroad tracks and landed in a mulberry bush."

His summer coach Gary Stone said, "It's the farthest and hardest I've seen a baseball hit."

Of course, Stone was already a big fan of Albert's. During a tournament the previous summer in which all the players had to use wood bats instead of aluminum, Stone noted that Albert would "have power even if he used a toothpick."

While Albert's talents on a baseball field were obvious to everybody who saw him play, he didn't attract the praise of many scouts. They didn't like Albert's footwork at shortstop and said that he lacked control on his throws.

Albert came back for his senior year in 1998 but earned enough credits to graduate early. He enrolled at Maple Woods Community College in Kansas City in January and started playing for the college team that spring.

Immediately, Albert proved he had the ability to play at the next level.

In his first game for the Monarchs, Albert turned an unassisted triple play at shortstop and hit a grand slam off Mark Buehrle (now a four-time major league All-Star who's thrown a no-hitter and a perfect game).

For the season, Albert hit .461 with 22 home runs and 80 RBIs.

When baseball's 1999 draft rolled around on June 2, Albert watched in anticipation. He knew his dream of making it to the pros was about to come true.

The Tampa Bay Devil Rays (now just the "Rays") selected Josh Hamilton first overall. Josh Beckett went second to the Florida Marlins. Nearly everybody close to baseball believed those two players would go right away. Albert figured he'd probably go in the first few rounds. The *Examiner* agreed, writing that he'd be drafted in the top three rounds. Other experts had him pegged to go anywhere from the fifth to eighth round. Scouts still didn't like Albert's throwing motion and worried because he'd gained a little weight in junior college.

After the first day of the draft was over, Albert's name was still on the board.

He had to wait until the morning of June 3 to hear that St Louis had drafted him in the *thirteenth* round with the 402nd pick.

Albert was devastated. His girlfriend at the time, Deidre Corona, said he cried like a baby. He even talked about quitting baseball.

Deidre persuaded him not to give up on his dream.

When St. Louis offered Albert a $10,000 signing bonus (Hamilton had been given $3.96 million), he turned it down because he

A HOME RUN HITTER WITH A HEART FOR OTHERS

felt like he was worth more.

To prove his worth, Albert went to the Jayhawk League, where college-aged players showcased their talent over the summer. In 55 games, Albert led the team in home runs and batting average. St. Louis came back and offered him $60,000. He took the deal and joined the team.

But the sting of being drafted in the thirteenth round didn't go away. Albert knew he had the talent and work ethic to make it in the pros, and he wanted to show his detractors they were wrong about him.

Albert had lived with doubters. But when coaches worked with him and saw his daily dedication, they often became his biggest fans.

"He's the best hitter I've coached or seen," said Marty Kilgore, Albert's coach at Maple Woods Community College. "But what impresses me most about Albert is his work ethic. A lot of coaches in the area told me he didn't have good work habits and that he was moody. I've seen just the opposite. He's the first player at practice, the last to leave, and when practice is over, he's heading over to the batting cage to take some more swings."

Albert developed his swing during his younger years and continued to hone it with countless repetitions. These days, he estimates that he takes between fifteen and twenty thousand practice swings a year in the batting cage. He works so hard to get his mechanics exactly right that it's no wonder he's earned the nickname "The Machine."

As it turns out, it was the scouts who didn't get a whole lot right in the 1999 draft. Only twenty-three of the fifty-one players drafted in the first round ever made it to the big leagues. Carl Crawford and

Justin Morneau went in the second round. Shane Victorino was selected with the 194th pick, and amazingly, Jake Peavy, a future Cy Young winner, was picked *after* Albert at the 472nd spot.

Being slighted in the draft has been a driving force for Albert—even to this day.

"I'll never, never get over it," he said.

With 401 reasons fueling his drive to succeed, Albert played just one year in the minor leagues. During that same time, he worked more on his physique, turning his body into a muscular 6-foot, 3-inch, 230-pound baseball-bashing machine.

Albert started the 2000 season with the Class A Peoria Chiefs in Illinois. After playing third base and being named the league's most valuable player, Albert had a brief stay at Double-A before jumping up to the Triple-A Memphis Redbirds.

The Redbirds were preparing to enter the Pacific Coast League playoffs. In Albert's first seven games, he hit .367 with two home runs. Then he helped lead Memphis past the Albuquerque Dukes and into the championship series against Salt Lake City. On September 15, 2000, the twenty-year-old showed no signs of nerves as he hit a walk-off home run in the thirteenth inning of Game 4 to give the Redbirds their first-ever PCL championship. For his efforts, Albert earned the league's Most Valuable Player award in the postseason.

In 2001, Albert entered spring training with the hopes of gaining a spot on the Cardinals' twenty-five-man roster. Most people close to the team figured Albert would spend another year with the Redbirds before he'd be ready for the majors. Albert wanted to prove them wrong. He took extra fielding practice to learn how to play first base and outfield, and he always looked strong at third.

A HOME RUN HITTER WITH A HEART FOR OTHERS

When the Opening Day lineup was announced, Albert found himself playing left field against the Colorado Rockies.

FIRM FOUNDATION

While Albert's baseball career was taking off, his personal life was doing the same.

In the summer of 1998, the teen went salsa dancing at a club in Kansas City, where he met a young woman named Deidre. It wasn't love at first sight, but the two became dancing buddies.

After several weeks, Albert worked up the courage to ask Deidre on a date. When they were out together, he admitted to lying to her about his age. He had told her that he was twenty-one when he was really only eighteen years old. Deidre also had a confession to make: she had just given birth to a baby girl with Down syndrome.

Instead of running away from the relationship, Albert wanted to meet Deidre's daughter. When Albert met Isabella for the first time, he didn't see her as child with Down syndrome. Instead, he just looked at her as a beautiful little girl.

Albert continued to date Deidre and to act as Isabella's occasional babysitter. Deidre had recently rededicated her life to Jesus Christ and encouraged Albert to attend church with her. She also explained the existence of heaven and hell to him and said the only way to heaven was through a personal relationship with Jesus Christ.

"I went to church every once in a while growing up," Albert said. "At that time, I didn't realize how important it was to go to church and have a relationship with Christ."

His grandmother had raised Albert to have good morals and

to be a good person. He didn't drink, smoke, or have any tattoos. But he also didn't know God or have a relationship with His Son.

Albert began attending church every week and learning more about Jesus. Once Albert understood the truth of the Gospel, he walked down the aisle and prayed to give his life to Christ on November 13, 1998.

"I wouldn't say it was easy and that the Lord starting turning things around [right away]," Albert said. "There were still challenges and still some tough times in my life, but the Lord was preparing me for the big things."

That included getting married and being successful in baseball.

Albert and Deidre were married on New Year's Day—January 1, 2000. When Albert was assigned to play in Peoria, Deidre and Isabella accompanied him.

Albert made around $125 a week playing baseball in the spring of 2000 (these days, his on-the-field salary is more than $280,000 a week, which doesn't include endorsement income). This wasn't enough money for a young family with a special needs child. The couple barely had enough money to pay rent or buy furniture. Albert remembers going to Walmart and purchasing a cheap card table and folding chairs so they could have a seating area.

When Albert made the jump to the majors in 2001, that all changed. His salary shot up to $200,000 for the year. And after Albert won NL Rookie of the Year honors by batting .329 with 37 home runs and 130 RBIs, his salary tripled to $600,000 the following year.

As Albert's statistics grew and his consistency became obvious—he was no one-season wonder!—the Cardinals kept rewarding him with larger contracts.

In 2005, his annual salary reached eight digits . . . $11 million to be exact. That was also the year that he and Deidre started the Pujols Family Foundation.

"I had been praying for God to be able to use Albert to share Jesus and wanted it to be bigger," Deidre said. "Todd Perry had been calling and presenting us with an idea [for the foundation]. It took about a year to get everybody in the same place. Our mission is faith, family, and others."

The Pujols Family Foundation helps families and children who live with Down syndrome and also works in the Dominican Republic to improve the quality of life of needy children. Perry has worked as the executive director from the beginning. Albert and Deidre don't just write a check and help raise money; they get physically involved with the people their organization touches.

One of the highlights of Albert's year is hosting a formal dance for teenagers with Down syndrome. The kids show up at this gala event in fancy dresses and tuxedos, walk the red carpet, and enjoy the prom-like atmosphere. And, of course, all the girls want to dance with Albert.

At the end of the 2010 celebration, Albert dripped with sweat but had a huge smile on his face.

"It must've been the highlight of the year for them," the *60 Minutes* reporter said to Albert during his interview.

"And for me, too," Albert quickly responded. "Every time I'm around them, I enjoy it and have a great time."

As the Pujols Family Foundation got going, Albert's own family was growing. Isabella got a little brother when Albert Jr. (known as A.J.) was born a couple of years after Albert and Deidre married. In 2005, Sophia came along, and more recently, Ezra was born.

"One thing I have learned is that it's not about me; it's about serving the Lord Jesus Christ," Albert said. "His plan was bigger than what I ever thought. I have a beautiful family and four beautiful kids."

Albert doesn't only want to be a role model to his own children, he hopes to positively influence other kids. During a recent season, the slugger had the opportunity to meet two young men who made an especially big impact on him.

One of them was Jacob Trammell, a fifteen-year-old who had been diagnosed with a cancerous tumor and had gone through chemotherapy and radiation. Through the Make-A-Wish Foundation, Jacob got to hang out with his idol. Albert showed Jacob around the Cardinals' clubhouse and took batting practice with him at Busch Stadium. ESPN recorded the events for its show "My Wish."

"He's like the best baseball player in baseball now," Jacob said about Albert. "He's a good Christian man. He's my role model because my dad had left."

The teenager, a good baseball player in his own right, dreamed of playing in the majors and got some hitting tips from Albert. With a few tweaks of his swing—such as keeping his hands high and swinging in one fluid motion—Jacob was smacking line drives all over the indoor hitting facility at Busch Stadium.

"That's the stroke I've been looking for all year," Albert quipped after Jacob stroked a streak of solid hits.

According to Jacob's mom, Debbie, it was the high point of Jacob's year.

"Albert is such a great player," she said. "Jacob likes his morals and the way he uses his Christian background, giving all the glory to God. Jacob is kind of like that, too."

A few weeks later, during the 2010 season, Albert lashed his 400th major league home run, making him the third youngest player to accomplish that feat. Only Alex Rodriguez and Ken Griffey Jr. reached that benchmark at a younger age.

Four days after reaching that milestone, Albert took the bat that hammered the historic home run and gave it to Brandon Johnson, a thirteen-year-old battling a malignant brain tumor at Texas Children's Hospital. Albert didn't go with a lot of fanfare or television cameras. He just quietly slipped away after the game with the Houston Astros, went to the hospital, prayed with Brandon, and stayed for about an hour.

Faith, family, and others. It's not just the mission of Albert's foundation—it's the foundation of his life.

MAKING HISTORY

While many of the best athletes in the world make headlines with little indiscretions or poor decisions, Albert makes headlines with the good he does—on and off the field. With a bat in his hands, he's put up numbers that are unparalleled in the long, storied history of baseball.

In his first eleven years in the big leagues, he hit more than 40 home runs and drove in better than 120 RBIs six times. He's won the National League's Most Valuable Player award three times (2005, 2008, and 2009). He led St. Louis to the World Series three times. The Cardinals lost to Boston in 2004, but the Redbirds came back two years later to beat Detroit. And during the recent 2011 campaign, Albert was at the front of the charge as St. Louis won its National League-leading eleventh World Series title.

The seven-game victory over Texas will be remembered as one of the most unlikely championships in baseball history. St. Louis was 10½ games back in the NL wild card race at the end of August when the Redbirds went on a tear in September. Albert hit .355 that month with five homers and 20 RBIs as St. Louis clinched the wild card spot on the final day of the regular season.

The underdog Cardinals defeated mighty Philadelphia in five games in the National League Divisional Series. Then they got past Milwaukee to set up the finale against the Rangers.

Albert had a slow start in the World Series, but then erupted for one of the best games ever by hitting three home runs and knocking in six RBIs in a 16–7 victory in Game 4. Albert's 14 total bases stand as a World Series record, and it marked the first time since 1977 that a player had hit three dingers in the Fall Classic. Only Reggie Jackson and Babe Ruth had accomplished the feat before.

"I'm glad it was him," the Hall of Famer Jackson said of Albert tying his record. "He's a fabulous representative of the game . . . I told him I admire the way he went about his business. I know he has a charity; I know he's a good, Christian man, a good team guy. He's got great focus."

Albert displayed that laser-like focus in the 2011 postseason by batting over .350 with five home runs and 16 RBIs.

"I think the last month of the season, that's where it started," Albert said. "Different guys were coming huge, getting big hits, and we carried that into the postseason and here we are, world champions."

Fans, sportswriters, opponents—even his manager—marvel at what Albert accomplishes on the diamond.

A HOME RUN HITTER WITH A HEART FOR OTHERS

"Enjoy it. Respect it. Appreciate it," said long-time Cardinals manager Tony La Russa, who retired following the 2011 World Series victory. "I'm left with just watching him. And if you watch him, he'll do something to show you how great he is."

His greatness shows in his consistency and versatility. After ten years in the sport, he'd won six Silver Slugger awards at three different positions—third base, outfield, and first base. He was also a two-time Gold Glove winner (2006 and 2010) at first base, proving that his fielding, throwing, and catching were also among the league's best.

But perhaps nothing showed Albert's ability better than an illustration that Fox Sports put on TV screens during one of Albert's World Series games. When a batter came to the plate, a graphic would flash on the screen to show where pitchers could throw the ball to get him out. Some batters couldn't get to a low-inside fastball. Others were susceptible to an outside curve. When Albert's graphic came up, there were no spots that pitchers could pitch to. He was capable of hitting any pitch at any count and making his opponents pay.

"Albert has no glaring weaknesses, and he doesn't chase many bad pitches," Hall of Famer Tony Gwynn said.

It's not just the hundreds of thousands of practice swings that have made Albert a great hitter. He has studied the game and worked on his weaknesses. He's spent hours talking with Cardinal pitchers about how they work certain batters and vary their pitches. This helps Albert get into the mind of a pitcher, so that he'll know what to expect in different situations.

All of his efforts have paid off. Albert hits for average, hits for power, and is known for coming through in the clutch. No

Cardinal has hit more grand slams than No. 5.

St. Louis teammate Lance Berkman said if he was managing an opposing team, he'd never pitch to Albert with the game on the line, even with the bases loaded. "I'd rather walk in a run than give up four," he said with a smile.

As of the end of the 2011 season, Albert had tallied 11 grand slams. He's nearly automatic with the bases loaded; in 2009 alone, he came to the plate with the bases full eight times and hit a home run on four occasions.

And his bat doesn't disappear during the postseason, when the pitching is better and the pressure ratchets up. Through the 2011 season, he's hit .330 in the playoffs with 18 home runs and 52 RBIs.

"He's the face of baseball," said ESPN baseball analyst Peter Gammons. "When we're looking at history, he's an icon. And we should appreciate him because he's never done anything that's stained his reputation."

During an era where baseball's best power hitters have been embroiled in steroid rumors, Albert has stayed above the fray. Despite his prolific numbers and prodigious physique, he's never failed a drug test and never been accused of using any kind of performance-enhancing drug. It gets his dander up, though, when people voice suspicions about his Hall-of-Fame-worthy statistics.

"I would never do any of that," Albert said about taking performance-enhancing drugs. "You think I'm going to ruin my relationship with God just because I want to get better in this game? You think I'm going to ruin everything because of steroids? . . . I want to be the person who represents God, represents my family, and represents the Cardinals the right way."

A HOME RUN HITTER WITH A HEART FOR OTHERS

On many occasions, Albert has invited baseball to test him every day. He has nothing to hide and wants people to know that he walks his talk.

In fact, Albert looks for ways to tell people about what God has done in his life. He's often said that God doesn't need him, but he needs God to live a successful life.

Since the early 1990s, the Cardinals have hosted a Christian Family Day when players share their testimonies with the fans at Busch Stadium after the conclusion of the game. From the time Albert joined the team, he and Deidre have become regulars at this event and others like it around the country.

The Christian Family Day organization also created a special testimony card for Albert and other members of the team. It looks like a baseball card, but instead of statistics on the back, it's packed with a player's personal story of accepting Jesus and a prayer that people can pray to invite Christ into their lives.

Albert signs the cards, and he and Deidre look for opportunities to pass them out to young fans.

Deidre has said that she sometimes feels like she's hitting a home run when she gives the card to people and sees the look on their faces. But when it comes to hitting balls out of major league parks, the former softball player leaves that up to her husband.

Even in 2011, when an early-season slump and fractured forearm hurt Albert's statistics, he managed to hit more than 30 home runs for the eleventh consecutive year.

Not surprisingly, no player in Cardinals history has put together more multiple home run games than Albert. During the 2011 season, he had hit two or more home runs in 42 games—breaking Stan Musial's record of 37. Mark McGwire was third on the list at

28 games. Albert has five career three-homer games (the most of any active player), and some say his record-setting 465-foot blast in Busch Stadium during the 2011 season still hasn't come down to earth.

Albert's fans often can't decide what's their favorite thing about a Pujols home run. Is it gawking at a towering drive as it leaves the yard for some distant destination? Or is it seeing him glide around the bases until he approaches home plate, where he does his trademark shuffle step as he looks up and points to heaven?

Albert doesn't point to the sky to disrespect his opponents. He does it to show his respect to his Savior.

Many experts have tried to dissect Albert's swing and figure out the secret to his success. But Albert already knows the answer.

"I don't believe in all that science stuff," Albert said. "I believe in Jesus Christ, who gave me the strength and power and talent to honor Him. You can always try to figure it out and be scientific and look for success. Not me. It's dedication, hard work, practice, and God."

The All-Star's plan for moving forward is simple: he'll keep working hard, keep swinging the way God created him to, and keep pointing to heaven.

Because Albert has even higher places to go.

7.

JOSH HAMILTON: BASEBALL'S BAT MAN COMES BACK FROM THE BRINK

Yankee Stadium in New York City has witnessed its share of historic events.

Babe Ruth hit the first home run in the ballpark on Opening Day in 1923. Lou Gehrig, after playing 2,130 consecutive games and being diagnosed with a deadly illness, delivered his "Luckiest Man on the Face of the Earth" speech in 1939. Pitcher Don Larsen threw a perfect game during the 1956 World Series. Roger Maris hit his sixty-first home run to break Ruth's record for most dingers in a season. One-handed pitcher Jim Abbott tossed a no-hitter in these fabled confines in 1993.

But perhaps no performance was more awe-producing than when Texas Rangers slugger Josh Hamilton stepped into the batter's box for the 2008 Home Run Derby. On baseball's biggest stage, the first-year All-Star came up big. No, make that huge.

From his first swing, the people packed into the stadium knew they were witnessing something special.

"Are you getting this?" a fan asked his buddy, who was videotaping the action on his cell phone.

"I am," his friend shouted back. "This is big time."

The rules for the Home Run Derby are simple. A player doesn't have to swing at every pitch. But if he does swing, the ball had better leave the yard. Any swing that doesn't produce a home run counts as an out. Ten outs and the round is over.

Some of baseball's most powerful hitters have left the batter's box with a goose egg. That wasn't the case for Josh.

Bending his knees a couple of times and breathing deep to relax, Josh sent ball after ball into the dark New York sky.

One, two.

Teammate Ian Kinsler ran over to wipe Josh's face with a towel after he crushed his second home run 502 feet. The two shared a laugh before Josh got back to work.

Three, four, five, six, seven, eight.

Almost immediately, New York's fickle-yet-intelligent fans started chanting his name.

"Ham-il-ton, Ham-il-ton, Ham-il-ton!"

The bat became a blur in his hands. *Nine, ten, eleven.*

With every swing of his arms and snap of his wrists, Josh hammered another ball into the stratosphere. Low pitch. *Smack.* A towering home run into the second-deck of right field. *Number twelve.* High pitch. *Crack.* A line drive home run that zoomed over the fence into a fan's glove. *Number thirteen.*

Josh smiled at his pitcher. Being an All-Star and hitting in Yankee Stadium may have been new to him, but seventy-one-year-old Clay Council was a familiar face. Council often threw batting practice for Josh during summer baseball when he was a teen in North Carolina. Now Council was watching Josh live up to all the promise he saw in the youngster years before.

Fourteen, fifteen, sixteen. Pretty soon Josh's opponents turned into cheerleaders. David "Big Papi" Ortiz laughed and pointed as yet another ball jetted over the fence. *Seventeen, eighteen, nineteen.*

Ridiculous. Like guided missiles, every ball found its target in the right field bleachers. Pretty soon Josh started laughing. Nobody had ever hit like this before. *Twenty, twenty-one, twenty-two.*

"What's the record?" a fan said.

"I have no idea," his friend answered.

The answer was 24. Bobby Abreu set that mark in the first round of 2005's Home Run Derby in Detroit's Comerica Park.

But it wasn't just Josh's total that amazed. It was the magnitude of his drives. Three of his home runs sailed over 500 feet— the longest estimated at a massive 518 feet.

Yankee Stadium started feeling like a party. Fans sensed history was taking place. Competitors shook their heads and smiled. Would it ever end? At one point, Josh hit thirteen home runs in a row. *Twenty-three, twenty-four, twenty-five!*

Rangers teammate Milton Bradley ran up and gave the slugger a little back massage. Josh was hot. Incredibly hot. Fans began bowing down to Josh in mock worship.

He still had two outs left. *Twenty-six, twenty-seven, twenty-eight.* Finally, his last two hits fell short of the fence. Fellow All-Star Michael Young gave Josh a hug. Sportswriters started saying fans had just witnessed twenty of the most exciting minutes in the history of baseball.

Before walking into Yankee Stadium on July 14, 2008, Josh

was a relatively unknown center fielder for the Rangers playing in his first full major league season. Stepping out of the batter's box, Josh effectively introduced himself to the baseball world. Actually, maybe it's better to say he *reintroduced* himself to baseball.

A long battle with drug and alcohol addiction had nearly erased Josh from baseball's memory. With twenty-eight swings, Josh announced he was back.

But more important to Josh than the media attention was the opportunity to talk about the difference Jesus Christ had made in his life. Before, his life was all about baseball. Now it focused on Jesus.

ONE GOAL

Just nine years before this historic night, baseball was abuzz with talk about Josh. As a 6-foot, 4-inch, 205-pound senior at Athens Drive High School in North Carolina, Josh was a can't-miss prospect. A five-tool player.

He could play outfield, first base, or pitch. He hit for power and still had a stunning batting average. And his arm in the outfield made opposing coaches think twice before trying to score a runner from second base.

During his senior year, Josh hit .529 with 13 home runs and 35 RBIs in 25 games. He struck out just seven times all year, while drawing 26 walks. His speed in the outfield allowed him to track down would-be base hits in the gap. He also stole 20 bases.

And pitching? His 95-mph fastball baffled hitters and amazed professional scouts. Josh tallied a 7–1 record his senior year with 91 strikeouts in just 56 innings.

At some games, more than fifty scouts would crowd together

to watch the two-time North Carolina Player of the Year show off his talents on the diamond.

Not that Josh was a showoff. Sure, he knew he was the best player on the field every time his size-19 cleats stepped onto the turf. But he stayed humble and didn't mock the opposing team.

It was Josh's humility that most impressed Dan Jennings, the Tampa Bay Devil Rays' director of scouting in 1999. That spring, Jennings traveled to Raleigh to watch Josh play in a home game for Athens Drive. Nearly sixty scouts watched wide-eyed as Josh crushed a home run well over four hundred feet.

"But that wasn't the amazing thing," Jennings said. "After [Hamilton] returns to the dugout, he comes back out and serves as the batboy for his teammates. And there was this mentally challenged kid [on the team], and Josh was treating him like his best friend."

Josh and Ashley Pittman were friends. Pittman had Down syndrome. At first, a high school baseball star and special education student might have seemed an unlikely pair. But both shared a love for baseball. Pittman worked as the team batboy, and Josh was impressed with his dedication to the game. Pittman rarely missed a practice, never missed a game, and always came looking professional in his team uniform.

The two often ate lunch together. Pittman called Josh by his nickname, "Hambone," and Josh referred to his friend as "Big Ash."

Big Ash was devastated when Athens Drive lost in the state semifinals during Josh's senior year, but the Jaguars' coach had a surprise at the year-end banquet. He was starting a special award to honor the player who best showed what the qualities of compassion and sportsmanship were all about.

The first winner of the Ashley Pittman Award was . . . of course, Josh Hamilton.

"I've gotten a lot of trophies over the years, but the Ashley Pittman Memorial Award is special to me," Josh wrote in his autobiography, *Beyond Belief.* "It's still prominently displayed in a case at my parents' house. More than any other trophy or newspaper clipping, it reminds me of who I was and how I lived at that point in my life."

Talent. Statistics. Size. Character. It was no surprise that Tampa Bay chose Josh with the first overall pick in the 1999 draft.

More than fifty family members, friends, and reporters were gathered at the Hamiltons' home on June 2 when Josh got the call from Jennings. With his selection, Josh became the first high school player to go number one since Alex Rodriguez went first in 1993.

"We've watched him for a long time," Tampa Bay general manager Chuck LaMar said. "Josh Hamilton withstood every test that we gave him, whether it be his performance on the field or questions we asked . . . we feel like he's the number-one player in this draft."

Josh felt like he was the top player, too. It wasn't pride. Josh had worked hard to get the most of his God-given abilities, and he was ready to make his mark on the major leagues.

After learning he was the first selection, he hugged his mom and dad. His father, Tony, had coached him from before he could attend school. His parents had rarely missed a game, often driving hundreds of miles to make it for the first pitch.

Then the giddy eighteen-year-old walked into his front yard

for his first press conference. When asked how he envisioned his career, Josh replied: "I'm thinking three years in the minors, then fifteen years in the big leagues." Josh paused for a moment before adding, "Then I'll have to wait five years to get into the Hall of Fame."

Everyone laughed, but Josh really wasn't kidding. He'd always felt special on a baseball field. He'd always had one goal—being a baseball All-Star.

People recognized Josh's talent when he was very young. He was just six when a scout came to watch him for the first time. Okay, maybe the word *scout* isn't quite right.

Josh was practicing with his brother Jason's eleven- and twelve-year-old team. Despite being half their age, Josh kept up with and often surpassed the older players with his baseball skills. The president of the Tar Heel League needed to decide what to do with the precocious elementary student who played like a middle schooler.

Playing with kids his own age certainly wasn't a challenge. Josh could hit farther and throw faster than any of his teammates. His skills were so advanced that other parents asked if Josh could be moved up because they were worried their sons could be hurt by one of Josh's hits or throws.

"Their fears became real in our first game," Josh wrote in *Beyond Belief.* "I fielded a ball at shortstop and threw it across the infield as hard as I could to get the runner. There was a problem, though—the first baseman either never saw the ball or didn't react fast enough to catch it. He stood there with his glove turned the wrong way as the ball smacked into his chest. He went down like a sniper got him . . . I felt terrible."

Shortly after, Josh was promoted to his brother's team. He turned seven on May 21, 1998, making him five years younger than his opponents.

But his talent bridged the gap. Batting ninth, Josh made his presence felt on the Hamilton Machine Little League team by hitting his first real home run. Just two weeks after turning seven, a twelve-year-old pitcher learned an important lesson: Don't throw Josh a fastball over the plate. The youngster cracked it over the left-center field fence.

It was the first of many home runs to come.

ON THE RIGHT PATH

When Josh hits a baseball, it just sounds different. The speed of his swing combined with the impact of the bat draws *oohs* and *ahs* from onlookers.

After Josh's post-draft celebration, he jumped into the car with Jason and went to the high school field to hit some baseballs.

A family with two young boys lived in a house beyond center field. They often watched Josh play games or take batting practice. On that evening, the father and his two boys walked up to the backstop.

"I didn't expect you'd be out here tonight," the dad said. "But I can always tell when you're hitting. It just sounds different inside my house when your bat hits the ball. From the first crack of the bat today, my boys said, 'Josh is hitting.' "

Josh's hitting impressed the Devil Rays as well. They signed him to a contract that included a $3.96 million signing bonus—a record at the time for a No. 1 pick. And despite the fact that Josh had a fastball that nearly reached triple digits, Tampa Bay wanted him to play outfield so he could hit every day.

With the major league season already underway, Josh was assigned to Tampa Bay's Class A Rookie League team in Princeton, West Virginia.

Josh had just turned eighteen, so he hopped in the car with his parents and drove to Princeton. In his first game, on June 19, 1999, Josh hit his first professional home run.

With his mom making sure her son had clean clothes and remained well fed, and his dad talking through at-bats and situations, Josh stayed fully focused on baseball.

Sure, the other rookies didn't have their parents traveling with them. But the other players probably weren't as close to their families and didn't have the means (i.e. nearly $4 million) that allowed them to come along.

Josh lived up to his hype in Princeton. In 56 games, he hit .347 with 10 home runs, 48 RBIs, and 49 runs scored.

Tampa Bay bumped Josh up to Class A Hudson Valley in New York in August. Instead of playing against rookies, he now faced second- and third-year professionals.

Hudson Valley was in the middle of a playoff race, and Josh was placed in the middle of its lineup. After struggling at first, he turned things around and helped the Renegades win the New York-Penn League championship by hitting .429 with two home runs and eight RBIs in the playoffs.

His rookie year had been a success. But during the season and back at home, he felt something was missing in his life. He had occasionally attended church with his aunt and uncle growing up, so he knew something about God. When he returned to North

Carolina, he visited his aunt and uncle's house to discuss some spiritual issues that he was wrestling with. He ended up praying to accept Jesus Christ into his life.

"I got saved when I was eighteen years old," Josh said. "I accepted Christ in my aunt and uncle's living room. But I didn't know how to grow spiritually. I didn't know how to get in the Word. I didn't know how to pray like I needed to. I didn't know how to fellowship with other people. I tell people that Satan comes after you a lot harder when you're a child of God."

Everything seemed to be going according to Josh's plan professionally when he reported to Tampa Bay for spring training in 2000. He had a strong spring and was assigned to the Class A Charleston RiverDogs in the South Atlantic League. Many of these players were more experienced, with three or four years of minor league baseball under their belts.

Again, Josh's parents came with him. They were at every home game, even showing up early to watch batting practice. They traveled with the team for road games, staying in the team's hotel. And Josh continued to flourish. Surrounded by people he loved and playing the game he loved, he was named co-MVP of the South Atlantic League. He was also honored as the Player of the Year in Class A baseball, and the Devil Rays named him their Minor League Player of the Year. Check out his stats: a .301 batting average, 13 home runs, 61 RBIs, and 62 runs scored.

Going into the 2001 campaign, Josh appeared to be ready to make the leap to the Big Show. If he wasn't going to be with the big league club to start the season, he certainly seemed destined to join the Devil Rays soon. But in a split second, everything changed.

ACCIDENTS AND BAD DECISIONS

On March 3, 2001, Josh and his parents were driving to their home in Bradenton, Florida, following an exhibition game. His mom, Linda, was behind the wheel of the family's Chevy Silverado, while Josh half-dozed in the front seat and his dad sat in the back. As the family drove through the intersection of Victory Road and U.S. 301, a dump truck ran a red light and barreled into the driver's side of the pickup.

Josh saw the whole thing about to happen and reached over to pull his mom to him. The impact sent the Hamiltons spinning in their truck for about a hundred feet.

The family was rushed to Memorial Hospital. Linda had neck pain. Tony was treated for a skull fracture. Josh had some pain in his back but was untreated and went back to spring training the next morning.

Over the next few days, however, the pain got worse. Doctors were baffled. They performed MRIs and CAT scans to diagnose the problem. Prescription painkillers didn't help much. Physically, everything looked fine, but Josh felt anything but okay.

With his parents recovering in North Carolina and playing baseball not an option, Josh started hanging out in a tattoo parlor.

He had shown up that spring with six tattoos. His first ink featured his nickname "Hambone" in all capital letters around his right bicep. Soon the word "Hammer" graced his other arm. He didn't have many friends in Florida, and without baseball, he didn't have anything to do, so pretty soon Kevin and Bill in the tattoo parlor became his "friends."

Josh would show up at the tattoo parlor and spend hours in the chair—sometimes getting two or three tattoos in a day.

The nineteen-year-old had six tattoos when his parents went to North Carolina. When they returned a few weeks later, he had twenty-one.

With doctors not finding a cause for his pain, Josh felt pressure to play. He was sent to Double-A Orlando to start the season, but he struggled. In 23 games, his stats were the worst of his professional career. He hit just .180 with no home runs and only four RBIs.

To make things worse, Josh tore his hamstring muscle running to first base in the first month of the season and was sent down to Charleston for an injury-rehabilitation assignment.

Josh's leg healed, but his back never felt right, so Tampa had him see a specialist in California. After doing an MRI, the doctor pointed to a white spot near the spine. It was a pocket of fluid pushing against a nerve. The doctor gave Josh a cortisone shot on the exact spot.

"He plunged the needle into my spine till it felt like it was grinding on bone," Josh said. "But as soon as the needle was removed, the pain was gone. I've never thanked a man so many times in my life."

Sporting a healthy back and renewed optimism, Josh headed into the 2002 season with something to prove. According to his timeline, this was the year he was supposed to break into the majors. Shortly after Christmas, he went to Florida to start training. He knew he had to make up for a disappointing year in 2001.

But one afternoon, he injured his back while training. The next morning he could barely get out of bed. Spring training was less than two weeks away. Depressed and disappointed, Josh returned to the comfort of the tattoo parlor.

His collection of ink continued to grow. Soon, he had a total of twenty-six tattoos. After hanging at the parlor one afternoon, Kevin and Bill asked Josh if he wanted to go out when the shop closed. Without thinking, he immediately said yes.

They took him to a strip club and ordered Josh a beer. He was still too young to legally drink and had never consumed alcohol before, but he downed that beer and a few more. Later, the trio went to Kevin's house where he was offered some cocaine.

A little drunk and not thinking straight, Josh inhaled the drug.

"I had a lot of 'firsts' that night," Josh said. "[The cocaine] gave the adrenaline rush that I wasn't getting by playing baseball."

At first, when Josh was playing baseball, he didn't do drugs. But like in so many cases, soon the drugs took over. For the next three-and-a-half years, drugs and alcohol ruled Josh's life.

Despite being plunged into a personal darkness, the light of his talent shined through from time to time.

Playing Class A ball for Bakersfield, California, during 2002, Josh produced a few highlights that have become things of legend. One evening, he hit an opposite-field home run in Sam Lynn Ballpark that smashed a digital display so hard that it stopped working—kind of like in the movie *The Natural*. Years later, the display still hadn't been fixed and was covered by a banner that promoted the team's website.

Josh also described a mammoth home run he hit that traveled 549 feet and landed in the Kern River. And another time, Josh showed his arm was still a weapon when he caught a fly ball on the warning track and threw to home plate, nailing a runner who had tagged up at third and tried to score.

But Bakersfield was also the first place Josh used drugs during the season. After 56 games, his numbers weren't bad—he hit .301 with nine home runs, 44 RBIs, and 23 runs scored. Elbow pain caused Josh's season to end early. Surgery in Alabama and rest in North Carolina cured the elbow pain, but not the drug problem.

Josh was using cocaine nearly every day while rehabilitating his injury with the Triple-A Durham Bulls. He knew there was a possibility of being randomly drug tested, but even when he was asked to do one, he remained in denial. The test came back positive and Josh was suspended from baseball for the first time.

Subsequent failed tests led to even longer suspensions until on March 19, 2004, Josh was suspended from baseball for one year for failing to comply with the MLB drug policy. Another failed drug test in August led to additional penalties.

In all, Josh played no professional baseball from the end of the 2002 season through most of 2006. Instead, he fell deeper into the darkness of drug addiction.

Not that everything was bleak in his life. During streaks of sobriety, he struck up a relationship with former high school classmate Katie Chadwick.

"Everybody knew who Josh was in high school," Katie said. "Everybody had a lot of respect for him, because he never did anything wrong."

Three years after graduating from high school, Josh was doing plenty of things wrong, but he called her out of the blue. She agreed to let him come to her house, and they ended up dating for three months. They broke things off but got back together in July

2004. Five months later, they were married.

Josh was attending Alcoholics Anonymous meetings and had convinced himself and Katie that his addictions were behind him. He had a slipup in January, but then on his twenty-fourth birthday, Josh went on a bender that led to a series a relapses.

Josh pulled himself together when the couple's first daughter, Sierra, was born on August 22, 2005. (Katie had another daughter from a previous relationship.) But three days later, Josh went to Walgreens to pick up his wife's prescription and ended up at a bar instead.

Over the next six weeks, he spent more than $100,000 on drugs.

By this time, Josh had turned to crack cocaine to get the high he used to get from the powder form of the drug. But while the highs were higher, the lows were lower.

Numerous times, Josh felt as if he might die—like his heart might thump its way out of his chest. He was never violent with Katie, but his erratic behavior caused her to get a restraining order against him. Trips to the emergency room weren't uncommon. Almost all of his nearly $4 million signing bonus was gone.

His life spiraled down until one night Josh found himself high, out of gas, and walking down a two-lane road.

"I was a shell of a human, a soulless being," Josh said. "I had stripped myself of self-respect and lost my ability to feel love or hope or joy or even pain."

On October 1, 2005, Josh showed up at his grandmother Mary Holt's house . . . at around two in the morning. He weighed 180 pounds and was almost unrecognizable.

"I was a wreck—dirty, twitchy, and barely coherent," Josh said.

Granny's house had always been a place of refuge for Josh growing up. He'd even kissed Granny, as Josh affectionately called her, on the cheek before playing every baseball game growing up. Now, when he had nowhere else to turn, he went to his grandmother's. She fed him and tucked him into bed.

Within a couple of days, Josh was using crack again—this time in Granny's house. After just five days under her roof, the seventy-two-year-old had seen enough. She confronted Josh in the hall.

Of course, Josh had seen and heard it all. He'd been in and out of eight rehabilitation centers, spent days on counselors' couches, and talked for hours with his father, mother, and wife. But there was something in the way that Granny looked at him with a mixture of sorrow and anger that pierced Josh's heart.

"I went back in the room where I'd just been using drugs, grabbed a Bible, and the first verse I read was James 4:7," Josh said, referring to the verse that says: "Submit yourselves, then, to God. Resist the devil, and he will flee from you".

At that moment, Josh recommitted his life to Christ. Unlike the first time he prayed to accept Christ, this time he followed through with action. His life began to change as he started reading his Bible, praying, and going to church with his aunt and uncle. Then a few weeks later, on the advice of her pastor, Katie called Josh and told him she forgave him.

BEING SECOND

After more than twenty-four years of putting himself first in his life, someone new was on the throne: Jesus Christ.

Josh started living and eating right. And God began restoring everything that Josh had nearly destroyed. He quickly gained back the fifty pounds of muscle he'd lost. His family rallied to his side. He reconciled with his wife. He started working—good, honest work with his brother's tree service.

Then on June 20, 2006, Josh got the call reinstating him to Major League Baseball.

Amazingly, after abusing his body for years, his skills hadn't diminished. He played 15 games for Hudson Valley that summer—the same Class A team he'd played for in 1999—with solid results. He hit .260 and scored seven runs.

One day that December, when he was trimming trees for his brother, Josh learned that the Cincinnati Reds had acquired him through the Rule 5 draft.

Instead of languishing in the minor leagues like he probably would've done with the Rays, guidelines in the Rule 5 draft required the Reds to give him the opportunity to make the big league club. And Josh wasn't about to ruin his second chance.

Josh became one of the Reds' best hitters in spring training. He batted .403 and made Cincinnati's roster as the fourth outfielder behind Adam Dunn, Ken Griffey Jr., and Ryan Freel.

On Opening Day, Josh received nearly as big an ovation as Griffey. The fans were immediately drawn to him and his story of overcoming addiction. Josh has said many times that standing on a major league field again—with his family, his parents, and his wife's family in the stands and everybody on their feet—nearly brought him to tears.

But he wanted to be a professional, so he fought back the lump in his throat. Like Tom Hanks said in the movie *A League of Their Own,* "There's no crying in baseball."

A week into the season, Josh got his first start and rewarded the Reds with his first major league hit—a home run. By the end of the month, Josh was named National League Rookie of the Month.

"Baseball is third in my life right now, behind my relationship with God and my family," Josh said at the time. "Without the first two, baseball isn't even in the picture. Believe me, I know."

The twenty-six-year-old rookie hit nearly .300 in his first season. He did end up on the disabled list twice during the year, once for a stomach ailment and once for a sprained wrist. He played eleven games at Triple-A Louisville, but he stayed clean the whole time—much in part to Cincinnati manager Jerry Narron's brother, Johnny.

Johnny had coached Josh when he was a teenager in North Carolina. The Reds hired the faithful man of God as their video coordinator and gave him the extra responsibility of keeping Josh accountable on the road.

Proving he could play at the big league level, Josh ended the 2007 season with a .290 batting average, 19 home runs, 47 RBIs, and 25 runs scored.

That offseason, though, Cincinnati traded Josh to Texas. The Rangers needed power in the outfield, and Cincinnati needed pitching. Johnny Narron came along, too, as an assistant hitting coach.

Texas fans and his new teammates immediately embraced Josh. He responded with monster numbers. Batting third for the Rangers, just ahead of Milton Bradley, Josh had 95 RBIs by the 2008 All-Star break.

In his first full major league season, Josh was voted onto the

All-Star team and made history at the Home Run Derby.

Before the derby, Katie prayed that Josh would hit at least one home run. He did much better than that. A lot of people were praying that night, including Josh and Council, who knelt down and prayed for God to be with them before stepping on the field for the first round.

And God answered big-time. All people remember from that July night in Yankee Stadium were Josh's 28 bombs in the first round. They don't remember that Justin Morneau beat Josh 5–3 in the finals. But Josh didn't care about losing—he'd already won because his story was being told on TV screens around the world.

"God has given me such a platform to share what He's done in my life," Josh said. While he was in one of the darkest, most drug-riddled parts of his life, he said, "My wife was telling me that God was going to allow me to get back into baseball. But it wasn't going to be about baseball. It was going to be about sharing how He brought me through the storm."

Josh stayed healthy the entire season, notching some impressive statistics. He hit .304 with 32 home runs, 130 RBIs, and 98 runs scored.

In the offseason, Josh wanted to prepare for an even better season in 2009. He went to Arizona to work out a month before spring training. But on January 21, 2009, he fell into old habits. Josh went into a restaurant that had a bar and ordered a drink.

"I was out there for three weeks and stopped praying, stopped doing my devotions, stopped reading the Word, stopped fellowshipping with my accountability partner," Josh said. "Doing all those things that had got me to where I was. I thought I could have one drink. And that thought doesn't work out too well with me. One leads to about twenty, and I don't remember half the stuff I do . . . immediately, it hit my heart why I'd done those things, and it's because I took God out of first position."

Josh woke up the next morning and immediately called his wife and told her what happened. He called the Texas Rangers. He called Major League Baseball.

News of Josh's escapade didn't surface for seven months, but when it did, the revelations included several rather risqué photos of him and three young women in the bar. Josh didn't shy away from the controversy of being an outspoken Christian who had just shown up in some compromising photos. He addressed it head-on.

"I'm embarrassed about it for my wife, Katie, for my kids, and for the organization," Josh wrote in a press release. "I'm not perfect. It's an ongoing struggle, and it's real. It's amazing how these things can creep back in. But I am human, and I have struggles."

Josh flew home right after the incident in January to get things right with his wife and with God. For her part, Katie knew things would be okay the moment Josh came in the house.

"When he walked in the door, and I [saw] how broken and repentant and remorseful he was, and how he was so upset at himself for the sin and for hurting me, I was just encouraged because I was looking at a transformed man," she said. "It just made it so easy to extend that grace to him again."

In the past when Josh had relapsed, his attitude was, *Oh well, I might as well keep doing it.* But now Josh was different. He was committed to God, to his family, and to staying clean.

He redoubled his efforts to keep Christ first in his life through a multilayered support system that was described by *The Dallas Morning News* as "rooted in his Christian beliefs and his rigorous daily devotions. Its primary components are his wife, his parents, and a host of 'accountability partners' that includes a Texas Rangers coach, pastors from three churches, his Christian sports agent, and his father-in-law."

Josh knew he was weak when he counted on his own strength, but he found power in the Holy Spirit to live according to God's commands.

The 2009 season proved to be forgettable for Josh, although the Rangers showed improvement by posting an 87–75 record. Injures limited him to just 89 games, and his statistics suffered accordingly. His batting average dropped to .260 and he hit just 10 home runs and drove in only 45 runs.

Despite his subpar year, Josh had an All-Star offseason. He and Katie made more than thirty appearances around the country, speaking about redemption and forgiveness through their foundation, Triple Play Ministries. Their ministry also hosted Christian sports camps, did community outreach, and helped support an orphanage in Uganda.

Early in the 2010 season, it was obvious that the Rangers and Josh were going to have a special year. In June, the team posted a 21–6 record—its best month in the franchise's fifty-year history.

By August, Josh had distinguished himself as the definitive choice for American League Most Valuable Player. He led the league in batting average at .362, slugging percentage (.634), and hits with 161. Tom Verducci pointed out on SI.com that the last three players to bat over .360 with a slugging percentage of more than .600 while playing centerfield were Mickey Mantle, Stan

Musial, and Joe DiMaggio. That's not bad company.

Verducci went on to describe a mid-August performance by Josh: "Just another night in the life of the best player in baseball went something like this: smash four hits all over the park; a single to left, a 440-foot bomb to center, a single and double to right; score from third base on a pop fly to deep shortstop/short left; score from second base on a ground ball to second; make a diving catch on the warning track and a leaping catch against the center field wall; cause the third-base coach to halt a runner from scoring from second on an otherwise routine run-scoring single to center field."

Being called the "best player in baseball" certainly felt better than being labeled one of the most disappointing No. 1 draft picks of all time. Josh was finally living up to his potential.

Despite missing nearly all the final month of the regular season with broken ribs, Josh helped Texas reach the playoffs with a 90–72 record. His gaudy 2010 statistics looked like this: a .359 batting average to go with 32 home runs and 100 RBIs.

Things were going great for Josh and the Rangers. But late in the season, on one of the best nights in team history, Josh was noticeably absent. It was September 25, 2010, and Texas had just clinched its first American League West title in more than a decade with a 4–3 win over Oakland. But instead of celebrating with his teammates, Josh chose to be alone.

It's a long-standing baseball tradition for teammates to spray each other with champagne after making it to the playoffs. Josh didn't want any part of the alcohol. He didn't even want it to touch his skin—it had caused that much pain in his life.

BASEBALL'S BAT MAN COMES BACK FROM THE BRINK

A few weeks later, on October 12, after Texas defeated Tampa 5–1 to advance to the American League Championship Series, Josh's teammates made sure he was part of the festivities. They grabbed him, gave him some eye goggles, and walked him into the clubhouse.

"Everybody yelled 'Ginger ale!' and I just jumped in the middle of the pile and they doused me with it," Josh said. "It was the coolest thing for my teammates to understand why I can't be a part of the celebration, and for them to adapt it for me to be a part of it says a lot about my teammates."

The Rangers faced the Yankees in the next round for the right to play in the World Series. Right away, Josh showed the Yankees that things would be different this time. He hit a three-run home run to open up the series.

When Texas won the second game 7–2, it broke a ten-game losing streak against New York in the playoffs. The Rangers eventually defeated the Yankees in the series, four games to two, to advance to the World Series for the first time in team history.

In the Fall Classic, the Texas offense struggled against San Francisco pitching, and the Giants claimed the title in five games.

About a month later, Josh won the American League Most Valuable Player Award. His 22 first-place votes and 358 points easily outdistanced Detroit's Miguel Cabrera's 262 points.

In February 2011, Josh was rewarded with a two-year, $24 million contract that included a $3 million signing bonus. He backed it up by hitting .298, knocking 25 home runs, and driving home 94 runners during the 2011 season, when the Rangers advanced to the World Series for the second straight year.

Josh nearly proved to be the hero of the Fall Classic when his two-run, tenth-inning home run in Game 6 put Texas just three outs away from its first world championship. The St. Louis Cardinals, however, rallied to tie the game in the tenth and win it in the eleventh on David Freese's dramatic walk-off home run. Even though the Redbirds went on to win the title in seven games, the Rangers proved they were among the game's elite teams.

In a similar fashion, Josh has made it to the top of the major leagues. His path hasn't been straight—like the Israelites wandering through the desert, it took him awhile to find the Promised Land. But Josh has said many times that he wouldn't change his past.

"Could I have reached people being that clean-cut kid coming out of high school?" Josh asked rhetorically during an interview. "Probably so. How many more people can I reach having tattoos, having an addiction problem? I've been through that . . . . And I've come back."

His comeback has inspired countless people who are fighting their own demons to give their lives to God. Josh's message to them is simple: *Put God first.*

"One thing I can't live without is, obviously, Jesus," Josh said. "When I don't put Him first, my decisions don't work out too well for me."

The Hall of Fame may still be well into the future, but with Jesus first and his priorities firmly in place, Josh Hamilton is finally on his way.

8.

MARIANO RIVERA:
THE CLOSER WHO GOT SAVED

Looking for a good argument? Just walk up to any die-hard baseball fan and start talking about the greatest players of all time.

Who's the best center fielder ever to play the game? Is it Willie Mays, Joe DiMaggio, Ty Cobb, Mickey Mantle, or Ken Griffey Jr.?

How about third basemen? Good cases can be made for Mike Schmidt, George Brett, Brooks Robinson, Alex Rodriguez, and Chipper Jones.

And don't even dare to bring up first basemen, where Lou Gehrig, Jimmie Foxx, and Albert Pujols top most lists.

The truth is, baseball fans love to argue the minutia of the sport and whether the bigger, stronger players of the modern era are better than the greats from the past. No other American sport has the history and voluminous statistics that baseball affords, so the debates over the "best ever" can be never ending.

But the position of closer is one where there's virtually no argument. When the bullpen gate swings open in the ninth inning with a game on the line, one player has dominated more than any other pitcher in history: Mariano Rivera.

In seventeen seasons since coming up with the New York Yankees in 1995, Mariano has earned 603 saves—the most in baseball history. Only he and Trevor Hoffman (601 saves) have passed the 600 mark . . . and that doesn't count Mariano's 42 postseason saves, which are also a major league record. When he's on the mound, the Yankees nearly always secure a victory. His save percentage is a hair under 90 percent—the best ever for pitchers who have had 250 or more save opportunities.

In the playoffs, where things really matter, Mariano has been nearly unhittable. And playing for the Yankees, he's had plenty of postseason experience. He has helped New York win five World Series titles and was named the Most Valuable Player of the 1999 World Series. His earned-run average in the playoffs is an unheard of 0.70.

Only twenty-one pitchers in the history of baseball have tallied *half* the number of saves that this slender hurler known as the "Hammer of God" has earned. Mariano has won the Rolaids Relief Man Award five times for the American League and has been voted an All-Star twelve times.

Despite the accolades and accomplishments, Mariano stays humble and firmly rooted in his Christian faith. He lets his actions, instead of his words, do the talking. Not exactly the demeanor of a typical big league closer.

Almost everything about Mariano is the opposite of what most people think of when they picture a relief pitcher. This normally high-strung bunch is known for their bushy beards, waxed moustaches, big rope necklaces, nervous tics, and unpredictable behavior on the mound.

"Look at Mo's delivery, look at how he repeats it," teammate Joba Chamberlain marveled. "He does the same exact thing every time. That's a very hard thing to do—I try, but I can't do it like Mo. There's never any added stress on his arm because all the parts move the same way every time."

If Mariano could be described in one word, it would be *predictable*. He warms up the same way before every appearance. He never looks rushed or worried. His demeanor is the same, whether it's a spring training game or the World Series. Even his signature pitch—the cut fastball—is predictable. Batters know it's coming, but they still can't hit it.

Jim Thome, who has hit more than 600 home runs in his career, called Mariano's cut fastball the greatest pitch in baseball history. Longtime Minnesota Twins manager Tom Kelly once said, "He needs to pitch in a higher league, if there is one. Ban him from baseball. He should be illegal."

When asked if being called the greatest closer ever embarrasses him, Mariano answered: "Yes, it does. It does make me uncomfortable because I don't like to talk about myself. I just want to be able to contribute as much as I can for the team. And the rest is just blessings from the Lord."

In reality, he doesn't have to say anything. Teammates, opponents, and sportscasters say it for him.

"You're seeing the greatest closer of all time," Yankee catcher Jorge Posada said. "I don't care about eras. There's nobody better. No one can even compare. His body doesn't change. He doesn't change. He's the same Mariano as he was as a setup man, as a closer, and as a friend."

Yankee shortstop Derek Jeter has equally high praise for the kind of person Mariano is. "He's like my brother," said Jeter, who came up in the minor leagues with Mariano. "Any time you play with someone that long, there's a connection there . . . . He's been the exact same person he was since the first day I met him."

That person is deeply committed to God, his family, and his teammates.

Mariano is the first to say that he never could've collected so many saves if his team hadn't put him in the right situation. In order to earn a save, a pitcher must record at least three outs with his team in the lead by no more than three runs. Every save opportunity brings pressure, but Mariano handles it with ease.

He appears strangely peaceful on the mound—and it's a peace that only comes from knowing the Prince of Peace.

"I don't know if we'll ever see it again," Yankee manager Joe Girardi said after Mariano notched his 600th career save. "This is a guy who I believe is the best closer that's ever been in the game, and I've had the fortune of catching him, coaching him, and managing him, and it's a treat."

Hitting against him is anything but a treat. However, Mariano has earned the respect of opposing batters, including Boston Red Sox great David Ortiz. "If you talk to him at an All-Star Game, it's like talking to somebody who just got called up," Ortiz said. "To him, everybody else is good. I don't get it. To him, everybody else is the best. It's unbelievable. And he is the greatest . . . . Good people, you want to do well."

And Mariano has done well. *Very* well, especially considering that when the Yankees first saw him, he was a *shortstop*, not a pitcher.

DEVELOPING THE MIRACLE PITCH

Kansas City Royals scout Herb Raybourn first witnessed Mariano on a baseball field in 1988. He was playing for Panamá Oeste

(Panama West) in the national championship game. At 6 feet, 2 inches and around 160 pounds, Mariano made an impact as a rangy shortstop with a good arm. His batting stroke, however, was less than impressive.

A year later, Panamá Oeste again qualified for the national tournament. But with his team's pitching floundering, Mariano volunteered to step onto the mound. He had thrown some growing up and, as a child, was always good at hurling rocks at a target.

Mariano wasn't overpowering as a pitcher, but he was accurate. So accurate, in fact, that he caught the eye of Chico Heron, a Yankees scout. Heron set up a tryout with Raybourn, who had since become the head of Latin American scouting for the Yankees.

Mariano traveled to Panama City for the audition. Raybourn immediately recognized him. The skinny shortstop took the ball and walked to the mound. He had thrown just nine pitches—all of which registered in the mid-80s on the speed gun—when Raybourn stopped him. Mariano thought he'd blown it. But Raybourn had seen enough.

"The radar wasn't really being lit up," Raybourn said. "But what I liked about Mariano was his looseness, a nice loose arm. And his fastball had a lot of movement. I could picture him pitching in the majors."

Raybourn figured that with some professional coaching and weight training, Mariano's fastball could gain some extra pop. He'd also have to learn a few other pitches.

The twenty-year-old signed with the Yankees on February 17, 1990, and received a $2,000 signing bonus. He had never thought about being a professional baseball player until he inked his name on the contract.

"Usually a player prepares for years," Mariano said. "Here I was signing, and I wasn't even [planning on becoming] a pitcher."

Even though Mariano didn't feel like a pitcher, he looked like one on the diamond. He was assigned to the Gulf Coast League Yankees, where he competed against other rookies. In 22 games, he pitched 52 innings and gave up one earned run while striking out 58 and walking just seven.

In 1991, he advanced to the Class A Greensboro Hornets (North Carolina). While his record (4–9) was subpar, he posted an impressive 2.75 ERA and 123-to-36 strikeouts-to-walks ratio. After the season, Mariano enjoyed a greater highlight when he flew home to Panama and married Clara Younce, whom he had known since elementary school.

Over the next several years, Mariano worked his way up to the Triple-A Columbus Clippers in Columbus, Ohio, but his 87-mile per hour fastball didn't impress the big league club.

Early in the 1995 season, though, injuries to several Yankees starters gave Mariano a chance to pitch in pinstripes for the first time. His major league debut turned out to be a dud when he gave up five runs and eight hits in just three innings to the California Angels. In his first four starts for the Yankees, he notched a 10.20 ERA and was quickly sent back to Columbus.

The Yankees still liked Mariano, but they wanted someone with more pop on his fastball. They considered trading him to the Detroit Tigers for David Wells. Then two weeks after Mariano shipped back to the minors, something amazing happened—he added ten miles an hour to his fastball.

On June 26, 1995, Mariano pitched a five-inning no-hitter against the Rochester Red Wings that ended early due to bad weather. But what impressed the Yankees organization most was that his fastball registered a smoking 96 miles per hour on the radar gun.

Nobody could explain where the extra speed came from, but Mariano had an answer: It was a gift from God.

The hurler had recently accepted Jesus Christ as his personal Savior. During his career in the minor leagues, Mariano had seen God show up for him time after time, often through the kindness of other people who would come forward to help at key moments. When his wife was in the hospital, a pitching coach offered to stay with the couple's first son so Mariano could be with her. Another time a lady in Panama helped out his wife while he had to play.

"Every time I was going through a hard time, somebody was there to help," Mariano said. "Even though I had nobody here, I was never alone. That made me accept Jesus as my Savior. I knew it wasn't a coincidence. It was the Lord putting someone there for me."

The extra oomph on his fastball earned Mariano a return trip to New York. This time he fared much better. On July 4, 1995, he struck out 11 in eight shutout innings against the Chicago White Sox.

In 1995, Major League Baseball's first season of expanded, four-teams-per-league playoffs, New York qualified for the play-offs as the wild card. Mariano made the postseason roster and earned a victory in Game 2 against Seattle. The Mariners won the series three games to two, but Mariano pitched well each time out—even striking out Mike Blowers in the eighth inning of Game 5 with the bases loaded.

By 1996, Joe Torre had taken over as manager of the Yankees, who were loaded with young talent, including Jorge Posada, Derek Jeter, Andy Pettitte, and Bernie Williams. With enough starting pitching, Torre knew he wanted Mariano coming out of the bullpen; he just didn't know what role Mariano would play.

The Yankees soon figured out that Mariano was the perfect setup man for closer John Wetteland. With Mariano and Wetteland coming out of the bullpen that year, the Yankees notched a 79-1 record in games in which they held a lead after seven innings.

After failing to win a World Series since 1978, the Yankees claimed the 1996 championship by defeating Atlanta four games to two. Wetteland earned Most Valuable Player honors in the Series, but everybody knew the season belonged to Mariano. He even finished third in Cy Young Award balloting, which goes to the best pitcher in each league. No setup man had ever finished that high.

A FASTBALL THAT'S A CUT ABOVE

If God had given Mariano a gift by adding extra zip to his fastball, He was about to perform a miracle that has kept Mariano at the top of the game for years.

The Yankees let the high-priced Wetteland go in the offseason and moved Mariano to closer. The decision seemed like a no-brainer. But after the 1997 season started, Mariano blew four of his first six save opportunities.

The slow start resulted in a meeting with Torre and Yankees pitching coach Mel Stottlemyre. Mariano felt terrible. He hated letting down the team.

"The harder I tried, the tougher it got," Mariano said. "It was like moving in quicksand. I kept sinking. Joe told me that, 'As long as you are here, you'll be the closer.' That's exactly what I needed to hear."

Shortly after the meeting, something remarkable happened. Mariano had made it into the majors with a four-seam fastball that sometimes had good movement. He got batters out with velocity and accuracy. But as he warmed up before a game with pitcher Ramiro Mendoza, Mariano tried holding the ball a bit differently as they played catch. Mariano noticed that his throws dipped and darted when he gripped the ball a certain way, moving so much that Mendoza had a tough time even catching them.

Mariano had always liked fiddling with how he held the baseball. His long fingers and flexible wrist were perfect for a pitcher. But now he had a problem . . . or did he?

At first, Stottlemyre tried working with Mariano to remove the cutting action and make the ball go straighter. But after discovering his new pitch, Mariano recorded the save that day. He converted his next three save opportunities, as well.

Suddenly, Mariano possessed a pitch that looked like a fastball but acted like a slider when it got close to the plate. And it wasn't long before Mariano developed perfect precision with his signature cut fastball. He controlled its location by putting different pressure on the ball with his fingers. Greater pressure with his middle finger made it move one way. Using the index finger a little more caused it to move another.

From a hitter's perspective, Mariano's delivery looked effortless. But in an instant, the ball exploded past the plate at more than 95 miles per hour.

Scientists have studied thousands of Mariano's pitches. What makes him so devastating is that he throws the cut fastball and four-seam fastball with the exact same motion. Contrary to popular belief, big league batters don't possess supernatural reflexes and reaction speeds. What allows a batter to hit a ball are visual cues and tons of practice. If a pitcher drops down in his delivery or flicks his wrist, a batter can anticipate where the ball is going to be.

"You can't see the spin on it," six-time All-Star Lance Berkman said about Mariano's cutter. "A four-seam fastball rotates a certain way. A slider or a cutter is going to spin a certain way—you see a red dot on the ball as it's coming at you from the seams as it spins. And once you see the rotation on it, you react a certain way. The good cutters, like Rivera's, rotate like a four-seamer—you don't see the red dot, you don't know it's going to come in on you until it's too late."

Batters often think they're seeing a hittable pitch over the plate, but by the time they make contact, the ball has moved several inches and is either in on their hands or hit off the end of the bat. Mariano has unofficially led the major leagues in broken bats every year since he developed his cut fastball. Some sportscasters have joked that bat-maker Louisville Slugger should pay Mariano a bonus because of all the business he's brought its way.

But this pitch is no joke to Mariano—it's a blessing.

"That is my miracle pitch," Mariano said. "That's what I call it, because it's God's gifting. I didn't have that pitch before and nobody taught me that. It came as a miracle."

Since mastering the pitch, Mariano throws his cutter more than 90 percent of the time. He might mix in an occasional two-seam fastball. And about four times a year, he'll throw a changeup just to keep batters honest.

Once Posada became the Yankees' everyday catcher, it got to

the point that he didn't flash signs to tell Mariano what pitch to throw. Posada would simply signal to throw the pitch over the inside or outside *corner* of the plate. Mariano rarely throws one down the middle. With pinpoint accuracy and a determination to win, Mariano goes after the black edges of the plate.

Unlike a lot of closers, Mariano doesn't resort to intimidation. He doesn't believe in throwing brushback pitches. One, because he isn't out there to show up hitters. And two, because that would waste a pitch. All Mariano wants to do is throw strikes.

"My mental approach is simple: Get three outs as quick as possible," he said. "If I can throw three, four pitches, the better it is. I don't care how I get you out, as long as I get you out."

HIS OLD MAN AND THE SEA

Mariano developed his workmanlike attitude as a child, thanks largely to his father.

Mariano was born on November 29, 1969, the son of a fisherman in the little town of Puerto Caimito, located about thirty miles north of Panama's capital, Panama City. His house sat about a hundred feet from the Pacific Ocean and consisted of concrete blocks and a corrugated tin roof.

Mariano's sport of choice as a child was soccer, but he also played baseball . . . if using a stick to hit a ball made of electrical tape wrapped around fish netting counts as a baseball.

During his early elementary years, Mariano and his friends would make a ball, cut a few straight tree branches for a bat, and form gloves and chest protectors out of cardboard. Games were played on a stretch of beach at low tide or in the streets.

When Mariano was twelve, his father bought him a real leather glove. The youngster was so excited that he slept with the glove and took it everywhere with him, even to school.

Mariano's father worked hard as a fisherman, earning around $50 a week, to provide for his four children. He was also a strict disciplinarian. Mariano remembers receiving a lot of spankings, but he knew his father punished him for his own good.

"My childhood was wonderful," Mariano said. "Basically, I didn't have anything. But what we had, I was happy."

As Mariano entered Pablo Sanchez High School, he dreamed of becoming a professional soccer player. He had quick feet and a smooth athleticism. What he didn't have was the ability to stay healthy. Numerous ankle injuries caused him to give up on his *fútbol* aspirations.

Instead of bending it like Beckham, Mariano was going to try to fish 'em like Roland Martin. Following his graduation from high school at sixteen, Mariano tried his hand at the family business. He wasn't afraid of hard work, but he soon realized that fishing wasn't for him. The boats would go out for six days a week. Everybody slept onboard, and sometimes it got dangerous when the seas were up. Once, his boat full of fish capsized and sent the crew into the ocean. Fortunately, everyone made it to the safety of a nearby vessel.

"It's hard. Extremely hard," Mariano said of being a fisherman. "I wanted to study to be a mechanic. Obviously, I didn't do it because the Lord had different plans for me."

While Mariano didn't follow his father's footsteps into fishing, he did pick up a lot from Mariano Sr.—including his strong character and generous spirit. If his father can help someone, he will, Mariano says—even if that means giving a person his last ten dollars. (Panama uses the American dollar as its currency.)

Mariano's generosity shows through in numerous ways. After making it with the Yankees, he always made sure to give back to his home country. Mariano purchased baseball equipment for local children. He donated medical equipment and supplies to a hospital. He sent Christmas presents. He honored area mothers by holding a party on Mother's Day (which is celebrated on December 8 in Panama) and giving away furniture and appliances. He even built a church in his hometown.

Mariano is also helping rebuild a church in his new home city. During the summer of 2011, Mariano and his fellow Spanish-speaking congregants at *Refugio de Esperanza*—Refuge of Hope—announced they were buying and restoring the historic North Avenue Church in New Rochelle, New York. Built in 1907, the church had been under public ownership for decades and fallen into disrepair. Renovation costs were estimated at $3 million.

Mariano fell in love with the building from the moment he saw it and has big plans for the church.

"We have a lot of goals to work with the youth," Mariano said. "That is my passion. We are working hard to make it open as soon as possible."

Mariano added that he plans to devote himself to the church full-time once he retires from baseball. Yankees fans, of course, hope that's years down the road, but it isn't the first time they've heard that kind of talk from their closer.

In July 1999, Mariano stood on the mound in Yankee Stadium as the Bronx Bombers hosted the Atlanta Braves. Between pitches, he heard something that he'd never heard before—a joyous, yet powerful sound. He described it as the voice of God telling him,

I am the One who has you here.

When the season ended and the Yankees had won their second straight World Series, Mariano went back home to Panama and spoke to a church, saying that he planned to play baseball four more years before retiring to become a minister.

Obviously, Mariano didn't end up walking away from baseball in 2003. But his desire to serve God hasn't changed.

"This was something special, and God wants me to concentrate on bringing Him to other people," Mariano said of the encounter. "That meant the only reason I'm here is because He's my strength. He put me here. Without Him, I'm nothing. I think it means that He has other plans for me, to deliver His Word."

Mariano is an extremely private man who's protective of his wife and three sons: Mariano Jr., Jafet, and Jaziel. But when it comes to his faith, he will boldly step out. He often reads his Bible in the Yankees locker room and is a regular at team chapel services.

Mariano also stays involved with a number of charities and was honored for his charity work with the 2003 Thurman Munson Award, named for the great Yankee catcher.

BIG MO

When it comes to great Yankees pitchers, Mariano already tops most lists—above other legends such as Lefty Gomez, Whitey Ford, Ron Guidry, Red Ruffing, and Goose Gossage.

At the end of the 2011 season, Mo—as his teammates call him—held twenty-nine MLB pitching records and eight career Yankee records, including a couple he set during an incredible streak from 1998 to 2000.

During those years, the Yankees won three consecutive World

Series—and Mariano was nearly unhittable. In 1999, Mariano actually recorded more saves (45) than hits he allowed (43) all season. That was also the year he won the World Series Most Valuable Player award. A week later, Panamanian president Mireya Moscoso gave him the Order of Manuel Amador Guerrero, one of the country's highest honors.

The following year, when Mariano notched the final out against the New York Mets in the World Series, it marked the first time in MLB history that the same pitcher had nailed down the last out in three straight Series.

Following their 2000 championship, the Yankees had to wait nine years before getting back on top. At times, Mariano carried some of the blame, like when he committed a throwing error on a bunt in the bottom of the ninth inning in Game 7 of the 2001 World Series against the Arizona Diamondbacks. Arizona capitalized by scoring two runs off broken-bat hits and winning the game 3–2, claiming the Series four games to three.

But even after the disappointment, Mariano saw God's hand at work. Had the Yankees won the game, a ticker tape parade was planned for the whole team. Without a championship, Yankees' teammate Enrique Wilson changed his plane flight and went home to the Dominican Republic early. He had originally planned to be on American Airlines Flight 587 on November 12, 2001. That plane crashed in Queens, New York, killing all 260 passengers on board.

"I'm glad we lost the World Series," Mariano said, "because it means that I still have a friend."

The Florida Marlins defeated the Yankees in the 2003 World Series, but New York earned its record twenty-seventh world championship on November 5, 2009. And who was on the mound when the Yankees recorded the decisive out against the Philadelphia Phillies? Mariano, of course. By his side were Jeter, Pettitte, and Posada—four players with five world championship rings apiece.

"That comes from God, having the ability to perform," Mariano said. "I always thank God that He has given me the chance to be part of a team like the New York Yankees and to be able to do my job every time I get there."

Mariano's consistency and dominance are truly amazing. Sportswriters have predicted his decline for years. After several blown saves early in one season, the *Albany Times Union* published the headline, "Rivera No Longer Mr. Automatic." That was in 2002. Since then, he's had some of his best years and has been every bit as automatic as he was in the late nineties.

In 2004, he earned a career-high 53 saves.

In 2011, at age forty-one, Mariano had one of his best seasons by amassing 44 saves, including two record-breaking performances.

On May 28, 2011, Mariano appeared in his 1,000th game as a Yankee. Fourteen pitchers before him had appeared in a thousand games, but he was the first one to do it with one team. His stats that night: four batters, three outs, and twelve pitches—ten of which were strikes.

On September 19, Mariano became baseball's all-time saves leader when he closed out a game against the Minnesota Twins. With a 6–4 lead in the ninth, Mariano took the mound, retired three batters, and preserved the win. The final out came in typical Mariano fashion. He started Minnesota's Chris Parmelee with a belt-high strike on the outside edge of the plate. Mariano followed with an inside strike that Parmelee fouled off, breaking his bat in the process. With new lumber in his hands, Parmelee could only watch as Mariano's signature cutter caught the outside corner for strike three.

Three pitches. Three strikes. One historic out.

Yankees fans and players jumped around with emotion as Mariano calmly took the game ball from catcher Russell Martin and smiled. After Mariano hugged his fellow Yankees, Posada nudged him back onto the mound to accept the adulation of the fans. He blew a kiss to the faithful at Yankee Stadium and took off his hat to thank the fans who had cheered for him for seventeen years. He looked almost embarrassed by the applause as he smiled and threw up his arms.

Immediately following the game, Mariano deflected attention away from himself and to his teammates and God.

"The whole organization, my whole teammates have been a pillar for me," Mariano said. "I always have to talk about God, because that's the most important thing in my life. Yes, there have been bumps in the road, but God gave me the strength."

Mariano credits his longevity to God's blessing and to living a clean lifestyle. After most games, he hurries home or to his hotel, where he's in bed about an hour after throwing the last pitch.

The fact that Mariano takes care of himself and has avoided major arm problems, following his elbow surgery in 1992, makes people believe that the closer may have a number of years ahead of him.

When asked about his future, Mariano joked that he could pitch until he's fifty. But more seriously, he said he's under contract for the 2012 season, and he'll evaluate how he feels and how much he can contribute after the season is over.

No matter what the future holds for Mariano on the mound, one thing is certain in the minds of many fans: they'll never see a pitcher like Mo again.

"When you talk about the greatest relievers of all time, there's only one guy," Yankees teammate Mark Teixeira said. "That conversation begins and ends with Mo."

Posada agreed. "Amazing that he's been able to do it with one pitch over and over again," the catcher said. "There will never be anybody like Mariano Rivera."

Mariano, on the other hand, honestly doesn't care where he'll be remembered in baseball history. He does hope, however, to be remembered for the impact he made on people.

"I don't pay too much attention to that," Mariano said when asked if he cared about being called the greatest relief pitcher who ever lived. "I just want to be the greatest person you've ever met. If I am, then I'm comfortable with that."

ABOUT THE AUTHORS

Mike Yorkey, a former *Focus on the Family* magazine editor and author, co-author or editor of more than seventy-five books, has written about sports all his life for a variety of publications, including *Breakaway, Brio, Focus on the Family Clubhouse, Tennis, Skiing*, and *City Sports* magazines.

Mike's a lifelong baseball fan, thanks to his parents, who are San Diego Padres season ticket holders. He has collaborated with former San Francisco Giants pitcher Dave Dravecky (*Called Up* and *Play Ball*) and is also the co-author of *Every Man's Battle* with Steve Arterburn and Fred Stoeker and ten other books in the *Every Man's Battle* series. He is also a novelist who, with Tricia Goyer, co-authored the World War II thriller *Chasing Mona Lisa*, which was released in early 2012.

Mike and his wife, Nicole, are the parents of two adult children, Andrea and Patrick. They make their home in Encinitas, California.

Mike's website is www.mikeyorkey.com.

Joshua Cooley, who assisted with the *Playing with Purpose: Baseball* project, is a former full-time sports editor/writer at *The Baltimore Examiner* and *The Gazette* newspapers in Maryland, who has worked in the sportswriting industry since 1996. His first book—*The One Year Sports Devotions for Kids* (Tyndale), a collaboration with Jesse Florea and Jeremy Jones—was published in October 2011.

Joshua currently works full-time at his church, Covenant Life, in Gaithersburg, Maryland, and freelances for a variety of publications. His freelance credits include *Sports Illustrated*, the *Atlanta Journal-Constitution*, the *Baltimore Sun*, the *Orlando Sentinel*, the *Pittsburgh Tribune-Review*, *Bethesda Magazine*, *Orioles Magazine*, and *Nationals Magazine*. He has also written for Christian publications such as *Sports Spectrum*, *Sharing the Victory*, *Breakaway*, *Brio*, *Focus on the Family Clubhouse*, and *Susie*. In 2006, he contributed to the International Bible Society's *"Path to Victory" Sports New Testament*.

Joshua bleeds Baltimore Orioles' black and orange, for better or worse. He and his wife, Kelly, are the parents of three children. The Cooleys make their home in Germantown, Maryland.

SOURCE MATERIAL

1. Tim Tebow: The Chosen One

"He's been called the NFL version's of a total solar eclipse . . ." "Fame, Fortune and Being Tim Tebow," by Johnette Howard, ESPN. com, April 22, 2010, and available at http://sports.espn.go.com/espn/commentary/news/story?page=howard/100422

"His agent, Jimmy Sexton, predicts Tim will become the best marketable athlete in history . . ." "Fame, Fortune and Being Tim Tebow," by Johnette Howard, ESPN.com, April 22, 2010, and available at http://sports.espn.go.com/espn/commentary/news/story?page=howard/100422

"The Davie-Brown Index . . ." "Not Even in NFL Yet, Tim Tebow Already a Marketing Trendsetter," Associated Press, April 19, 2010, and available at http://www.usatoday.com/sports/football/nfl/2010-04-19-tim-tebow-marketing_N.htm?utm_source=moggy&utm_medium=twitter&utm_campaign=GatorWire&utm_source=GatorWire&utm_medium=twitter&utm_campaign=MoggySocialMedia

"Growing up, I knew my goal was to get a job and make a million dollars . . ." "Tebow's Family Vision Runs Much Deeper Than Just TDs," by Dave Curtis, *South Florida Sun-Sentinel*, August 8, 2008, and available at http://www.sunsentinel.com/sports/other/sfl-flsptebowdad08sbaug08,0,5446800.story

"Bob and Pam became friends, and their first date came a year after they met . . . " "Coaching Character," by Suzy A. Richardson, *Gainesville Sun,* October 7, 2007, and available at http://www.gainesville.com/article/ 20071007/NEWS/710060317?p =all&tc=pgall

"It wasn't always easy, but it was a wonderful time for our family . . ." "Coaching Character," by Suzy A. Richardson, *Gainesville Sun,* October 7, 2007, and available at http://www.gainesville. com/article/20071007/NEWS/710060317?p =all&tc=pgall

"I was weeping over the millions of babies being [aborted] in America . . ." "You Gotta Love Tim Tebow," by Austin Murphy, *Sports Illustrated,* July 27, 2009, and available at http://sportsillustrated.cnn.com/vault/article/ magazine/MAG1158168/index.htm

"Dysentery is common in developing and tropical countries like the Philippines. . ." "Amoebic Dysentery: How Common Is It?" the British Medical Journal Group in association with the *Guardian* newspaper, March 9, 2010, and available at http://www.guardian.co.uk/lifeandstyle/besttreatments/amoebic-dysenteryhow-common

"They didn't really give me a choice. That was the only option they gave me . . ." "Mothering Tebow," by Joni B. Hannigan, *Florida Baptist Witness*, January 8, 2009, and available at http://gofbw.com/News.asp?ID=9758

"It was amazing that God spared him, but we knew God had His hand on his life . . . " "Mothering Tebow," by Joni B. Hannigan, *Florida Baptist Witness*, January 8, 2009, and available at http://gofbw.com/News.asp?ID=9758

"If I could get my kids to the age of 25 and they know God and serve God . . ." "Tebows to Headline Evangelism Conference Sessions," *Florida Baptist Witness*, January 29, 2008, and available at http://www.gofbw.com/news.asp?ID=8334

"But the Tebows *were* into competition . . ." "Competitive Fire Fuels Tebow," by Guerry Smith, Rivals.com Web site, December 8, 2007, and available at http://collegefootball.rivals.com/content.asp?cid=748732

"Some of his teammates were picking at the ground without even paying attention . . ." "Competitive Fire Fuels Tebow," by Guerry Smith, Rivals.com Web site, December 8, 2007, and available at http://collegefootball.rivals.com/content.asp?cid=748732

"One time, Tim wrote a report on why athletes' bodies need more protein . . ." "Pam Tebow's Labor of Love," by Lindsay H. Jones, *Denver Post*, May 10, 2010, and available at http://www.gainesville.com/article/20100510/ARTICLES/100519941?p=all&tc=pgall&tc=ar

"Guess that's my claim to fame . . ." "Tebow Caused a Stir Even as a Youngster," by Dave Curtis, *Orlando Sentinel*, December 5, 2007, and available at http://articles.orlandosentinel.com/2007-12-05/sports/tebowthekid05_1_quarterback-tim-tebow-hess-allen

"That's not what Bob Tebow wanted for his son, though . . ." "Team Tebow," by Robbie Andreu, *Gainesville Sun*, January 31, 2006, and available at http://www.gainesville.com/article /20060131/GATORS 01/201310351?p=all&tc=pgall&tc=ar

"We wanted to give Tim the opportunity to develop his God-given talent . . ." "Parents, High School Officials at Odds Over Motivation for Athletes' Transfers," by Ray Glier, *USA Today*, November 21, 2006, and available at http://www.usatoday.com/sports/preps/2006-11-21-transfers-cover_x.htm

"We were willing to make that sacrifice. We have made sacrifices for all our children . . ." "QB Facing College Challenges Grounded in Christ," by Barbara Denman, *Florida Baptist Witness*, January 17, 2006, and available at http://www.gofbw.com/news.asp?ID=5351

"People can always lead with words but not always with actions . . ." "A Gator for God," by Suzy Richardson, *Charisma*, October 2008, and available at http://www.charismamag.com/index.php/features/2008/october/17874-agator-for-god

"We had six road games my sophomore year . . ." "Tim Tebow Draws from High School Days at Nease," by Mitch Stephens at MaxPreps.com, February 16, 2010, and available at http://www.maxpreps.com/news/AmVWLhtREd-UswAcxJTdpg/tim-tebow-draws-from-high-school-daysat-nease.htm

"Chris Leak is our quarterback . . . " "Orange Defeats Blue in a Less Than Spectacular Spring Finale," by Dennis Culver, *Gainesville Sun*, April 26, 2006, and available at http://www.gainesville.com/article/20060422/GATORS0108/60422003?p=all&tc=pgall

"There's room for another one next year, Timmy Tebow . . ." "Leak, Wuerffel Share Lifetime Gator Bond," by Pat Dooley, *Gainesville Sun*, January 14, 2007, and available at http://www.gainesville.com/article/20070114/GATORS24/70114040?p=all&tc=pgall&tc=ar

"The story noted that Tim had sung 'She Thinks My Tractor's Sexy' . . . " "A Florida Folk Hero Prepares to Face Reality," by Pete Thamel, *New York Times*, September 1, 2007, and available at http://www. nytimes.com/2007/09/01/sports/ncaafootball/01florida.html?_r=1
"It makes you realize that everything that happens in this game doesn't really mean that much in the grand scheme of things . . ."

"Notebook: UF's Tebow Takes Losses Hard, Gains Perspective," by Brandon Zimmerman, *Gainesville Sun*, October 30, 2007, and available at http://www.gainesville.com/ar-ticle/20071030/NEWS/710300310?tc=ar

"Tim took some hits from the media . . . " "John 3:16—Latest Bible Verse to Be Featured on Tim Tebow's Eye Black," by Tom Herrera, *NCAA Football Fanhouse*, January 9, 2009, and available at http://ncaafoot-ball.fanhouse.com/2009/01/09/john-3-16-latest-bible-verse-to-be-featured-on-tim-tebow/

"He's just an amazing young man, an amazing football player . . . " "Tebow Wins Wuerffel Award," by Robbie Andreu, *Gainesville Sun*, December 9, 2008, and available at http://www.gainesville.com/article/20081209/NEWS/812090943
"You knew he was going to lead us to victory . . . " "Tebow Engineers Comeback," by Kevin Brockway, *Gainesville Sun*, December 7, 2008, and available at http://www.gainesville.com/article/20081207/NEWS/812060925

"I was pretty excited . . . " "Best Player Ever? I'll Take Tebow" by Pat Dooley, *Gainesville Sun*, January 9, 2009, and available at http://www.gainesville.com/article/20090109/COLUMNISTS/901090279?p=all&tc=pgall&tc=ar

" 'It's simple,' said one NFL scout . . ." "Tim Tebow Senior Bowl: Disaster or First Step to NFL?" by Mark Sappenfield, *Christian Science Monitor*, January 31, 2010, and available at http://www. csmonitor.com/USA/Society/2010/0131/Tim-Tebow-Senior-Bowl-Disaster-or-first-step-to-NFL

"Scouts Inc. gave Tim a D+ grade . . ." "2010 Senior Bowl: Tim Tebow's Performance Adds to His Plummeting NFL Draft Stock," by Daniel Wolf, Bleacher Report.com, January 30, 2010, and available at http://bleacherreport.com/articles/336387-tim-tebow-senior-bowl-performanceadds-to-plummeting-nfl-draft-stock

"No mention of abortion . . . because they were a division winner" "Tim Tebow's Brilliant Fake Leads to Pro-Life Score," by David Gibson, PoliticsDaily.com, February 7, 2007, and available at http://www.politicsdaily.com/2010/02/07/tim-tebows-brilliant-fake-leads-to-pro-life-score/

"It's more of a tweak . . ." "Tim Tebow's New Team Honing His Technique," by Sam Farmer, *Los Angeles Times*, February 27, 2010, and available at http://articles.latimes.com/2010/feb/27/sports/la-sp-nfl-combine27-2010feb27

"Kurt Hester, the corporate director of training at D1 . . ." "What's It Like to Help Tim Tebow Prepare for the NFL? D1's Kurt Hester Is Here to Tell You," by Ben Volin, *Palm Beach Post*, February 22, 2010, and available at http://blogs.palmbeachpost.com/gatorbytes/2010/02/22/whats-it-like-to-helptim-tebow-prepare-for-the-nfl-d1s-kurt-hester-is-here-to-tell-you/

"For all the television time, Internet bandwidth . . ." "Florida's Pro Day Was a True Circus, with Tim Tebow Front and Center," by Andy Staples, SI.com, March 18, 2010, and available at http://sportsillustrated.cnn.com/2010/writers/andy_staples/03/17/tim.tebow.pro.day/index.html

"The 15 minutes passed by way too quickly . . ." "Tebow Quickly Impressed McDaniels, Broncos as a Genuine Gem," by Lindsay H. Jones, *The Denver Post*, April 25, 2010, and available at http://www.denverpost.com/broncos/ci_14953999

"When quarterbacks Peyton Manning and Ryan Leaf were in the running . . ." "Leaf's Pro Career: Short and Unhappy," by Damon Hack, *New York Times*, August 4, 2002, and available at http://www.nytimes.com/2002/08/04/sports/profootball-leaf-s-pro-career-short-and-unhappy.html

"It would have been exciting to be here . . ." "Tebow Declines Invitations to Attend Draft, Decides to Return Home," by Jason La Canfora, NFL.com, April 21, 2010, and available at http://www.nfl.com/draft/story?id=09000d5d817aa5ce&template=with-video-withcomments&confirm=true

"Tim's former teammate at Florida, Cincinnati Bengals wide receiver Andre Caldwell . . ." "Bengals' Andre Caldwell: Right Spot to Pick Tim Tebow Is 'Late Second Round,'" *USA Today*'s The Huddle, March 31, 2010, and available at http://content.usatoday.com/communities/thehuddle/post/2010/03/bengals-andrecaldwell-right-spot-to-pick-tim-tebow-is-late-second-round/1

"Miami Dolphins quarterback Chad Henne . . ." "Dolphins' Chad Henne on Tim Tebow: 'He's Not an NFL Quarterback,' " *USA Today*'s The Huddle, March 18, 2010, and available at http://content.usatoday.com/communities/thehuddle/post/2010/03/dolphins-chad-henne-hes-not-annfl-quarterback/1

" . . . Tim did an interview on ESPN Radio with host Freddie Coleman . . ." "Time Tebow Does Not Take Mel Kiper's Criticism Kindly, Calls Him Out on Air," by Will Brinson, NCAA Football Fanhouse, December 19, 2008, and available at http://ncaafootball.fanhouse.com/2008/12/19/tim-tebow-does-not-takemel-kipers-criticism-kindly-calls-him/

"On the morning of the NFL draft . . . " "Tim Tebow: Is He a Miracle Worker, or Just an Average QB?" by Jon Saraceno, *USA Today*, April 22, 2010, and available at http://www.usatoday.com/sports/football/nfl/2010-04-21-tim-tebow_N.htm

"If you want Tim to be on your football team . . ." "Great Tebow Draft Debate Will Finally Be Answered," by Robbie Andreu, *Gainesville Sun*, April 21, 2010, and available at http://www.gainesville.com/article/20100421/ARTICLES/100429878?p=all&tc=pgall&tc=ar

"Kiper and his ESPN sidekick, Todd McShay, stuck to their guns . . ." "Great Tebow Draft Debate Will Finally Be Answered," by Robbie Andreu, *Gainesville Sun*, April 21, 2010, and available at http://www.gainesville.com/article/20100421/ARTICLES/100429878?p=all&tc=pgall&tc=ar

"And that's when Tim's cell phone rang with a 303 area code . . ." "Tim Tebow Drafted by Denver Broncos in First Round of NFL Draft," by Jeremy Fowler, *South Florida Sun-Sentinel,* April 23, 2010, and available at http://articles.sun-sentinel.com/2010-04-23/sports/ sfl-tim-tebow-broncos-10_1_tim-tebow-25th-selection-later-round

"Coach McDaniels was on the line, but he didn't seem at all in a hurry . . ." "Mile-High on Tebow," by Robbie Andreu, *Gainesville Sun,* April 23, 2010, and available at http://www.gainesville.com/ article/20100423/ARTICLES/4231012?p=all&tc=pgall&tc=ar

"I just think I showed them [the Broncos] I was willing to do whatever it took . . ." "Tim Tebow Drafted by the Denver Broncos," Alligator Army website, April 22, 2010, and available at http://www.alligatorarmy. com/2010/4/22/1437123/tim-tebow-drafted-by-the-denver

"Tim Tebow is a lightning rod . . ." "Colorado Evangelicals Singing Praises of McDaniels' QB Pick Tebow," by Electa Draper, *The Denver Post,* April 24, 2010, and available at http://www.denverpost. com/news/ci_14948943

"Tim needs to work on the fundamentals of being a pocket passer . . ." "Elway Says Young QB Tebow Needs Work as a Pocket Passer," by Lindsay H. Jones, *The Denver Post,* January 6, 2011, available at http://www.denverpost.com/broncos/ci_17021315

"Most people wait until they're at least 24 . . ." "Tim Tebow Shows Charisma on MSNBC's Morning Joe," *Orlando Sentinel,* June 3, 2011, and available at http://blogs.orlandosentinel.com/sports-sentinel-sports-now/2011/06/03/tim-tebow-shows-charisma-on-msnbcs-morning-joe-video/

"Nice kid, sincere as a first kiss . . ." "Tim Tebow Not Ready for Prime Time," by Rick Reilly, espn.com, August 9, 2011, and available at http://espn.go.com/espn/story/_/id/6846531/tim-tebow-not-ready-prime-time

"He makes plays, you can't deny that . . ." "Chargers Hold Off Tebow-Inspired Broncos, 29-24," Associated Press, October 9, 2011, and available at http://sportsillustrated.cnn.com/football/nfl/gameflash/2011/10/09/4472_recap.html

"Tim needed to 'put everything behind him' . . ." "John Elway Has Advice for Tim Tebow," Associated Press, January 5, 2012, and available at http://goo.gl/SaZaF

"When I saw him scoring . . ." "Behind Tebow's Magic, Broncos Stun Steelers in Overtime Thriller," by CBS Channel 4 Denver, January 8, 2012, and available at http://denver.cbslocal.com/2012/01/08/broncos-stun-steelers-in-overtime-thriller/

"I really like him . . . " "Jeremy Lin + Tim Tebow = Cutest Sports Bromance Ever," by Jill Baughman, Cafemom.com, February 23, 2012, and available at http://thestir.cafemom.com/sports/133481/jeremy_lin_tim_tebow_cutest

"One of the reasons I get on a knee . . ." "Tebow's Appearance at Vegas Church Draws 20,000," Associated Press, March 5, 2012, and available at http://lasvegas.cbslocal.com/2012/03/05/tebows-appearance-at-vegas-church-draws-20000/

2. Jeremy Lin: Welcome to the Show

"Jeremy has a better skill set than anyone I've seen at his age . . . ."
"Harvard's Hoops Star Is Asian. Why's That a Problem?" by Sean
Gregory, *Time* magazine, December 31, 2009, and available at
http://www.time.com/time/nation/article/0,8599,1951044,00.html

"He knew exactly what needed to be done at every point in the
basketball game . . ." "An All-Around Talent, Obscured by His
Pedigree," by Chuck Culpepper, *New York Times*, September 14,
2010, and available at http://www.nytimes.com/2010/09/15/sports/
basketball/15nba.html

"Many college-age Christians lose interest in their faith . . ." "NBA
Rising Star Jeremy Lin Not Too Busy to Pray," by Gordon Govier,
Charisma News, February 15, 2012, and available at http://charismanews.
com/culture/32833-nba-rising-star-jeremy-lin-not-too-busy-to-pray

"Jeremy Lin is probably one of the best players in the country you
don't know about . . ." from "What They're Saying About Harvard
Basketball and Jeremy," Harvard sports website, December 11, 2009,
and available at http://www.gocrimson.com/sports/mbkb/2009-10/
releases/091210_MBB_Quotes

"This fascinating interview between Lacob and *San Jose Mercury
News* columnist Tim Kawakami . . ." from "Lacob Interview, Part
3: On Jeremy Lin, Ellison, Larry Riley, Bold Moves, and Poker"
conducted by Tim Kawakami on the Talking Points website,
August 17, 2010, and available at http://blogs.mercurynews.com/
kawakami/2010/08/17/lacob-interview-part-3-on-jeremy-lin-
ellison-larry-riley-bold-moves-and-poker/

"His schedule was Navy SEAL Team 6 material . . ." "Jeremy Lin's HS Coach Is Surprised, too," by Tim Keown at espn.com, February 14, 2012, and available at http://goo.gl/0wbQU

"At the time, I was thinking if this doesn't work out . . ." "Exclusive: Jeremy Lin Says 'Lin-Sanity' Was Triggered by Leap of Faith," by Marcus Thompson II, *Silicon Valley Mercury News*, February 13, 2012, and available at http://www.mercurynews.com/jeremy-lin/ci_19954877

"The Knicks offense didn't get a huge boost Tuesday . . ." "Knicks Claim Harvard Grad Off Waivers," by Sean Brennan, *New York Daily News,* December 27, 2011, and available at http://goo.gl/lGhQm

"I had no opportunity to prove myself . . . " "Exclusive: Jeremy Lin Says 'Lin-Sanity' Was Triggered by Leap of Faith," by Marcus Thompson II, *Silicon Valley Mercury News*, February 13, 2012, and available at http://www.mercurynews.com/jeremy-lin/ci_19954877

"I think they messed up their coverage . . . " "Lin, Knicks Scale Wall's Wizards in Washington," by Frank Isola, *New York Daily News*, February 8, 2012, and available at http://goo.gl/FGH8o

"The fluke no longer looks so flukey . . ." "Lin Leads Again as Knicks Win 3rd in a Row," by Howard Beck, *New York Times*, February 8, 2012, and available at http://goo.gl/9eD9I

"So we wanted to go out there and do something that was lighthearted and not too serious . . ." "Jeremy Lin's Religious Pregame Ritual," thestar.com website, February 13, 2012, and available at http://goo.gl/CeKvW

3. Luke Ridnour: Heir to Pistol Pete

"Really, when I started reading the Word with my chaplain, everything changed . . ." from "Super Sonic: Seattle's Luke Ridnour Talks Small Towns and Big Faith," by Jill Ewert, *Sharing the Victory* magazine, a publication of Fellowship of Christian Athletes, and available at http://www.sharingthevictory.com/vsItemDisplay.lsp?method=display&objectid=F10AF9D8-5E91-416A-959F5BAC3AA6B942

"Coach Kent summed up his point guard's contribution this way . . ." from "Cool Hand Luke" by Jeanne Halsey, *Sports Spectrum* magazine, and available at http://faithsite.com/content.asp?SID=808&CID=59253

"My mom wouldn't be too happy about it . . ." from "The Inside Track," the *Los Angeles Times*, December 17, 2002, and available at http://articles.latimes.com/2002/dec/17/sports/sp-quotebook17

"You must have made a big impression on him, then . . ." from "Super Couple: Kate Ridnour Q&A," by Jill Ewert, *Sharing the Victory* magazine, a publication of Fellowship of Christian Athletes, and available at http://www.sharingthevictory.com/vsItemDisplay.lsp&objectID=E22C67AB-BE6F-4326-86C9D58F7DC1BC2B&method=display

4. Stephen Curry, Nenê, Reggie Williams, Nick Collison, Kevin Durant, Greivis Vasquez: They're Playing with Purpose in the NBA, Too

"It turns out that Dr. Orsino is a blogger . . ." from a blog called "End of Me" by Guy Stanton, April 21, 2008, and available at http://stantonmarcfreyendofme.blogspot.com/2008/04/stephen-curry-i-can-do-all-things.html

"I have like a deal for my pastor . . ." from "Brazil's Nene Vows to Retire by 2016 Olympics to Focus on Religion," by Chris Tomassen, *AOL News*, October 4, 2009, and available at http://www.aolnews.com/2009/10/04/brazils-nene-vows-to-retire-by-2016-olympics-to-focus-on-religi/

"It was scary, but I believe in God . . ." from "Nene 'a Survivor' After Cancerous Testicle Removed," by Benjamin Hockman, the *Denver Post*, March 8, 2008, and available at http://webcache.googleusercontent.com/search?q=cache:asPckLRh0aAJ:www.denverpost.com/ci_8498637%3Fsource%3Dbb+nene+a+survivor+after+cancerous+testicle+removed&cd=2&hl=en&ct=clnk&gl=us&source=www.google.com

"It's a good play for our defense . . . " from "Feisty Nick Collison Takes Charge," by Mike Baldwin, *The Oklahoman* newspaper, March 9, 2010, and available at http://newsok.com/fiesty-nick-collison-takes-charge/article/3444923

"In short, Kevin Durant is endorsement gold right now . . ." from "Kevin Durant is D'Man: An Endorsement Diamond in the Midwestern Rough," by Patrick Rishe, *Forbes* magazine, May 20, 2011, and available at http://blogs.forbes.com/sportsmoney/2011/05/20/kevin-durant-is-dman-an-endorsement-diamond-in-the-midwestern-rough/

"It's tough, man. I can't lie about that . . ." from "NBA All-Star Kevin Durant on Faith, Family, and Fame" by Chad Bonham of *Inspiring Athletes*, and available at http://blog.beliefnet.com/inspiringathletes/2011/05/nba-all-star-kevin-durant-on-faith-family-and-fame.html

"I'm keeping strong at it, just trying to make my walk with faith a little better . . ." from "Thunder's Kevin Durant Commits to Daily Bible Reading," by Darnell Mayberry, *The Oklahoman* newspaper, April 21, 2011, and available at http://newsok.com/thunders-kevin-durant-commits-to-daily-bible-reading/article/3560862

"I've got Jesus in my heart . . . " from "Bill Sorrell: Faith Sustains Young Griz Players," by Bill Sorrell, published on the FaithinMemphis website on April 8, 2011, and available at http://faithinmemphis.com/2011/04/08/bill-sorrell-faith-sustains-young-griz-players/

"It helps me in every aspect of my life . . ." from "NBA Rookie in the Habit of Thanking God," by Lee Warren, *Christian Post*, May 11, 2011, and available at http://www.christianpost.com/news/nba-rookie-in-the-habit-of-thanking-god-50190/

5. Clayton Kershaw: Standing on the Precipice of Greatness

All quotations used are from personal interviews between co-author Joshua Cooley and Clayton Kershaw, except the following:

"Probably the best in the world . . . " from "Clayton Kershaw's Great Expectations" by Jeff Passan, *Yahoo! Sports*, May 14, 2008, and available at http://sports.yahoo.com/mlb/news?slug=jp-kershaw051408

"Might as well go by Zeus . . ." and "These guys don't come along often . . ." from "Kershaw Takes the Stage" by Jeff Passan, *Yahoo! Sports*, May 26, 2008, and available at http://sports.yahoo.com/mlb/news?slug=jp-kershaw052608

"Ceiling? There is no ceiling . . ." from "Kershaw Looking Ahead to Life Without Limits" by Ken Gurnick, *MLB.com*, February 23, 2010, and available at http://losangeles.dodgers.mlb.com/news/article.jsp?ymd=20100223&content_id=8120062&vkey=news_la&fext=.jsp&c_id=la

"There's no reason to really set limits . . ." from "Dodgers' Clayton Kershaw Continues to Shine" by Ben Bolch, *The Los Angeles Times*, August 13, 2011, and available at http://www.latimes.com/sports/la-sp-0814-dodgers-astros-20110814,0,6852499.story

6. Albert Pujols: A Home Run Hitter with a Heart for Others

"That was me twenty-five years ago . . ." from the *60 Minutes* segment, "The Incredible Mr. Pujols," that aired on April 10, 2011, on CBS, and available at http://www.cbsnews.com/video/watch/?id=7362328n

"Believe it or not, baseball is not the chief ambition of my life . . ." from "A Message of Faith from Albert Pujols" by the Pujols Family Foundation and available at http://www.pujolsfamilyfoundation.org/faith/

"Growing up in the Dominican, that's pretty much all I did is play baseball . . ." from "Albert and Dee Pujols: Giving Honor to God," *Focus on the Family*, Daily Radio Digest, August 15–16, 2006.

"It's the farthest and hardest I've seen a baseball hit . . ." from "Albert Pujols: Revisiting the Early Years" by Arne Christensen, *The Hardball Times*, June 15, 2010, and available at http://www. hardballtimes.com/main/article/albert-pujols-revisiting-the-early-years/

"Have power even if he used a toothpick . . ." from "Albert Pujols: Revisiting the Early Years" by Arne Christensen, *The Hardball Times*, June 15, 2010, and available at http://www.hardballtimes. com/main/article/albert-pujols-revisiting-the-early-years/

"He's the best hitter I've coached or seen . . ." from "Albert Pujols: Revisiting the Early Years" by Arne Christensen, *The Hardball Times*, June 15, 2010, and available at http://www.hardballtimes. com/main/article/albert-pujols-revisiting-the-early-years/

"I'll never, never get over it . . ." from the *60 Minutes* segment, "The Incredible Mr. Pujols," that aired on April 10, 2011 on CBS, and available at http://www.cbsnews.com/video/watch/?id=7362328n

"I went to church every once in awhile growing up . . ." from "Albert Pujols Testimony," Baseball Chapel video, July 20, 2011, and available at http://www.youtube.com/watch?v=n9yz9inU5XY&feature=youtube_gdata_player

"I wouldn't say it was easy and that the Lord starting turning things around [right away] . . ." from "Albert Pujols Testimony," Baseball Chapel video, July 20, 2011, and available at http://www.youtube. com/watch?v=n9yz9inU5XY&feature=youtube_gdata_player

"I had been praying for God to be able to use Albert to share Jesus and wanted it to be bigger . . ." from "Albert and Dee Pujols: Giving Honor to God," *Focus on the Family,* Daily Radio Digest, August 15–16, 2006.

"It must've been the highlight of the year for them . . ." from the *60 Minutes* segment, "The Incredible Mr. Pujols," that aired on April 10, 2011 on CBS, and available at http://www.cbsnews.com/video/watch/?id=7362328n

"One thing I have learned is that it's not about me; it's about serving the Lord Jesus Christ . . ." from "Albert Pujols Testimony," Baseball Chapel video, July 20, 2011, and available at http://www.youtube.com/watch?v=n9yz9inU5XY&feature=youtube_gdata_player

"He's like the best baseball player in baseball now . . ." from "My Wish: Albert Pujols," *ESPN Sports Center: My Wish,* July 19, 2010, and available at http://espn.go.com/video/clip?id=5392781

"Albert is such a great player . . ." from "My Wish Q&A: Debbie Trammel," by Scott Miller, *ESPN.com,* July 21, 2010, and available at http://sports.espn.go.com/espn/features/mywish/news/story?id=5367335

"I'm glad it was him . . ." from "For Pujols, a Game for the Ages," by Tyler Kepner, *The New York Times,* October 23, 2011, and available at http://www.nytimes.com/2011/10/24/sports/baseball/for-albert-pujols-of-st-louis-3-home-runs-for-a-record-night.html

"I think the last month of the season . . ." from "Cards Win World Series, Beat Texas 6–2 in Game 7," Associated Press, October 28, 2011, and available at http://sportsillustrated.cnn.com/baseball/mlb/gameflash/2011/10/28/40004_recap.html

"Enjoy it. Respect it. Appreciate it . . ." from "Pujols Is a Faith-Based Mystery," by Jeff Passan, *Yahoo! Sports,* July 14, 2009, and available at http://sports.yahoo.com/mlb/news?slug=jp-pujols071409

"Albert has no glaring weaknesses, and he doesn't chase many bad pitches . . ." from "Albert Pujols Quotes," *Baseball Almanac,* and available at http://www.baseball-almanac.com/quotes/albert_pujols_quotes.shtml

"I'd rather walk in a run than give up four . . ." from the *60 Minutes* segment, "The Incredible Mr. Pujols," that aired on April 10, 2011, on CBS, and available at http://www.cbsnews.com/video/watch/?id=7362328n

"He's the face of baseball . . ." from the *60 Minutes* segment, "The Incredible Mr. Pujols," that aired on April 10, 2011, on CBS, and available at http://www.cbsnews.com/video/watch/?id=7362328n

"I would never do any of that . . ." from "Cardinals Slugger Albert Pujols Is Batting Cleanup for Baseball," by Bob Nightengale, *USA Today,* July 13, 2009, and available at http://www.usatoday.com/sports/baseball/nl/cardinals/2009-07-12-pujols-cover_N.htm

"I don't believe in all that science stuff . . ." from "Pujols Is a Faith-Based Mystery," by Jeff Passan, *Yahoo! Sports,* July 14, 2009, and available at http://sports.yahoo.com/mlb/news?slug=jp-pujols071409

7. Josh Hamilton: Baseball's Bat Man Comes Back from the Brink

"But that wasn't the amazing thing . . ." from "180 Degrees of Separation" by Jeff Pearlman, *Sports Illustrated,* April 12, 2004, and available at http://sportsillustrated.cnn.com/vault/article/magazine/MAG1031772/index.htm

"I've gotten a lot of trophies over the years, but the Ashley Pittman Memorial Award is special to me . . ." from *Beyond Belief: Finding the Strength to Come Back* by Josh Hamilton with Tim Keown (New York: Hachette Book Group, 2008), page 33.

"We've watched him for a long time . . ." from "Rays Feel Hamilton Has Makings of a Star," CNNSI.com, June 2, 1999, and available at http://sportsillustrated.cnn.com/baseball/mlb/1999/draft/news/1999/06/02/hamilton_lamar/

"I'm thinking three years in the minors, then fifteen years in the big leagues . . ." from *Beyond Belief: Finding the Strength to Come Back* by Josh Hamilton with Tim Keown (New York: Hachette Book Group, 2008), page 37.

"Their fears became real in our first game . . ." from *Beyond Belief: Finding the Strength to Come Back* by Josh Hamilton with Tim Keown (New York: Hachette Book Group, 2008), pages 7–8.

"I didn't expect you'd be out here tonight . . ." from *Beyond Belief: Finding the Strength to Come Back* by Josh Hamilton with Tim Keown (New York: Hachette Book Group, 2008), page 38.

"I got saved when I was eighteen years old. . ." from the *Larry King Live* show on CNN, October 28, 2008, and available at http://www.youtube.com/watch?v=rJ2xN_xHT0g

"He plunged the needle into my spine till it felt like it was grinding on bone . . ." from *Beyond Belief: Finding the Strength to Come Back* by Josh Hamilton with Tim Keown (New York: Hachette Book Group, 2008), page 76.

"I had a lot of 'firsts' that night . . ." from the *Larry King Live* show on CNN, October 28, 2008, and available at http://www.youtube.com/watch?v=rJ2xN_xHT0g

"The display still hadn't been fixed and was covered by a banner that promoted the team's website . . ." from "If You Build it, They Will Come, or Will They?" by Matt Martz, Bakersfield.com, October 17, 2008, and available at http://people.bakersfield.com/home/ViewPost/78184

"Everybody knew who Josh was in high school . . ." from "Josh and Kate Hamilton, Parts 1–3 Live Interview, February 14, 2010," West Lonsdale Baptist Church, February 14, 2010, and available at http://www.youtube.com/watch?v=dM_M8JTjkvM&feature=related

"I was a shell of a human, a soulless being . . ." from *Beyond Belief: Finding the Strength to Come Back* by Josh Hamilton with Tim Keown (New York: Hachette Book Group, 2008), page 150.

"I was a wreck—dirty, twitchy, barely coherent . . ." from *Beyond Belief: Finding the Strength to Come Back* by Josh Hamilton with Tim Keown (New York: Hachette Book Group, 2008), page 154.

"I went back in the room where I'd just been using drugs, grabbed a Bible, and the first verse I read James 4:7 . . ." from "Josh and Kate Hamilton, Parts 1–3 Live Interview, February 14, 2010," West Lonsdale Baptist Church, February 14, 2010, and available at http://www.youtube.com/watch?v=dM_M8JTjkvM&feature=related

"Baseball is third in my life right now, behind my relationship with God and my family . . ." from "I'm Proof That Hope Is Never Lost," an excerpt from *Beyond Belief* by Josh Hamilton with Tim Keown, *ESPN, The Magazine,* July 5, 2007, and available at http://sports.espn.go.com/mlb/news/story?id=2926447

"God has given me such a platform to share what He's done in my life . . ." from "Hamilton's Drug Comeback 'Beyond Belief,'" Associated Press, October 19, 2008, and available at http://www.youtube.com/watch?v=942OxgJT0ec&feature=relmfu

"I was out there for three weeks and stopped praying, stopped doing my devotions, stopped reading the Word . . ." from "Josh and Kate Hamilton, Parts 1–3 Live Interview, February 14, 2010," West Lonsdale Baptist Church, February 14, 2010, and available at http://www.youtube.com/watch?v=dM_M8JTjkvM&feature=related

"I'm embarrassed about it for my wife, Katie, for my kids, and for the organization . . ." from "Hamilton Admits to Relapse with Alcohol" by Joe Resnick of the Associated Press, August 8, 2009, and available at http://www.breitbart.com/article.php?id=D99UTUGG1&show_article=1

"When he walked in the door, and I [saw] how broken and repentant and remorseful he was . . ." from "Josh and Kate

Hamilton, Parts 1–3 Live Interview, February 14, 2010," West Lonsdale Baptist Church, February 14, 2010, and available at http://www.youtube.com/watch?v=dM_M8JTjkvM&feature=related

"Rooted in his Christian beliefs and his rigorous daily devotions . . ." from "Josh Hamilton Finds Strength after Misstep in Recovery from Addiction" by S.C. Gywnne, *Dallas Morning News*, October 4, 2010, and available at http://www.dallasnews.com/incoming/20101003-Josh-Hamilton-finds-strength-after-misstep-1474.ece

"Just another night in the life of the best player in baseball went something like this . . ." from "Hamilton Leaving No Doubt He Is the Best Player in Baseball" by Tom Verducci, SI.com, August 17, 2010, and available at http://sportsillustrated.cnn.com/vault/article/web/COM1173399/index.htm

"Everybody yelled 'Ginger ale!' and I just jumped in the middle of the pile and they doused me with it . . ." from "Josh Hamilton Included in Celebration" by Richard Durrett, ESPNDallas.com, October 12, 2010, and available at http://sports.espn.go.com/dallas/mlb/news/story?id=5679952

"Could I have reached people being that clean-cut kid coming out of high school?" from "Hamilton's Drug Comeback 'Beyond Belief,'" Associated Press, October 19, 2008, and available at http://www.youtube.com/watch?v=942OxgJT0ec&feature=relmfu

"One thing I can't live without is obviously Jesus . . ." from "Josh and Kate Hamilton, Parts 1–3 Live Interview, February 14, 2010," West Lonsdale Baptist Church, February 14, 2010, and available at http://www.youtube.com/watch?v=dM_M8JTjkvM&feature=related

8. Mariano River: The Closer Who Got Saved

"He needs to pitch in a higher league, if there is one . . ." from "Mariano River's a True Yankee, Almost Mythical in His Dominance" by Joe Posnanski, SI.com, July 2, 2009, and available at http://sportsillustrated.cnn.com/2009/writers/joe_posnanski/07/01/rivera/index.html

"Yes, it does. It does make me uncomfortable, because I don't like to talk about myself . . ." from "The Michael Kay Show," ESPN New York (1050 AM) podcast, September 16, 2011, and available at http://espn.go.com/new-york/radio/archive?id=2693958

"You're seeing the greatest closer of all time . . ." from "Mariano Saves" by Tom Verducci, *Sports Illustrated,* October 5, 2009, and available at http://sportsillustrated.cnn.com/vault/article/magazine/MAG1160757/index.htm

"He's like my brother . . ." from "Modern Yankee Heroes: From Humble Beginnings, Mariano Rivera Becomes Greatest Closer in MLB History" by Christian Red, *New York Daily News,* March 13, 2010, and available at http://articles.nydailynews.com/2010-03-13/sports/27058930_1_puerto-caimito-cardboard-cousin

"I don't know if we'll ever see it again . . ." from "Mariano Rivera gets 600th save" by Andrew Marchand, ESPNNewYork.com, September 14, 2011, and available at http://m.espn.go.com/mlb/story?w=1b0rl&storyId=6968238&i=TOP&wjb=

"If you talk to him at an All-Star Game, it's like talking to somebody who just got called up . . ." from "Mariano Saves" by Tom Verducci,

Sports Illustrated, October 5, 2009, and available at http://
sportsillustrated.cnn.com/vault/article/magazine/MAG1160757/
index.htm

"The radar wasn't really being lit up . . ." from "Modern Yankee
Heroes: From Humble Beginnings, Mariano Rivera Becomes
Greatest Closer in MLB History" by Christian Red, *New York Daily
News*, March 13, 2010, and available at http://articles.nydailynews.
com/2010-03-13/sports/27058930_1_puerto-caimito-cardboard-
cousin

"Usually a player prepares for years . . ." from *Mariano Rivera* by
Judith Levin (New York: Checkmark Books, 2008), page 18.

"Every time I was going through a hard time, somebody was there
to help . . ." from "The Secret of Mariano Rivera's Success" by Peter
Schiller, baseballreflections.com, November 7, 2009, and available
at http://baseballreflections.com/2009/11/07/the-secret-of-
mariano-riveras-success/

"The harder I tried, the tougher it got . . ." from "Yanks' Rivera
Continues to Learn" by Mel Antonen, *USA Today*, October 9, 2006,
and available at http://www.usatoday.com/sports/soac/2006-10-09-
rivera_x.htm

"You can't see the spin on it . . ." from "This Is the Game Changer,"
by Albert Chen, *Sports Illustrated*, June 13, 2011, and available
at http://sportsillustrated.cnn.com/vault/article/magazine/
MAG1187105/index.htm

"That is my miracle pitch . . ." from "Mariano River's Cutter 'The Miracle Pitch,'" interview with Pastor Dewey Friedel, courtesy the Trinity Broadcasting Network, and available at http://www.youtube.com/watch?v=L0tTLssCKZU

"My mental approach is simple: Get three outs as quick as possible . . ." from "Mariano Saves" by Tom Verducci, *Sports Illustrated,* October 5, 2009, and available at http://sportsillustrated.cnn.com/vault/article/magazine/MAG1160757/index.htm

"My childhood was wonderful . . ." from "Modern Yankee Heroes: From Humble Beginnings, Mariano Rivera Becomes Greatest Closer in MLB History" by Christian Red, *New York Daily News,* March 13, 2010, and available at http://articles.nydailynews.com/2010-03-13/sports/27058930_1_puerto-caimito-cardboard-cousin

"It's hard. Extremely hard . . ." from "Modern Yankee Heroes: From Humble Beginnings, Mariano Rivera Becomes Greatest Closer in MLB History" by Christian Red, *New York Daily News,* March 13, 2010, and available at http://articles.nydailynews.com/2010-03-13/sports/27058930_1_puerto-caimito-cardboard-cousin

"We have a lot of goals to work with the youth . . ." from "Yankees Pitcher to Open Church" by Danielle De Souza, *New Rochelle Patch,* June 28, 2011, and available at http://newrochelle.patch.com/articles/yankees-pitcher-to-open-church

"This was something special, and God wants me to concentrate on bringing Him to other people . . ." from "Baseball; Love of God Outweighs Love of the Game" by Jack Curry, *New York*

Times, December 10, 1999, and available at http://www.nytimes.com/1999/12/10/sports/baseball-love-of-god-outweighs-love-of-the-game.html

"I'm glad we lost the World Series . . ." from "The Confidence Man" by Buster Olney, *New York Magazine,* May 21, 2005, and available at http://nymag.com/nymetro/news/sports/features/9375/index2.html

"That comes from God, having the ability to perform . . ." from "World Baseball Classic Pool D: San Juan," an interview with Mariano Rivera by ASAP Sports, March 7, 2009, and available at http://www.asapsports.com/show_interview.php?id=54723

"Look at Mo's delivery, look at how he repeats it . . ." from "Mariano Rivera Pitches in 1,000th Game for Yanks and Has a Lot of Mo" by Bob Klapisch, *The Record,* May 28, 2011, and available at http://www.post-gazette.com/pg/11148/1150003-63-0.stm?cmpid=sports.xml

"The whole organization, my whole teammates have been a pillar for me . . ." from "Mariano Rivera Gets 602 to Become All-Time Saves Leader" by Bryan Llenas, *Fox New Latino,* September 19, 2011, and available at http://latino.foxnews.com/latino/sports/2011/09/19/mariano-rivera-gets-number-602-to-become-all-time-saves-leader/

"When you talk about the greatest relievers of all time, there's only one guy . . ." from "Mariano Rivera: Saving with Grace" by Kevin Baxter, *Los Angeles Times,* September 17, 2011, and available at http://articles.latimes.com/2011/sep/17/sports/la-sp-0918-down-the-line-20110918

"Amazing that he's been able to do it with one pitch over and over again . . ." from "Modern Yankee Heroes: From Humble Beginnings, Mariano Rivera Becomes Greatest Closer in MLB History" by Christian Red, *New York Daily News,* March 13, 2010, and available at http://articles.nydailynews.com/2010-03-13/sports/27058930_1_puerto-caimito-cardboard-cousin

"I don't pay too much attention to that . . ." from "The Michael Kay Show," ESPN New York (1050 AM) podcast, September 16, 2011, and available at http://espn.go.com/new-york/radio/archive?id=2693958